State, Society and National Security

Challenges and Opportunities in the 21st Century

State, Society and National Security

Challenges and Opportunities in the 21st Century

Edited by

Shashi Jayakumar

S. Rajaratnam School of International Studies, NTU, Singapore

World Scientific

NEW JERSEY · LONDON · SINGAPORE · BEIJING · SHANGHAI · HONG KONG · TAIPEI · CHENNAI · TOKYO

Published by

World Scientific Publishing Co. Pte. Ltd.

5 Toh Tuck Link, Singapore 596224

USA office: 27 Warren Street, Suite 401-402, Hackensack, NJ 07601

UK office: 57 Shelton Street, Covent Garden, London WC2H 9HE

National Library Board, Singapore Cataloguing-in-Publication Data
Names: Jayakumar, Shashi.
Title: State, society and national security : challenges and opportunities in the 21st century /
    Shashi Jayakumar.
Description: Singapore : World Scientific Publishing Co. Pte. Ltd., [2016] |
    Includes bibliographic references and index.
Identifiers: OCN 940529203 | ISBN 978-981-31-0998-8 (hardcover) |
    ISBN 978-981-3109-99-5 (paperback)
Subjects: LCSH: National security--21st century. | Radicalism--21st century. |
    Cyberspace--Security measures--21st century.
Classification: LCC HV6429 | DDC 363.3--dc23

Image on cover courtesy of:
Wilson Wong
WilzWorkz / Techgoondu / The Photographers' Guild /
Singapore Photography Interest Network
MOB: 91502799

Desk Editor: Shreya Gopi

Typeset by Stallion Press
Email: enquiries@stallionpress.com

Contents

Part II   Resilience

Part III   Radicalisation and Extremism

Part IV   Strategic and Crisis Communications

Acknowledgements

Several individuals and agencies have played a major part in the development of CENS, and have supported the present book. These include: Ambassador Barry Desker, Distinguished Fellow (and former Dean) RSIS, who gave strong support to CENS from the very beginning. This support has continued by Executive Deputy Chairman of RSIS, Ambassador Ong Keng Yong. The support of the National Security Coordination Secretariat, and especially the Permanent Secretaries (National Security and Intelligence Coordination) has also been critical. Two of the Permanent Secretaries, Mr Benny Lim and Mr Peter Ho (present and past, respectively), have also taken the time to contribute to this volume. We are grateful to them, as we are to all contributors who have found the time to collectively make possible this volume.

A sincere thank you to all these individuals and agencies (as well as many others who cannot be named here) for being part of the CENS journey.

The Editor wishes to thank Cameron Sumpter (Senior Analyst, CENS) for his assistance throughout the preparation of this volume.

Minor corrections have been made for the second printing.

About the Contributors

Andrew Silke is among the world's leading experts on the psychology of terrorism, radicalisation, and the broader field of terrorism studies. He is Head of Criminology and Director of Terrorism Studies at the University of East London, and has delivered lectures and talks at universities and conferences throughout the world. Professor Silke has authored over one hundred papers and journal articles on terrorism, counter-terrorism, crime, policing, and conflict, as well as producing a number of books such as the recent works, *Terrorism: All That Matters* (Hodder and Stoughton, 2014) and the edited volume, *Prisons, Terrorism and Extremism* (Routledge, 2014). Beyond his important contributions to the study of terrorism, Silke has also produced incisive observations and critiques of the developing field, which have been cited widely and have assisted in stimulating the growth of multidisciplinary collaborations and research based on empirical evidence. He has advised various governments and international organisations on counter-terrorism and preventing violent extremism, and presides on the United Nations Roster of Terrorism Experts and the European Commission's European Network of Experts on Radicalisation.

Professor Silke was a CENS Distinguished Visitor in September 2015.

Benny Lim is the Permanent Secretary for National Security and Intelligence Coordination. He concurrently holds the appointments of Permanent Secretary in the Prime Minister's Office and of the Ministry of

National Development. Prior to his current appointments, he was the Director of the Internal Security Department (1997 to 2004) and Permanent Secretary of the Ministry of Home Affairs (2005 to 2011). He was Chairman of the Homefront Crisis Executive Group from 2004 to 2011 which oversees the management of national crisis incidents. Mr Lim started his career in the public service as a Police constable in 1975 and rose to the rank of Deputy Commissioner of Police in 1997. He left the Police Force in 2001 and joined the Administrative Service. He read English as an undergraduate at the National University of Singapore and later pursued postgraduate studies in political sociology at the London School of Economics and Political Science. He was awarded the Meritorious Service Medal in 2010.

Caitríona Heinl joined the Centre of Excellence for National Security (CENS) at RSIS as Research Fellow responsible for cyber-related matters in October 2012. She has published peer-reviewed articles and policy advisory reports on topics that include international and regional cooperation, country case studies, national security implications of emerging technologies such as cyber capabilities and increasingly autonomous technologies, public-private partnerships, and cyber defence. She currently holds a non-resident international fellowship with the ASPI International Cyber Policy Centre, Canberra. Caitríona previously led the Justice and Home Affairs policy group and Justice Steering Committee at the Institute of International and European Affairs (IIEA), Ireland. In this position, she covered transnational crime, fundamental rights, data privacy and data protection, police/judicial cooperation, counter-terrorism, international security and cybercrime. She qualified as a U.K. trained Solicitor (non-practising) and she is admitted as an Attorney-at-Law in New York. She holds an MPhil in International Relations from the University of Cambridge. She graduated in both commerce and law at University College Dublin and the Leopold Franzens University of Innsbruck Austria with First Class Honours.

Christian-Marc Lifländer assumed his duties as a Deputy Head for Policy at the Cyber Defence Section of the Emerging Security Challenges Division at the NATO Headquarters in November 2015. Prior to this Lifländer served as a Policy Advisor at the Cyber Defence Section of the

Emerging Security Challenges Division. Before joining NATO International Staff, Lifländer served a career in the Estonian Ministry of Defence. He held several executive and senior advisory level positions early in his career, including serving as Deputy Undersecretary for Defence Policy, Director of Policy Planning, and Adviser to the Minister of Defence. Lifländer also served as Defence Counselor at the Embassy of the Republic of Estonia in the United States and Defence Counselor at the Delegation of the Republic of Estonia to NATO. He earned a B.Sc. from United States Military Academy, West Point and an M.A. from Georgetown University in Washington, DC. Mr Lifländer has been awarded with Estonian Defence Forces Distinguished Service Decoration as well as Distinguished Service Decorations of the Estonian Ministry of Defence (gold and silver).

Lifländer presented at APPSNO VII (2013).

Damien D. Cheong is a Research Fellow at the Centre of Excellence for National Security (CENS), S. Rajaratnam School of International Studies, Nanyang Technological University, Singapore. He has researched and written on a variety of issues related to homeland defence, strategic communication, security studies, political violence, and Middle East politics. Dr Cheong obtained his PhD in Politics from Monash University (Australia). Prior to joining CENS, Cheong was an adjunct research fellow at the Global Terrorism Research Centre (GTReC). He also lectured in strategic communications at Monash University from 2009–2010 and has published work such as 'Security', in Webinger & Schahbasi (eds.) *Stable States: Rethinking Social Cohesion and Good Governance* (Austrian Federal Ministry of the Interior, 2014); 'The Instrumental Use of Jihad: Explaining the Palestinian Islamic Jihad's Suicide Attacks during 2005–2006', in Mansouri & Akbarzadeh (eds.) *Political Islam and Human Security* (Cambridge Scholar Press, 2006).

David F. Heyman was until May 2014 Assistant Secretary of Policy for the United States Department of Homeland Security (DHS), where he managed a diverse portfolio involving the agency's five core areas of counter-terrorism, border security, immigration, cyber security, and strengthening resilience to natural disasters. Heyman established various domestic and international initiatives designed to reinforce U.S. security, including the cultivation of the nation's first Quadrennial Homeland Security Reviews (QHSR). Following the terrorist attacks on September 11, 2001, Heyman began working with the influential think tank, the Center for Strategic and International Studies (CSIS), where he worked on a number of pertinent national security issues, such as radicalisation, bio-terrorism, and aviation security. Heyman has worked as a senior national security advisor in the White House and has provided expert testimony to a number of Congressional committees. He has published extensively, producing works such as *DHS 2.0: Rethinking the Department of Homeland Security* (2004) and *America's Domestic Security Five Years After 9/11* (2006).

Heyman presented at APPSNO I (2007), APPSNO II (2008), and APPSNO IX (2015).

Professor Sir David Omand is former director of the United Kingdom's Government Communication Headquarters (GCHQ) and currently serves as a commissioner for the Global Commission on Internet Governance. He has held a range of high-level positions within the British Government, including Permanent Secretary of the Home Office and Deputy Under Secretary of State for Policy in the Ministry of Defence, as well as serving for seven years on the Joint Intelligence Committee. Sir Omand is a Visiting Professor at King's College London, where his work and lecturing focus on national security and counter-terrorism strategy, intelligence analysis and assessment, and developing the concepts of national resilience and crisis management. Author of the critically well-received book, *Securing the State* (Columbia University Press, 2010), Sir Omand has penned a number of articles and book chapters, including 'What should be the Limits of Counter-Terrorism Policy', in English (ed.) *Illusions of Terrorism and Counter-Terrorism* (Oxford University Press, 2015); 'The Domestic Balance', in Johnston, *Wars and Peace* (RUSI, 2014); and 'The future of intelligence', in Duyvestayn, de Jong & van Reijn (eds.) *The Future of Intelligence* (Routledge, 2014).

Professor Sir David Omand was a CENS Distinguished Visitor in October 2012.

Ilan Mizrahi is a former National Security Advisor and headed Israel's National Security Council, during the Ehud Olmert premiership from 2006 to 2008. Having also served as Deputy Head of Israel's primary intelligence collection agency, Mossad, Mizrahi is now President and CEO of the private security and intelligence firm, TATOOM Consulting Pte Ltd. Mizrahi held various responsibilities during his thirty-year career at Mossad, including the leadership of the Anti-Terror department, Recruitment and Operations, and the Human Intelligence division. After leaving the agency in 2003, Mizrahi was appointed CEO of the non-governmental organisation, Keren Yaniv, which works with vulnerable youth, and also advised technology and defence companies on security. Fluent in Arabic and versed in the history of Islam, Mizrahi holds a double degree in Political Science and Middle Eastern History from Tel Aviv University, and a Master's degree in Political Science from The University of Haifa.

Mizrahi was a CENS Distinguished Visitor in May 2008 and a speaker at CENS' Global Futures Forum in September 2010.

Katherine Brown is a lecturer of Islamic Studies in the Department of Theology and Religion at the University of Birmingham, having recently moved from King's College London where she lectured for eight years in the Defence Studies Department. Dr Brown's research focuses on resistance, gender and political Islam and particularly the ways in which gendered jihadi narratives motivate people and combine with everyday experiences of living and politics. She is currently writing a monograph investigating the gendered nature of counter-terrorism and counter-radicalisation strategies and the differential gendered impact they have on their subjects. Dr Brown holds a PhD from the University of Southampton and has published widely. Her works include: 'Radicalization and counter-radicalization at British universities: Muslim encounters and alternatives', *Journal of Ethnic and Racial Studies* (2014); 'Gender and Counter Radicalisation: women and emerging counter-terrorism measures', in Satterthwaite & Huckerby (eds.) *Gender, National Security and Counter Terrorism: a human rights perspective* (2012); and 'Influencing Political

Islam: Moderation, Resilience and De-Radicalization in UK domestic Counter-Terrorism policies (2005–2011)' in Tuck and Kennedy (eds.) *British Propaganda and Wars of Empire: Influencing Friend and Foe 1900–2010* (Ashgate, 2014).

John, Lord Alderdice FRCPsych is a Liberal Democrat member of the House of Lords, Senior Research Fellow and Director of the Centre for the Resolution of Intractable Conflict at Harris Manchester College, Oxford and Chairman of the Centre for Democracy and Peace Building in Belfast. Leader of the Alliance Party of Northern Ireland for eleven years from 1987, he played a significant role in negotiating the 1998 Good Friday Agreement, was first Speaker of the Northern Ireland Assembly and from 2004 appointed by the British and Irish Governments one of four international commissioners overseeing security normalization and terrorist demobilization. The First and Deputy First Ministers of Northern Ireland have recently appointed him to help produce a strategy for disbanding paramilitary groups. Formerly President of Liberal International (the global federation of more than 100 liberal political parties), he is now Presidente d'Honneur. In 2010 he retired as senior psychiatrist at the Centre for Psychotherapy, Senior Lecturer at Queen's University, Belfast and Visiting Professor at the University of Virginia. He continues consulting, mediating, negotiating, teaching and writing on fundamentalism, radicalisation and violent political conflict around the world. He has been recognized with many honorary degrees and prizes including the International Psychoanalytic Association Award for Extraordinarily Meritorious Service to Psychoanalysis, the World Federation of Scientists Prize for the application of Science to the Cause of Peace and Liberal International's Prize for Freedom.

Lord Alderdice presented at APPSNO II (2008) and APPSNO IV (2011).

Kumar Ramakrishna is an Associate Professor and Head of Policy Studies in the Office of the Executive Deputy Chairman, S. Rajaratnam School of International Studies, Singapore. He was previously Head of the Centre of Excellence for National Security (April 2006–March 2015). His current research interests include British propaganda in the Malayan Emergency; propaganda theory and practice; history of strategic thought; and counter-terrorism with a focus on radicalisation. Assoc Prof Ramakrishna has been a frequent speaker on counter-terrorism before local and international audiences, a regular media commentator on counter-terrorism, and an established author in numerous internationally refereed journals. His book, Radical Pathways: Understanding Muslim Radicalisation in Indonesia (2009), was featured as one of the top 150 books on terrorism and counter-terrorism in a May 2012 article published in the respected journal Perspectives of Terrorism, where Assoc Prof Ramakrishna was said to be "one of Southeast Asia's leading counterterrorism experts" and Radical Pathways "an important and insightful case study on the pathways to extremism and violent jihad in Indonesia". His latest single-authored books are *Islamist Terrorism and Militancy in Indonesia: The Power of the Manichean Mindset* (2015) and *Original Sin? Revising the Revisionist Critique of the 1963 Operation Coldstore in Singapore* (2015).

Marc Sageman is an independent researcher on radicalisation and terrorism and the founding president of Sageman Consulting LLC. He is the author of *Understanding Terror Networks* (University of Pennsylvania Press, 2004) and *Leaderless Jihad* (University of Pennsylvania Press, 2008) which were based on a comprehensive database created by the author at a time when empirical studies on the subject were limited. The books provided important early illustrations of the social nature of radicalisation and are among the most cited works in the field of terrorism studies. Sageman attended Harvard University before obtaining his MD and PhD in sociology from New York University. In 1984, Sageman joined the United States Central Intelligence Agency (CIA) and spent time in Central and South Asia where he led U.S. multilateral programs with the Afghan Mujahidin. After leaving the agency in the early 1990s, Sageman began practicing as a clinical psychiatrist, which informed and guided his research on terrorism. Various governments, including those of the United Kingdom, France, Canada, Australia, and Spain have called upon Sageman's expertise, and he has presented extensively at universities and conferences throughout the world. Sageman's 2014 journal article, *The Stagnation in Terrorism Research*, incited a lively debate within the field.

Sageman was a CENS Distinguished Visitor in November 2009.

Norman Vasu is Senior Fellow and Deputy Head of the Centre of Excellence for National Security (CENS) at the S. Rajaratnam School of International Studies (RSIS), Singapore. Within CENS, he also coordinates the Social Resilience Programme — one of four research programmes in the Centre. Vasu received his PhD in International Politics from the University of Wales at Aberystwyth in 2004 and was a Fulbright Visiting Fellow with the Center for Strategic Communication, Hugh Downs School of Human Communication, Arizona State University in 2012. He is the author of *How Diasporic Peoples Maintain their Identity in Multicultural Societies: Chinese, Africans, and Jews* (Edwin Mellen Press, 2008), editor of *Social Resilience in Singapore: Reflections from the London Bombings* (Select Publishing, 2007), co-editor of Nations, National Narratives and Communities in the Asia Pacific, (Routledge, 2014), and co-editor of *Immigration in Singapore* (Amsterdam University Press, 2014). His research on multiculturalism, ethnic relations, narratives of governance, citizenship, immigration and national security have been published in journals such as Asian Survey, Asian Ethnicity, The Round Table, Journal of Comparative Asian Development and The Copenhagen Journal of Asian Studies and in a number of edited volumes.

Peter Ho is the Senior Advisor to the Centre for Strategic Futures, a Senior Fellow in the Civil Service College, an Adjunct Professor at the S. Rajaratnam School of International Studies, and a Visiting Fellow at the Lee Kuan Yew School of Public Policy. Peter Ho is Chairman of the Urban Development Authority of Singapore, Chairman of the Social Science Research Council, and Chairman of the Singapore Centre on Environmental Life Sciences Engineering. He is a member of the National University Board of Trustees, a board member of the Lee Kuan Yew Exchange Fellowship, a member of the S. Rajaratnam School of International Studies' Board of Governors, and a council member of the International Institute of Strategic Studies. He is also a member of Statoil's Strategy Advisory Council, and the McKinsey Center for Government Advisory Council. When he retired from the Singapore Administrative Service in 2010 after a career in the Public Service stretching more than 34 years, he was Head, Civil Service, concurrent with his other appointments of Permanent Secretary (Foreign Affairs), Permanent Secretary (National Security and Intelligence

Coordination), and Permanent Secretary (Special Duties) in the Prime Minister's Office. Before that, he was Permanent Secretary (Defence).

Shashi Jayakumar assumed the appointment as Head, Centre of Excellence for National Security (CENS) on 1 April 2015. Dr Jayakumar was educated at Oxford University where he studied History (BA 1997, D.Phil, 2001). He has been a member of the Singapore Administrative Service since 2002. During this time, he was posted to various Ministries, including the Ministries of Defence, Manpower, Information and the Arts, and Community Development, Youth and Sports. He was from August 2011–July 2014 a Senior Visiting Research Fellow at the Lee Kuan Yew School of Public Policy. The main focus of his research and writing there has been local society and politics. He is currently working on two book projects relating to local politics (forthcoming, 2016). His other interests include extremism, social resilience, and homeland defence.

Steven R. Corman is a Professor in the Hugh Downs School of Human Communication and Director of the Center for Strategic Communication at Arizona State University. Since 2001 he has served as an invited participant on numerous national and international workshops and symposia on counterterrorism, strategic communication and public diplomacy. In 2011 he was a Distinguished Visiting Fellow at the Centre of Excellence for National Security, Nanyang Technological University (Singapore) and Senior Consortium Research Fellow at the U.S. Army Research Institute. In 2003–2005 he was a member of the Scientist Panel for the Strategic Operations Working Group at U.S. Special Operations Command. He has given invited presentations and briefings for, U.S. MISOC, NATO SACEUR, the NATO 2012 Strategic Communication Conference, the NATO Center of Excellence for Defense Against Terrorism, USJFCOM/USSOCOM. Corman is author, editor and/or co-editor of the books, *Narrating the Exit from Afghanistan* (CSC, Spring 2013) and *Master Narratives of Islamist Extremism* (Palgrave, Spring 2011), Weapons of Mass Persuasion: Strategic Communication to Combat Violent Extremism (Peter Lang, 2008).

Corman presented at APPSNO II (2008) and was a CENS Distinguished Visitor in September 2011.

Stephen E. Flynn is Professor of Political Science and Director, Center for Resilience Studies, at Northeastern University. He is the bestselling author of *America the Vulnerable* (HarperCollins 2004) and *The Edge of Disaster: Rebuilding a Resilient Nation* (Random House, 2007). He holds research affiliations with the Wharton School's Risk Management and Decision Processes Center, and the Homeland Security Studies and Analysis Institute. In 2014, U.S. Secretary of Homeland Security Jeh Johnson appointed him to serve on the Homeland Security Science and Technology Advisory Council. He is also a member of the National Security Advisory Board for Argonne National Laboratory. Before arriving at Northeastern in 2011, he was President of the Center for National Policy and spent a decade as Senior Fellow for National Security Studies at the Council on Foreign Relations. In 2008 he served as the lead homeland security policy adviser for the Presidential Transition Team for President Barack Obama. Dr. Flynn was a highly decorated commissioned officer in the U.S. Coast Guard for 20 years, including two tours as commanding officer at sea. He holds the M.A.L.D. and Ph.D. degrees from the Fletcher School of Law and Diplomacy, Tufts University, and B.S. from the U.S. Coast Guard Academy.

Flynn was a CENS Distinguished Visitor in April 2014.

W. Timothy Coombs is a full professor in the Department of Communication at Texas A&M University. He is also an honorary professor in the Department of Business Communication at Aarhus University. Dr Coombs researches in the area of crisis communication and his works appear in *Management Communication Quarterly, Corporate Communication: An International Journal, Public Relations Review, Business Horizons*, and the *Journal of Communication Management*. He has authored two books on crisis communication, *Ongoing Crisis Communication* and *Code Red in the Boardroom* as well as being co-editor of the Handbook of Crisis Communication and numerous book chapters on the topic. He has received the 2002 recipient of Jackson, Jackson & Wagner Behavioral Science Prize from the Public Relations Society of America and the 2013 Pathfinder Award from the Institute of Public Relations in recognition of his research contributions to the field and to the practice. Dr Coombs has worked with governments, corporations, and consulting firms in the U.S., Asia, and Europe on ways to improve crisis communication efforts for themselves and their clients. He is also the current editor for *Corporation Communication: An International Journal.*

Coombs presented at APPSNO VI (2012).

Wong Yu Han leads the strategy function for the Cyber Security Agency of Singapore (CSA) established on 1 April 2015, facilitating plans and policies for the operation, international collaboration, technology and industry development, and education and outreach work for Singapore's cyber security. Prior to his current appointment, he served for 24 years in the Singapore Armed Forces, holding successful command appointments up to the Division level, leading the Singaporean contingent in Afghanistan in 2011, serving as military attaché in Jakarta, and holding various staff appointments in the armed forces and Ministry of Defence. From 2011 to 2015, he sat on the board of Unicorn International.

Foreword

This publication marks the 10th anniversary of the formation of the Centre of Excellence for National Security (CENS). It is also the 10th edition of its milestone programme, the Asia Pacific Programme for Senior National Security Officers (APPSNO).

It is a rare privilege for me indeed to be able to pen the foreword to this volume.

When CENS was formed in 2006, in partnership with the National Security Coordination Secretariat in the Prime Minister's Office, certain key events — terrorist attacks of September 2001, the subsequent uncovering of a terrorist Jemaah Islamiah cell in Singapore, SARS in 2003 — were still relatively fresh in the minds of those working in the security realm in Singapore.

A major review of Singapore's security architecture, the Strategic Framework for National Security, had been completed in July 2004. Our thinking at the time was to supplement the Strategic Framework by increasing the intellectual capital available to analyse national security issues.

We knew that we could not consistently avoid strategic surprise but we could better deal with it if and when it came, if we had the benefit of fresh thinking about the impact and implications of trends before its occurrence.

We knew that the government could not have all the answers.

We recognised that what was needed was a centre that could solicit and harness the insights of academia, both international and local experts, to make security assessments that could enrich and inform the perspectives of policymakers. We did not need an in-house think tank to tell the government what it already knew; we wanted to and needed to hear the things that had not been thought about or thought about enough; to receive perspectives not heard of before or which ran against orthodox wisdom or the prevailing conventional view.

From the get-go, the decision was taken to ensure that the CENS team would be multi-national in composition, comprising both Singaporean and foreign analysts who are specialists in various aspects of national and homeland security affairs. And while key academics and practitioners are invited to come to Singapore as part of CENS' events and workshops, CENS itself ranges far afield, establishing contacts with a range of similar think-tanks around the world that are engaged in similar work. Indeed, a crucial source of CENS's strength and success over the years has been its formidable and still growing collaborative network of experts and practitioners.

Through the years, friends of CENS have been very generous in sharing their knowledge, coming to Singapore to take part in our workshops, distinguished visitor schemes and the annual Asia-Pacific Programme for Senior National Security Officers (APPSNO). These members of the CENS alumni are our richest resource.

I am heartened by the fact that so many friends of CENS — in many cases the foremost authorities in their respective fields — have agreed to contribute to this book, marking the 10th anniversary of CENS' foundation, as well as the 10th edition of APPSNO.

Reading through the various contributions, I am glad, too, that the contributors have revisited arguments they have made on earlier occasions (as CENS' Distinguished Visitors, or at earlier APPSNOs). In some cases, contributors have refined their arguments; in others, there is a looking forward to give some sense of likely future developments.

CENS at 10 is a young man with a great future; this will be so if it stays nimble, able to continue proactively engaging established as well as up and coming experts in various disciplines. It will have to keep key milestones like APPSNO fresh even as it explores nascent trends which may point the direction to future programmes.

What will be the shape and directions of our security realm in the future? What will matter more and how will it impact Singapore? Climate change and national security? The security impact of human migration? Time will tell — but hopefully, CENS will tell us first.

Mr Benny Lim
Permanent Secretary (National Security & Intelligence
Coordination) and Permanent Secretary for National
Development (Prime Minister's Office)

Part I

National Security

Introduction

Few could have envisaged the directions that the Centre of Excellence for National Security (CENS) would eventually take when it began its journey on April 1, 2006. As Permanent Secretary (National Security and Intelligence Coordination) Mr Benny Lim makes clear in his generous foreword, there was the sense that government did not have the answers and needed deeper insights into key national security domains. But beyond this, the remit was not precisely defined. This was intentional: our partner in government then and now, the National Security Coordination Secretariat (NSCS) and its successive Permanent Secretaries (Mr Peter Ho, Mr Peter Ong and Mr Benny Lim) have always made it a point to allow CENS room to experiment with research directions and to engage with new ideas, however unconventional they might be.

This latitude to roam freely (intellectually as well as geographically) has meant that over the past decade a valuable databank of contacts comprising local and international experts across a whole range of issues has been built, mirroring the cosmopolitan make-up of CENS itself. Many of these contacts are leading world experts in various security domains and have been an integral part of the CENS journey. In fact, CENS could not be successful in producing thoughtful, timely and policy-relevant research without these collaborations and contacts.

This volume marks the 10th anniversary of CENS, and also the 10th edition of our milestone event, The Asia-Pacific Programme for Senior

National Security Officers (APPSNO) which has over time developed into a premier national security conference in Asia, bringing together practitioners, policymakers and academics from all parts of the world for an intensive, one-week discussion on salient national security trends.

In order to put together this volume, we reached out to these friends of CENS who have over the years been generous in sharing their knowledge by coming to Singapore to speak at APPSNO, or who have been CENS' Distinguished Visitors in the past.[1] It is enormously gratifying that we received positive responses from all whom we approached. The contributors are a good mix of practitioners, policy experts and academics, all at the apex of their respective fields. CENS programme coordinators have also contributed. The book is divided into sections mirroring CENS' research domains (radicalisation, resilience, cyber and homeland security — the latter including strategic communications). There is also an introductory, overarching section on national security.

We made it a point not to be prescriptive: contributors were simply asked to cast their minds back over developments, over the past decade, and to revisit appropriate key trends, and, where possible, to look back at their own arguments and conclusions when they presented at APPSNO or during the course of talks given as part of our Distinguished Visitor series. But some care has been taken to maintain a connecting thread. Where feasible, contributors have attempted to shed light on what has changed in security discourse, what has worked (as well as what has not), and what potential further evolutions within each domain can and should be. It is a broad remit and we are delighted that contributors have chosen to range freely within it.

Even as CENS reaches the 10 year mark, grappling with pressing questions in each of our key domains has become increasingly complex. The book provides a chance for CENS and its international network to address some of these complexities, and it is also a reminder that 10 years' worth of thinking and talking about national security imperatives has generated insights with meaning and impact. It is therefore not meant as a simple commemorative anniversary book; the contributions will repay close attention, whether the reader is a policymaker, security practitioner, academic or interested individual.

National Security

The introductory National Security section that underpins the book sees contributions from longstanding friends of CENS, who have had considerable experience across multiple security domains. We asked them simply to cast their minds across these domains and to pen their thoughts on key developments, as well as what we might expect to see in future. The opening contribution sees the editor engaging in a conversation (in reality several conversations over lunch, taking place between December 2015–January 2016) with former Head of Civil Service **Mr Peter Ho** and **Mr Benny Lim** (Permanent Secretary, Prime Minister's Office, and also Permanent Secretary for National Development as well as National Security and Intelligence Coordination) on issues pertaining to national security and the future of Singapore's security. Ho (who has been the Permanent Secretary of several key Ministries, including Defence and Foreign Affairs, as well as being a past holder of the National Security and Intelligence Coordination portfolio) and Lim (whose past appointments include Permanent Secretary, Ministry of Home Affairs) are well known as being profound thinkers on security matters. This is the first time that they have engaged in a "trilogue" of this type in print. The discussion covers the main themes in the book (terrorism, resilience, communication, cyber), but also ranges far beyond these issues. They share their views on scenarios, complexity and the Singapore security architecture, pulling no punches in their views on how it has to evolve. Tellingly, a key preoccupation of Ho (who is currently the Advisor for the Centre for Strategic Futures under the Prime Minister's Office) is with cyberissues and what the future holds for us in this domain. He points out (in an echo of the contribution from Wong Yu Han from Singapore's CSA) that there are both risks and opportunities inherent in current cyberchallenges: these cannot be avoided and deep thinking, as well as policy action, are required to avoid being caught behind in getting to grips with issues such as the Internet of Things. Lim, who was Director of the Internal Security Department at the time of the September 11, 2001 terrorist attacks and the subsequent arrests of Jemaah Islamiyah extremists in Singapore that year, makes the observation that the self-radicalisation we are seeing in

Singapore and elsewhere reflects a clear and present danger. Both agree on a key point: rather than trying to proof Singapore against an attack (which may be well-nigh impossible), it is the post-event scenarios that should be examined. Lim observes that competence shown by the government and security services has had an unintended effect: a lack of preparedness on the part of the public. For his part, Ho argues that we should move away from vulnerability to discussions in which resilience (a concept everyone can understand) is central.

In his treatment of national security, **Professor Sir David Omand** (former Director of the United Kingdom's Government Communication Headquarters, GCHQ) makes the important point that with the advent of "whole new categories of risk" such as cybercrime and the increasing presence of non-state actors (terror groups), the goal of national security strategy is increasingly seen as the maintenance of conditions of normality, providing confidence to the public that the many major risks — threats and hazards — can be managed so normal everyday life can continue. This citizen centricity is a very important theme not adequately talked about in national security discourse; and, as Omand observes, this is to frame national security as a psychological construct as much as a physical one. The public must have confidence in the ability of the authorities to manage the risks. Omand observes that in recent years much experience has been gained in planning for resilience, or improving the ability of a nation to withstand shocks. Whether one considers "sudden impact" and "rising tide" scenarios, the public must have the evidence to merit confidence that they are part of a society that will be resilient to the shocks and surprises the future will bring. Nations, he says, may have no choice but to get used to the idea that it will be necessary to invest in the requisite preparations to make a success of a world full of surprises, threats and hazards. And we have to accept, as Omand notes, that while causes of conflict later in the 21st century are thus unlikely to be dissimilar from those of previous centuries, the *way* these conflicts are expressed will be different, not least because of the exploitation of cyberspace.

Ilan Mizrahi (former Head of the Israeli National Security Council) begins by noting that the broad range of threats nations now face — from nuclear proliferation and weapons of mass destruction, to sophisticated terrorists, financial crises, popular uprisings, the disintegration of states and the flows of illegal immigrants which follow. Echoing Sir David Omand's contribution, he notes there is as a result greater uncertainty and complexity which often lead to strategic surprises. But the questions Mizrahi raises are markedly different: who is the enemy in a changing world of disintegrating nation states and shifting alliances? Should the definition of National Security in light of growing internal threats (such as terrorism and in some countries, illegal immigration) be changed? Mizrahi also makes the point (made also by Mr Peter Ho) that it will increasingly prove expedient for intelligence agencies to collaborate with the private sector and academia in order to come to better assessments. Mirazhi also gives no easy answers when tackling the question of how intelligence assessments should be crafted in an age when policymakers want to know what will happen. It is worth bearing in mind, however, his point that not all the answers will come from technology: a special effort should still be made to recruit and train talented and daring analysts, with open access to the pyramid heads of the agency.

David Heyman (former Assistant Secretary for Policy at the United States Department of Homeland Security), in his contribution titled "The Velocity of Change", enumerates the conventional and unconventional challenges we face, but makes the point that what is more pernicious than any of the particular challenges is the sheer *rate* of change in which we experience global security challenges in society today. Put simply: the velocity of change may be increasing beyond our ability to adapt and overcome rising threats. Even as the defining principles of this new emergent (and technologically interconnected) order fall into place, Heyman avers that the new order has brought with it new vulnerabilities and opportunities that international criminals, terrorists and even state actors can exploit. These groups, while distributed globally, are able to insinuate themselves locally, by inspiring and operating over the internet and through social media. Therein, Heyman argues, lies the problem: in spite of these significant and growing new threats, the fundamental security architecture of governments (with one or two notable exceptions) has remained locked into institutions developed earlier. In the face of these new threats, traditional national security institutions become less useful. New institutions and new governance are therefore needed.

Resilience

A word on CENS' approach to resilience is in order before proceeding to the contributions to the section in question. The approach in CENS (and indeed in Singapore generally) to addressing the resilience question was in the early years to take a hard approach — "resistance", so to speak, rather than "resilience". Over time, however, think tanks and government agencies alike agreed that a more holistic understanding had to be conceived; one that encompassed absorptive capacity as well as the ability to thrive after a crisis. It is no exaggeration to say that CENS was thinking and talking about "resilience" before it became fashionable. This transformation in thinking took place for a reason. Other countries "do" resilience for particular reasons. In some cases, central governments push the concept simply because they cannot help quickly enough, or on the required scale, when a crisis hits the nation's extremities. The premise in Singapore was (and is) of course quite different. Public awareness of the resilience concept was low. We started from an imperfect understanding of the very concept of resilience: it was in many ways our underbelly. After seeing, and studying what had happened with the aftermaths of terror attacks in Madrid (2004) and London (2007), as well as various natural disasters (such as the Christchurch earthquake in 2011) we realised that important lessons and comparisons had to be drawn in terms of the very cohering of society after the event. Failure to cohere post event, in Singapore's case, could well be an existential issue (although some, including Peter Ho in his input to the contribution in the national security section, might disagree).

Stephen E. Flynn (Professor of Political Science and Director of the Center for Resilience Studies at Northeastern University) draws on an interesting and often overlooked sidelight to the terrorist attacks of September 11, 2001. Mariners from all around New York harbour came together that day in a spontaneous armada to help organise and carry out what turned out to be the largest sea evacuation in history: the 9/11 boatlift. This was, as Flynn observes, entirely spontaneous and unplanned. It has to be understood, however, that what took place was in fact shaped by well-established attitudes and capabilities within the maritime community. Flynn also deals with the events of April 15, 2013, when two IEDs were detonated near the finish line of the Boston Marathon. The Boston medical response had deep roots in formal and informal preparedness. Because of frequent training and exercises, Boston hospitals were well prepared to handle mass casualty events. As Flynn observes, The "Boston Strong" story demonstrates the importance of preparedness when it comes to mitigating damage and harm associated with a terrorist attack. It also highlights the importance of creating conditions in which the general community is both encouraged and empowered to volunteer their skills and resources to respond to these events. Communities must invest time and resources in preparing to withstand, respond to, and bounce back from these attacks. What is required is a serious commitment to conducting planning and training for when things go wrong, on the precise assumption that they *will* go wrong at some point. And this type of preparation would, as Flynn suggests, make adversaries such as terrorists think twice before acting: terrorism is only an appealing weapon when a certain degree of disruption can be generated, and the adversary in question would need to possess significant capability if hoping to cause disruption in a community that is truly resilient. Resilience is therefore in and of itself a deterrent.

John, Lord Alderdice has over the decades garnered a near-unparalleled knowledge of the development of the Irish Peace Process. He was from 1989 until 1998 the leader of the cross-community political party called Alliance. During the implementation of the Good Friday Agreement he was appointed as the first Speaker of the Northern Ireland Assembly, a position he held until 2004. This makes him uniquely qualified to comment on the case study of the Irish peace process, as well as to draw out some aspects deserving wider attention. Alderdice suggests that feelings of injustice or humiliation weaken social resilience and are conducive to the formation of extremist groups. If one is excluded (through discrimination or the feeling that nothing can be gained through civic participation) then this leads to a toxic milieu — the beginnings of an "uncivil society". Based on his first-hand experience, Alderdice stresses the need to build respectful behaviour between different sections of the community. These types of positive values have the effect of contributing greatly to societies being able to bounce back.

Rounding off the section on resilience is the contribution from **Norman Vasu**, Senior Fellow, Deputy Head of CENS and the Coordinator for

CENS' Social Resilience Programme. Vasu observes that resilience became the *du jour* term to describe a society's ability to return to normal life post-crisis after the London bombings in 2005. The term is naturally appealing to those working in the field of national security owing to the general belief that society cannot be protected from all threats — be they man-made or natural. His contribution unpacks the term resilience into two forms — conservative and dynamic — and he argues that dynamic resilience, a resilience comfortable with adaptation and change, may be the optimal approach when responding to challenges arising from an increasingly complex global environment.

Radicalisation and Extremism

The contributions for the radicalisation section are united by common conceptual threads — threads which are topical for academics and relevant to practitioners. All three contributions engage to some degree with the distinction between (and disentangling of) "radicalisation" and "extremism". In their conclusion, all three make observations or recommendations that practitioners and those responsible for designing "deradicalisation" programmes would do well to heed.

Marc Sageman, independent scholar and longstanding friend of CENS, reminds us of something we often forget — how new the organised study of "radicalisation" actually is. But now, despite such a vast literature on the concept, our understanding of the term has reached a state of stagnation. Sageman dissects key theories of radicalisation — and points out their flaws. All the main theories make assumptions that remain unexamined and are often uncritically accepted. Ideology is of course important, but as Sageman observes, this has become mixed in with a new "politically correct phrase", countering violent extremism (CVE) which is itself problematic. A critical conclusion that Sageman arrives at is that the process of radicalisation takes place in the context of an escalation of conflict between political challengers and the state or society. This escalation of conflict may turn to violence when certain conditions are fulfilled: political dissenters' disillusionment with peaceful political processes, and moral outrage at state aggression against their group. Sageman's views — uncomfortable reading as they might be for some in the field — command respect given the sheer number of politically violent individuals he has come face to face with and interviewed. These were, by Sageman's own account, individuals who "viewed themselves as soldiers for their respective comrades and cause". This carries with it the implication (in another of his key conclusions) that the number of terrorists is not stable but strongly dependent on the actions of the state. If one understands the conflict between the state and challengers, then one understands Radicalisation.

Associate Prof Kumar Ramakrishna, Head of Policy Studies at RSIS and the immediate past Head of CENS, similarly opens with the theoretical meanings of radicalisation and extremism, engaging first with the myriad contending interpretations of "radicalisation". Where he departs from Sageman is in offering a synthesis of the process of radicalisation into violent extremism (RIVE). He argues that cognitive radicalisation should be seen as the process of *drastic identity simplification* on the part of in-group members that perceive themselves to be under collective threat by an out-group. Dr Ramakrishna argues persuasively that the real threat of violence emanates not from radicals but rather extremists — "One may say that the intensity with which the extremist clings to his beliefs significantly exceeds that of the radical." This is not mere semantics: the concern on the part of practitioners and policymakers in his view should not really be radicalisation into radicalism *per se*, but rather radicalisation into extremism, with the attendant potential for violence. This would of course (as Ramakrishna observes) also have implications for national and regional counter-terrorist and rehabilitation programmes.

Prof Andrew Silke (Head of Criminology and Director of Terrorism Studies at the University of East London) and **Dr Katherine Brown** (Lecturer in Islamic Studies at the University of Birmingham) take an entry point into the subject matter not altogether dissimilar from the other contributions in the section, reviewing at the outset the major developments in and significant issues connected with our understanding of radicalisation. Like Sageman, they point out that ultimately the emergence of the term "radicalisation" to describe this process of deepening involvement in radical violent causes and activism is a very recent phenomenon, but by 2007, it had effectively taken over policy and research discourse on this subject, replacing the earlier commonplace of "recruitment" into terrorist organisations. In their review of some of the key "models" of radicalisation, Silke and Brown observe that getting from radicalisation to violent extremism can be an "erratic" experience. A second major observation made — conceptually similar to a key argument made by Kumar Ramakrishna in his contribution — is that it is all too easy to assume that "radicalisation" as a phenomenon is the major root cause of terrorism. But the authors argue that radicalisation should more accurately be seen as part of recruitment processes. Other factors drive these processes, and it is these deeper underlying causes (and not the headline "radicalisation") which merit attention and intervention, particularly when designing models for counter-terrorism and CVE.

Strategic and Crisis Communications

CENS' Homeland Security pillar devotes a great deal of its attention to the issue of strategic and crisis communications, with particular reference to the role of new media. Those who have been invited to contribute to this section, all longstanding friends of CENS, are experts in these domains. **Steven R. Corman** (Herberger Professor and Director of the Center for Strategic Communication at Arizona State University) argues that trends in strategic communication have in recent years developed in a manner that poses particular challenges to state actors. Non-state actors have also entered the strategic communications game, and in the case of the latter, asymmetric advantages accrue (for example, in terms of recruiting and maintaining a support base). This has serious implications from a policy perspective, Corman argues. State communicators need to embrace uncertainty (as well as complexity) and need a different, more fluid approach to strategic communication.

   W. Timothy Coombs (Professor at the Nicholson School of Communication, University of Central Florida) identifies key ways that those responding to disasters and those affected by disasters can utilise social media. Coombs stresses the importance of "digital naturals" (that is, those who have grown up with the media and become habituated to it) and how their use of social media has led to a re-thinking of disaster communications. The rise of this generation of digital naturals has unavoidable implications for how governments approach emergency management and communication. As Coombs observes, nowhere is this better evidenced than by how people around the world have been using social media during disasters. This in and of itself has implications for how governments and NGOs need to adapt. Disaster communications must establish a social media presence and voice well before a crisis begins. Coombs also stresses (and these are points which should be taken on board by all policymakers dealing with emergency response) that social media is helpful in recruiting and organising actual volunteers, but neither should the government forget the role of digital (as opposed to real-world) volunteers. Digital volunteers perform the valuable role of collecting, synthesising and sharing disaster-related information.

The third contribution in this section sees **Damien D. Cheong**, (Coordinator of CENS' Homeland Security Programme and Research Fellow) examining the development and transformation of social media within the national security domain. He observes that while social media was developed and conceptualised originally as an alternative medium for communication, the data from social media communications has become extremely useful for analyses and investigations related to national security. He also explores how data from social media can be used in the future in the field of predictive analysis, and concludes with a brief examination of the challenges and policy implications of this development.

Cyber

CENS' Cyber pillar is a comparatively recent (2015) addition, but already in the short span of its existence has been able to make its mark through networking, quality research, and a very fruitful collaboration with Singapore's Cyber Security Agency (CSA; an agency itself of recent vintage).

Christian Lifländer (Policy Advisor in the Cyber Defense Section of NATO HQ) opens his contribution with the stark message that cyberattacks are taking place at a faster rate than defences can be built. Lifländer suggests that this might in fact only be the beginnings of the problem. As the Internet of Things becomes part of our everyday life, an entire mesh (buildings, objects, vehicles) will become part of our everyday lives — and this will bring with it vulnerability. Lifländer stresses that no one actor, however powerful, can afford to go it alone when dealing with these challenges. Collaborations and networks are crucial and Lifländer provides examples of useful platforms and networks that have been developed, sometimes as collaborations between industry and government. Lifländer also gives an important reminder that discussions in international fora that attempt to set down "rules of the road" are also vital in order to govern the behaviour of states and individuals. Few would be better placed that Lifländer to make the observation that the Tallinn Manual, a touchstone at the intersection of state behaviour, international law and cybernorms, needs a proper successor in the form of the (still ongoing and eagerly awaited) Tallinn 2.0 manual, which will expand on the original and will also pertain to the international legal framework for cyberactions in peacetime. Lifländer does not of course suggest that this alone will be a panacea. Indeed, there are wider issues of internet sovereignty on which major powers are far from seeing eye-to-eye. These differences are "likely to have an impact not only on the future of the Internet, but also for the future of how conflict and acts of war may be defined". Lifländer concludes by noting that this will be a long road, and where we end up may have very little to do with the starting point.

The contribution in this section (specially solicited for the volume) is from **Wong Yu Han**, Director for Strategy at CSA. As Yu Han points out, it would be a mistake to see cybersecurity as a purely technical issue: there are interrelated technological, economic, political and social components (which very much chimes with CENS' own approach to the cyberdomain). Like Lifländer, the author points to the explosive growth of the internet and the corresponding exponential increase in cyberthreats, which are bound to grow further given greater interconnections and interdependencies in networks. The vulnerabilities, of course, are not simply through the front door: organisations are also exposed through supply chain and vendor networks. To cope, some level of citizen awareness, cyberdiscipline and good governance is needed. But perhaps more importantly, there has to be a ramping up of cyberskills within the workforce, which would be a *sine qua non* of a truly Smart Nation. If the effort succeeds, we will end up not just with a Smart Nation, but with a country that can aspire to be a hub for cyberinnovation and a locus for partnerships.

The final contribution to this section (and to the volume) comes from Caitríona Heinl, CENS Research Fellow with responsibility for cyber issues. Heinl outlines several developments relating to cybersecurity that are unique to Southeast Asia and the wider Asia Pacific region, all of which impact on the formulation cyber-related policies. Heinl does not simply survey the ground: she provides several applied policy recommendations to deal with the increasingly cross-border nature of future cyber issues. Her key conclusion: while there have been many recent developments in the right direction, there is still a great deal of room for deeper collaboration involving all concerned actors that might facilitate the implementation of relevant policy at both the national and regional levels.

"Deeper collaboration" is perhaps a fitting note on which to close out this volume. This is something that is all too easily talked and written about. It is hoped, however, that the contributions to this volume do indeed convey some sense of this deeper collaboration: a flavour of the interaction and intellectual cross-pollination amongst CENS, its friends, and elements of the national security ecosystem it has developed around itself over the past ten years. In a small way, too, this volume makes a case for saying that these interactions have contributed to shaping the thinking underpinning Singapore's national security.

Shashi Jayakumar

Endnote

1. The one exception is the piece from Wong Yu Han, Director of Strategy at Singapore's Cyber Security Agency (CSA), in a contribution specially solicited for this volume. Another contribution in the radicalisation section of the book, by Prof Andrew Silke (a CENS Distinguished Visitor in 2015) has been written in collaboration with Dr Katherine Brown from the University of Birmingham.

Chapter 1

Securing the State: A Conversation with Peter Ho and Benny Lim

Security & Foresight

Shashi Jayakumar (SJ) — When 9/11 happened, where were you, and what were you doing?

Peter Ho (PH) — I was driving from Tysons Corner, going to see Jim Kelly, who was then the Assistant Secretary of East Asia and the Pacific. We were driving along the I-95 (Interstate 95), and were about to pass under a bridge. I saw this silver coloured AA75 (American Airlines No. 75, which crashed into the Pentagon). It was flying very low and I thought this was strange.

Then we went under the bridge. When we came out of the bridge, there was a big plume of black smoke. So I said, the plane must have crashed.

Peter Ho is the Senior Advisor to the Centre for Strategic Futures, a Senior Fellow in the Civil Service College, an Adjunct Professor at the S Rajaratnam School of International Studies, and a Visiting Fellow at the Lee Kuan Yew School of Public Policy;

Benny Lim is the Permanent Secretary for National Security and Intelligence Coordination and also concurrently Permanent Secretary (National Development) and Permanent Secretary (Prime Minister's Office);

Shashi Jayakumar is the Head of CENS.

I didn't know it had crashed into the Pentagon. We didn't have the slightest notion of what was going on in New York. Then we started to get phone calls repeating all sorts of other rumours: The State Department has been car-bombed, and then something's happening in New York. So we say, oh this is not very good — it sounded as if they were all connected.

We went straight to the Singapore Embassy. Of course, there was absolute chaos. People didn't know what exactly was going on. By the time we got there, only one of the Twin Towers had been hit. We saw the plane going in for the second one, and we also saw on TV the tragedy unfolding. Then we saw the first tower collapsing. I will never forget these images.

And by the way — the day before, in the evening, I had been in the part of the Pentagon that had been hit by the aircraft. So all this is fate, I suppose.

Then, at the Embassy, I got a very urgent call from a very senior official back home. First, he asked me what was going on. I told him that I only knew what I was seeing on TV. Then he said there were a lot of worries in Singapore about this, and sought my views on what we should do to tighten security. He asked me what I thought about the proposal to post guards around all the tall buildings. So I told him that was the most idiotic idea in my view. You post a guard around the tall building, and the threat was going to come from crashing aeroplanes. What was he supposed to do? Find the aircraft that's coming? Or, say, stop, stop — don't come near here? I said, if I were you, I wouldn't do it because you guys would become the laughing stock.

Benny Lim (BL) – I was watching the news on TV when I saw the footage of the planes crashing into the Twin Towers. It felt surreal. We immediately activated the stepping up of all operational security forces on the ground, and at all our entry/exit points.

I was then the Director of ISD. I remember clearly that we could not get any updates or substantive intelligence through our liaison channels. The bandwidth of our American counterparts was fully absorbed by their crisis situation at hand. Our other liaison services did not have much to share that could throw more light on the incident and the forward threat situation. I remember being recalled to attend an urgently convened Homefront Crisis Executive Group (HCEG) meeting at midnight. When I arrived, I was asked by someone what the latest intelligence was. I said, not in jest, watch CNN. Peter observes that what we knew was just about what everyone else knew from the news media. Quite so: that was our feeling here in Singapore at the time too.

Our own domestic intelligence did not surface any specific terrorist threats against us. I double-checked. No change. However, given the circumstances of the moment, we had to operate on the assumption that the threat may come completely from outside us, bypassing any early intelligence triggers or indicators we had inside the country. We needed to accept that there may be a terror wave, and it may hit us in the same form or otherwise.

In such a situation, where information was so lacking, what we had to do was to be as prepared operationally as we could to respond to any contingency. We had to step up our intelligence surveillance and collection on the ground, talk closely with our partners, especially our neighbours and brace ourselves for the worst, even as we hoped for the best.

SJ — 9/11 triggered a lot of thinking about building capabilities — not to forecast these types of events, which is impossible, but to get people looking in the right direction. Is there a link with your trip, Peter, to the U.S. in the following year, 2002, when you met up with John Poindexter. You wanted to know more about his Total Information Awareness program. So clearly, some of this thinking was going on even then.

PH — Yes, I mean it's not unconnected. You'll remember that the JI network was discovered by accident. It wasn't as if they were looking for these guys. They just happened to get the right information.

And so, I was already thinking about these issues, and wondering whether there was something we could do in terms of looking for these little anomalies in the data. I had heard about the work done by John Poindexter. I asked if I could see him, since we knew DARPA very well. He sat me down in his small office for two hours to explain his concept of total information awareness, which now when you think back, was a big data system — trawling through huge amounts of data. But at that time, the technology was not as developed as it is today. So after speaking with him, I was convinced that the technology existed. That was really the start of my thinking that it was possible to do something like RAHS. I said if we could pull these concepts together, maybe we could have something that would help us better deal with these emerging threats and weak signals. I don't think we even framed it that way. It was just an idea that, you know you've got these problems, lots of data, lots of weak signals. You have to separate the weak signals from other noises, and why not try to use computer systems to do it?

SJ — You have subsequently explained elsewhere: if this concept had been used let's say to look out for an event or crisis like SARS, before it actually hit Singapore in 2003 .... you were quite encouraged by what the results would have told you.

PH — Yes, so retrospectively we knew. But obviously it was never meant to be simply a crystal ball. It requires you, in the first place, to be aware of some of the types of things you should be looking for.

SJ — To be in the right ballpark.

PH — If you're not looking for it, you won't find it. And you might see all this stuff, but it doesn't mean anything will happen.

SJ — We have agencies that are set up specifically to look at problems that would otherwise fall through inter-agency cracks. We also have the government foresight enterprise, especially RAHS. Still, the concern is that at some point, we're going to be blindsided, and the resilience of our systems and our agencies will be called into question.

PH — You should attend my lectures. I say you cannot eliminate surprise. You will always be surprised by black swans and other strategic shocks. But through this process of foresight/futures thinking tools like RAHS, you can reduce the frequency of these shocks, so that you are shocked less often. Second, if you are shocked, the amplitude of the shock is not as great, because you were half expecting something to happen. You might not know how bad it is, but you are half prepared for it. So, it's different from when you're totally unprepared for it. This goes into a point that often comes up in my lectures — that part of it has to do with political skill of the leadership. If you don't engage in some kind of adult conversation early, there are things that could create shock and social disruption.

BL — I'd like to follow up on a point Peter is making here and this is really about mental frameworks. We need people who have minds that are always prepared to entertain the counterfactual. These are minds that are kind of half expecting something to happen even when what the event might in fact be is uncertain. Really, crisis leaders need that kind of dynamic and adaptive mental framework to operate more effectively in complex environments.

We can accept that we can't in today's complex environment avoid surprise. Surprise may be unavoidable, but you need not be resigned to react to it like a deer frozen when caught between headlights. You can do what you can to mitigate the full impact of nasty surprises upstream and downstream. Upstream, such as the kind of work we do with RAHS, and also with inter-dependency analysis; downstream, such as developing modularity in response capabilities and redundancy-buffer in resource capacities relevant to those areas you value most: human life for example. This then allows you the discretionary space needed to adjust and adapt, so as to steer and navigate through an unanticipated crisis.

SJ — But are there ways of doing more, or doing things differently to examine and mitigate surprise? I mean, in your own view, are our agencies/ministries set up in the right way? We have the intelligence agencies. We now have the Strategy Group under the Prime Minister's Office, which is meant to look at issues that might otherwise fall between the cracks. How do we make sure each agency has skin in the game?

PH — If one understands complexity, it teaches you that you will be surprised all the time. If you have one big surprise, such as the one that hit America in 2001, which convinced them to create the Department of Homeland Security, the next big surprise won't be in the area of homeland security. It will be something else. And also, you can't create a new, complex department, as budgeting and manpower constraints will limit the capabilities of the department. The only sensible option is to set up a coordinating body to oversee incidents that you think will last a long time. Essentially, thinking about national security as a cross-agency coordination function. Thinking along these lines is not exactly new, but in Singapore's context it's not exactly old either. Let's go back to something that worried us in 1997 and 1998. I'm afraid I can't reveal the exact context, but it had to do with the climate in the region. It wasn't exactly a threat, but it was certainly non-traditional, and we assessed that this would be a large security challenge for our agencies. There were all sorts of details and contingency planning, but the upshot was we discovered that we needed to have a proper national security set up. So that was actually the genesis of setting up a National Security Secretariat (NSS) in 1997. The contingency planning happened before, but the Secretariat was set up in 1999. Agencies had to cough up people for the Secretariat. But because the contingency for which it was set up did not happen, nobody took it that seriously. Nothing happened until 2001. Then we had 9/11, and then JI. That started another round of more serious thinking, because this time it was more of a real threat; it was a clear and present danger. So, that eventually led to the transformation of the NSS, which was morphed into the National Security Coordination Secretariat, with the Joint Counter-Terrorism Centre (JCTC) and the National Security Coordination Centre (NSCC) in the Prime Minister's Office. So that's the real evolution.

But anyway, back to my point. You can't of course wholly prevent strategic surprise. But there are things you can do to mitigate these surprises. I am a big believer in net assessment, where you take information from all sources. Intelligence agencies should not be over-reliant on information from sensitive sources. Just because it's sensitive, it doesn't mean you're going to read the situation correctly. Either you've been fed crap, or you're only seeing part of the picture. Net assessment is very different. You take everything together, which is why I told a close friend once because he posed me the question: why did we fail to foresee the Arab Spring? What could we have done better? I replied that there was, and is, a fundamental structural problem in intelligence agencies. They tend to rely on certain types of sources of information, in particular, privileged information. The breakout of the Arab Spring was in my view a type of spontaneous combustion that had very complex societal and economic factors at its core. Intelligence agencies are not structured to take in all of this type of information, especially the social parts. But the social parts were core to the Arab Spring. Whereas the net assessment takes in everything — what the business community, sociologists, anthropologists say or think. But that's very difficult to achieve. There are only two outfits who do it well: the U.S. Net Assessment Office in the

Department of Defense under Andy Marshall — he spotted the rise of China very, very early, and I think he focuses on the right things; and the Australian Office of National Assessments.

SJ — Could there be a case to be made that we might need something like that here, or are we too small for that?

PH — I've made this argument to our security and intelligence agencies. They should have more engagement with business leaders in the private sector, as they would be able to give accurate readings on the ground in the present environment. I also explained why I thought they should not be prisoners of the need-to-know doctrine. So, you only share secrets with people who need to know. But how do you know what they need to know until they've seen the information? On the other hand, why are you so scared of talking to some of these people on the outside who might have interesting views? I'm of the view that intelligence agencies need to rethink their roles. I actually think they need to be looking at things from a broader perspective. I'm not saying they shouldn't do what they're doing now, but in addition to that, they should be elevating their view of things to a broader level.

What I am not entirely convinced of is whether we need entirely new complex structures to analyse something to death, when the key problems are staring at you in the face. By the way, I've got a new metaphor for it — have you heard of the black elephant?

SJ — Clearly a relative of the Black Swan.

PH — It's a cross between the black swan and the elephant in the room. You see that the black elephant is in the room, but you hope that it will go away and disappear. You pretend to ignore it. Then when it really starts to trample on things, you say: "Oh my God, this is a black swan". Actually it was staring at you all the time, but you pretended it wasn't there.

SJ — If it somehow does exist, you pretend it never existed.

PH — Yeah you pretend, and that's your dearest wish; that it will disappear. The more I think about it, the more I think we are confronting a lot of these black elephants. Why do you need to analyse these things to death? It's staring at you — just go and do something about it. Assign a task force to do something about it. Don't be paralysed by the analysis. When we set up NSS, the problem we had been preparing for did not actually materialise, but that didn't stop us from going ahead and putting the structures in place.

BL — I like Peter's black elephant idea. On one level, it reminds me of what an Israeli friend once told me, when I asked him why something that was very obvious was persistently ignored until it exploded. He simply said: "Denial is not just the name of a river in Egypt. It is a common feature of human nature". Peter talks about the black elephant and the danger of something that is closely related: paralysis by analysis. This is a disability which is cultivated, so to speak. It is rooted to a culture of risk aversion, something typical in bureaucracies. We need to be aware, and to guard against this dangerous habit of discussion *ad nauseum*, capped by a chronic inability to take a decision. We cannot afford this in leadership; it is a vulnerability, a weakness that can sink us.

A Mossad chief once told me that good staff work does not naturally lead to good decisions. Good staff work avoids bad decisions, but can only bring you to the edge where leadership makes a judgement, takes a decision. In a dynamic, inter-connected complex terrain, you will never get all the facts before deciding. You take a decision on the best information available, even if elliptical, and then you adjust and take sequential decisions along the way, as you navigate and operationalise it. No single answer; no magic bullet solution. Tediously protracted analysis of the issue will not change that. In fact, it only gets worse because the problematic situation at hand mutates, morphs and grows unrecognisable, even as you dither in endless pontification.

* * *

Cyber

PH — We better start worrying now about the Internet of Things.

SJ — And start securitising it.

PH — Because the Internet of Things has absolutely no security today, we are beginning to see some of the dangers, like how these hackers are able to get into these cars and take control of them. It would be a nightmare if we could hack into a flying aeroplane.

SJ — They're starting to try.

PH — People can now hack into cars — they know how to do it. I didn't drive in today — there's something wrong with my car. The workshop said we need a computer to go in and do the fault finding. Now it's not your machinery; it's the electronics and computers that control your car. You don't know what's going on. Suppose some malicious thing is planted in your car, and instead of solving your problem, it adds other problems. I got a little certificate when I was younger, because I attended this adult education programme. I can maintain old cars, but I can't maintain new cars, because it's a black box and instead of spark plugs and you've got this electronic ignition.

SJ — But certain kinds of cars — the Tesla I believe — have superb security architecture, so it is possible to engineer them in this way.

PH — It is, but whether people are prepared to invest in keeping their cars secured is quite another thing. Most things, they don't even think about it. So we think about these so-called smart homes that everybody's trying to develop — where's the security?

SJ — Are we in danger of seriously falling behind? I mean when it comes to a holistic understanding of both risks and opportunities inherent in the Internet of Things.

PH — My own guess is we have an opportunity to move; if not first mover, then 1.5 mover. We can have 1.5 mover advantage, but it won't last for very long. Almost all governments are behind. They can barely swallow the current problem. Your computers, laptops and smartphones have some basic security provisions, but everything else has nothing. Why? Because it takes money to insert security into a refrigerator or a television control system. If for some reason the hacker decides that he's unhappy with a system or person, he gets into that person's fridge system and causes it to burn down. That might just be a problem or inconvenience. But if you do this on a large scale, you've got a different kind of problem.

We are on the cusp of change, which would have seemed unimaginable not all that long ago. We've got innovations in areas like artificial intelligence, 3D printing, predictive analytics, big data, cloud computing, the Internet of Things. All companies are organised in a particular way to take advantage of the current wave. Old technologies of 5–10 years ago are no longer relevant. That's contributing a lot to this turbulence. I think you're going to see a lot of turbulence because new ideas, new products, new concepts, are going to emerge from all of this. That's why I'm a very strong believer in looking at these new waves. If you want to position yourself to be ahead of the curve, you should also be looking at the implications of artificial intelligence, 3D printing, predictive analytics, cloud computing. Actually, this predictive analytics is very interesting. One of my people showed me an article. Hitachi says that by looking at data, it can now predict when a crime is going to be committed. You're going to see a lot more of this. One of the other interesting things that's happening already in the U.S., again in the legal area — they're using predictive analytics to calculate your chances of winning a court case. I presume there are hundreds of thousands of precedents. You give it the basic elements of your issue and it will tell you your chances of winning the case. You can then decide whether you want to spend the money to go ahead with your court case. So, a lot of these things are happening, which will have an interesting but potentially disruptive impact on legal and policy issues.

SJ — The broader question is this: in the Singapore security policy set up, are we in danger of falling behind the curve? Is there something we don't get?

PH — The mistake that people are making is that many are more interested in technologies than they are in the policy and strategic aspects of things. In the Singapore set up, I think we are in danger of making the mistake of being too focused on the technology. That doesn't cover what some people wrongly describe as the "soft aspects of policy". The real point, of course, is that when you develop the technological and industrial eco-system, it is the basic guiding policies that really underpin it. The policy should guide the technology, not vice-versa.

People don't think deeply enough about these issues. For the cybersphere, I would say that we need to decide first what we value in society. There's the security part, which is very large as you can see. Then there's the issue of privacy, which is almost opposing but also part of the same problem. People want to protect their data. All of us are defined in cyberspace. The more you use the internet, your smart phone, the more you are defined. There's a lot of information there. You talk to some of the people who are very good at data analytics, they tell you they can finger all of you. You can't hide if they are very determined to find you. So, you want to protect that. But if you over-do it, you run into this problem of data. Data in today's environment is actually a very powerful tool for governance. To plan things, you need data, and where's the data going to come from? So we have to make decisions at the policy level about what we want. We have this ambition of being a smart nation. What does it mean to be a smart nation? Being a smart nation means you have to expose some of your data. You have to keep it open and accessible, and you have to have things like your remotely driven cars — self-driving cars or autonomous vehicles, which can potentially be hijacked by hackers. So, you can't have it both ways. If you decide you want to go there, then you just have to manage the risk. But these are big policy issues. Our people should be wary of getting to the point of being paralysed because they want perfection. You can't have perfection.

National security policy has to find the balance and decide the risk that has to be managed. Remember what Emerson said: "A foolish consistency is the hobgoblin of a feeble mind". Don't go around looking for consistency. You'll never find consistency in a complex world. You have to take a very experimental approach.

See, our people start from the opposite end. Data has to be protected, and then what can we release? Then we will play it safe, and that's not necessarily a good thing. I think that's a big issue for us. I think you can't have your cake and eat it. If you want to be absolutely safe and secure, then you shut everything down. Pull up the draw bridges and then cut yourself off from the rest of the world. But you know first that's not what Singapore is. Secondly, even if you do that, it will still be penetrated.

SJ — This was what I was going to ask about. We are pushing to be a smart nation, but can we be a secure smart nation?

PH — You can to a point, but it requires a certain mentality of risk management. People don't necessarily understand risk management. If you know that no matter what you do, there will be vulnerabilities; then you have to take a risk management approach which means red-teaming and random checks. Once you know where the weak points are, you go and check those quite often. If you know the Scada system has a weak point, you go and randomly red team the Scada systems. And then you know there are obvious systemic problems which you discover along the way; so you put in the money to resolve these issues. If you don't do these kinds of studies, then you don't understand where your vulnerabilities are.

SJ — The failure to securitise Singapore's Smart Nation could lead to a huge cost down the line. So, Smart Nation — securitising it — who pays?

PH — This is a tricky issue because some organisations take it far more seriously than others. If we take the banking sector, you don't need the government to worry about it. If they are brought down, then the critical part, which is public trust and confidence, is lost. That loses them the business and they can calculate how much they can lose, so they are prepared to invest. When I was in Mindef, this was the basic approach and rule of thumb — most complex organisations will spend about 10 percent of their capital and operational budget on IT-cybersystems. I'm not sure if 10 percent is actually enough. But actually you should be spending more. My own guess is it's closer to 30 percent now, given the kind of threats they are facing. It's not just the systems protection. It's the operational part, which are the checks, the red-teaming, getting penetrations and so on. So the cost is actually quite a lot.

But there are ways to be more effective in this game. One of the things you have to think very carefully about when you design systems is whether you want to deliberately build into your system some diversity. Because if one part goes down, at least you have other parts which are up and running. So must everything be based on Microsoft Windows? Or you want to have Linux, and also Apple. Why not some type of a mixture? If everyone uses the same bundle, there's one single point of failure. Why are Microsoft systems hacked so much more than Apple ones?

SJ — Because it wasn't worth attacking them?

PH — Because it's not worth attacking them! Microsoft has the market share, and if you're a hacker, you go after them. So, if you are looking at it from a national point of view, too much central control itself is bad. You must have some diversity, so there's not a single point of failure.

I must tell you a real story, about diversity and inter-operability, and there's an object lesson here. Years ago, when I was younger and more naïve — and this was the time when I was helping the government out, not just on cybersecurity, but on e-commerce and various things — I was asked to try to get the restructured hospitals to share data. It was a long time ago. They were very unwilling to do it. And what was the basic argument? It was about having different operating systems which are incompatible. They also cited an issue of data privacy concerns. But basically, what was happening was that hospitals just didn't want other hospitals to know what they were doing. The second part of the story is this. After having listened to all these stories which they were telling me and swallowing it hook, line and sinker, 2003 happened. 2003 was the SARS crisis. If you remember, during the SARS crisis, it suddenly became critical that we would have the ability to share data for things like contact tracing. And then, obviously you'll have to, in very quick time, connect all the hospitals electronically. It's true that we started off with different operating systems. So I brought in the people from Mindef. Within two weeks, they solved the problem. The system was up and running, and the hospitals were exchanging data.

So what was going on was that the Mindef people didn't even begin to try changing the operating systems. They just super-imposed on that some kind of over-arching system that can suck up the data in a particular type of format, reorganise it, process it and then pump it up and redistribute the information. So it's possible. Now I know it's a red herring when people say that different operating systems cannot be done, and that common standards are needed. You can't manage. There are too many different things out there, and sometimes you buy certain systems to meet certain specific requirements, which others are not interested in. So don't be like me in the 90s .... getting side-tracked into believing all these stories.

* * * *

Radicalisation, Vulberability, Resilience

SJ — Singapore's rehabilitation and counter-ideology strategies — these have been generally effective so far. The question is where do we go from here?

BL — Well, my view is that the rehabilitation of individuals indoctrinated, or self-radicalised by extremist ideologies to support or carry out terrorist violence, is really not an option. It's necessary because the alternative is to lock up the person indefinitely in order to prevent him from posing a violent threat to society.

So long as the individual believes he is religiously bound to support or undertake acts of terrorist violence against others, and has shown a proclivity to act on it, he remains a security threat. Engagement through rehabilitation gives us a chance to change that.

Religious rehabilitation is necessary because given the religious cloak donned by extremist ideologies, you need engagement bearing a religious dimension. If a chap takes a sacred oath or *bai'ah*, he often feels locked to observe it no matter what, and perhaps a religious key to unlock it is the way to go. So for reasons of competency and legitimacy in this regard, such engagement must involve participation of a religious authority. Hence, the vital role of the azatizahs and their Religious Rehabilitation Programme.

I feel that religious rehabilitation is a crucial part of our overall effort to engage and rehabilitate the individual. But that's not all. It can't be all. Rehabilitation needs to go beyond religious counselling, and must involve addressing other aspects of the individual's psyche or personal situation that makes him vulnerable or at risk. A rehabilitation program for any of these radicalised individuals therefore need to be composed in terms of the whole and unique person.

SJ — Have we been effective?

BL — Yes. It is true, however, that we have had detainees who have returned to their old ways. They have been re-arrested and re-detained. On the other hand, such cases of recidivism are the exception rather than the norm. This suggests we haven't done too badly.

My own take is that the war against jihadist terrorism, and its potent ideological allure, is far from over. We must continue to persevere, in order to counter the distortions of Islam, which such elements purvey to support their agenda, and to do so in cogent ways. But so long as this threat continues — morphing and evolving but persisting — we must assume that vulnerable individuals who had succumbed to it before, may very well relapse.

SJ — This is a little gloomy as a prognosis. A really difficult task — to rehabilitate, to persevere with those who have been through rehabilitation as well as to engage with those at risk of recidivism?

BL — I think this is fairly common in the rehabilitation process of at-risk individuals and it applies beyond the domain of terrorist extremists. I would not necessarily therefore be so pessimistic even if it means accepting that there can be no permanent guarantees against backsliding and recidivism. Hence, I am convinced of the critical need for post-release engagement programmes for such individuals, to ensure that they are assisted to re-integrate into the community and mainstream society. We need to ensure that they do not falter for whatever reason; and if they show signs of such, that this is detected early enough for proactive intervention. This would be a necessary on-going part of any comprehensive strategy for counter-radicalisation.

al-Qaeda was a resilient and persistent threat, precisely because of its ideological appeal across borders. But I think the appeal of ISIS is even more potent than AQ. It goes beyond a narrative of defending the ummah against infidel oppression so as to create a caliphate. Instead, it is about joining the caliphate that has already arrived in ISIS-held territory, and take part in fulfilling the end of times prophecy that it heralds. The imagery and iconography of this narrative has great potency, and cannot be underestimated.

I think that what we are seeing in Singapore and elsewhere, about self-radicalised individuals, reflects a problem that never went away; and which in fact, has evolved and morphed into something potentially even more potent.

SJ — To what extent is Singapore ready and prepared for a crisis like a terrorist attack?

BL — I remember how the salience of preventive security changed overnight between pre-9/11 and post-9/11. In the months that followed 9/11, a flurry of security policies and measures rushed through for many organisations. We were playing catch-up for the long years of peace enjoyed wherein preventive security advice had frequently taken a backseat to overriding concerns of organisational costs and efficiency. People who didn't care to talk to ISD's protective security unit were suddenly calling up to ask them to do security audits of their outfits in double-quick time. So in this area, we have done reasonably well over the last 10–15 years.

I tend to think that now it is not so much a matter of what new additional things our agencies can do in Singapore, but perhaps more about prioritising, reviewing, energising and enhancing, where appropriate, what we have been or are doing. We can do this with for instance border security, with reviewing our operational responses to specific scenarios like *fedayeen* attacks, with revitalising our community engagement programmes for vigilance and social resilience. We need to constantly test our response capabilities against the prevailing threat forms.

All this fundamentally has to do with the level of system preparedness, which is generally high in Singapore. The picture seems to be one of strong resilience at the organisational and system level. This has translated into high public support for and confidence in the Government's ability to handle a crisis. Trust in our institutions like the SAF, Police and SCDF is very high.

SJ — It's difficult to disagree with what you say. But what about after the event, so to speak. If one looks at the discourse that the leadership has been using on Singaporeans in the last couple of years, there's a notable shift. They're basically saying: look, something's going to happen; get ready for it. Surely the real issue, besides the event itself, is the bouncing back of society after an event.

BL — You are right. All that I've just talked about relates to how well the public regard the Government agencies and their readiness to anticipate and respond effectively to the threat. But paradoxically, this high confidence in Government has also given rise to a high dependency on the Government, and a lack of preparedness on the part of the public. This means a weaker resilience at the people level. The level of individual preparedness is relatively low.

PH — The question I have in my mind concerns what happened in Europe, particularly in France, last year, which must have been a very challenging year for them. First, the Charlie Hebdo incident, and then these terrible mass attacks in Paris. What for me has been very interesting, apart from feeling that these were really unconscionable acts of violence, was how the system bounced back from all of this. Of course, people feel angry and upset, and the casualty levels — particularly in the Paris attacks, but even Madrid in 2004 — were actually very high. But very quickly, all of them go back to business as usual. I think not business as usual for the security forces, because they have to be much more alert. But the people as a whole kind of said, okay, this is part of life, and we just have to carry on, we're not going to be held hostage. Now, the question is — never mind about what the politicians say — what will our society's reaction be to this?

BL — I think that while individual resilience certainly matters, what we hope to achieve over time through our public communications and engagement programmes like the "Let's Stand Together" campaign or the Community Engagement Programme, is a societal resilience that is greater than the sum of the resilience of its individuals. Whether this is done through building networks of trust across communities, or raising levels of preparedness for emergencies across sectors and demographics — we have persevered at this goal for some years now. And I think we've done reasonably well. Will we be able to stand the test if and when it comes? I suppose no one knows for sure until it happens.

PH — Could I pick up on something Benny said — the point about resilience. This is absolutely critical. Paris had *Je Suis Charlie*, and the British after the 7/7 attacks were able to quickly show a return to normal — a sort of sangfroid — in a way proving that they can't be cowed. This is not the government telling them to do things. So the question is for me, of course government must say that we have certain vulnerabilities, and that the population needs to stand together and all that, but I think we shouldn't over-do that part.

BL — Agree; short of cranking up the threat level all the time, which of course risks making it a bogey or making everyone a bundle of neurotic anxieties, we need to accept that pushing the vulnerability narrative for security has limits beyond which the outcomes can be dysfunctional. To me, shifting the narrative to resilience is much more interesting and fruitful than simply dwelling on vulnerability.

PH — Yes. So that's why I think a new framework should centre on something like resilience, rather than vulnerabilities. It's not so easy to argue about Singapore's vulnerability when you look at the recent successes of Singapore through the young generation, which has grown up in affluence essentially. Vulnerability means nothing to them as a concept, because they have not lived through that period of vulnerability, unlike my generation. So that's why — in a way — we should move away from vulnerability to discussions where resilience is central. Resilience is a concept which everybody can understand: it takes you away to something which I think you can make a better intellectual case.

Part of the dilemma I think we are facing right now, is something couched in almost existential terms. If Singapore gets hit by a terrorist attack, will society crumble or will it cohere and so on. Then of course people have in their minds that this is an existential challenge, and therefore their responses are existential. Whereas many other countries say we'll just get on with business and of course find the people who did this. So they don't frame it in the same terms as we do.

If one wanted really to push the argument: to benchmark the performance of society according to how they react immediately after an attack may be setting ourselves up for failure. In Singapore's case, are we framing things too sharply? Maybe it might be better to emphasise a few important issues and then trust that the system will have its own self-correcting capacity. To frame the issue in the expectation that the kind of worst case scenario may eventuate, and saying therefore we have to start making all these dire warnings beforehand, may be a bit too much. Maybe some of the reactions have to happen spontaneously.

SJ — Yes. In the aftermath of the recent Jakarta attacks, the Indonesian government doesn't even come close to telling people what to think. But still, after the Jakarta attacks, you've got this *Kami Tidak Takut* campaign.

Not all of this should be coming from the government, surely. Nor indeed seen to be coming from the government.

BL —Take the British again. They have the attitudinal attributes — the ability to hold together and maintain a kind of normalcy in times of crisis. The British public faced challenges like the Blitz in the Second World War and stood up to it; that generation had a history of facing challenges with a certain degree of what I suppose the British call a stiff upper lip. We don't have this history; don't forget we are a young country. One could argue that in Singapore our public have become too accustomed to the "supernormal", viz. lowest crime rate, no natural disasters, etc. So the issue and the challenge for our thinkers and policymakers is how to cultivate this type of toughness and resilience, ideally ground up, even in "supernormal" conditions.

SJ — Just to pick up on that. One of CENS' friends, Sir David Omand, has said on a number of occasions that the goal of national security strategies will increasingly be seen by governments as simply to maintain the conditions of normality; in providing confidence to the public, and the idea that major hazards and risks are being managed so that everyday life can continue. This is interesting in that it frames national security just as much as a psychological construct as a physical one. Do you think that this will become the prime business of government, given the current situation of the world in which we live in?

PH — I agree with Benny that the cultural context is very important.

But really, if you think about the larger equation, the business of both government and increasingly, people, should be about thinking through the big strategic approaches, as the very concept of national security is evolving. Is national security today still about the concept of hard national security, i.e. defence, or is there an increasing focus on the softer aspects such as psychological or social defence? Thanks to Total Defence there is public buy-in of the idea that dealing with security is a national effort, and not just the Government's problem. To me, national security is about thinking and conceptualising ideas, and perhaps we do not spend enough time thinking about such issues.

SJ — Agencies have their own drawer plans to deal with crises. What more do we need? What more should we be thinking about?

PH — We don't look enough at non-traditional types of situations, which are actually in a sense more likely to happen. One dimension will be resilience against things like climate change — there could be climate change refugees. I mean, this is not going to happen straight away. But what happens 50 years down the road, when the South Pacific Islands start to disappear, or Bangladesh starts to go under water? They might look towards Malaysia, Myanmar and Singapore, and then there's a national security dimension. Looking back, many of Singapore's national security challenges are quite varied. Besides the JI threat, we had the Asian Financial Crisis and SARS. And also, we should not be trapped into viewing national security through the lens of recent events or threats. The assumption that future challenges will be caused by terrorism is naïve. Future problems could be caused by climate change, for all we know. The government can commission RSIS and CENS to do research studies in these areas, and to help the government think strategically on these issues.

BL — I agree with Peter. In fact we should take this further. We should crowd-source for ideas and insights from all quarters on how to do this better than how we have done so far. It's clear that we can benefit from not only a more active, but a better informed public, who understand the security challenges we face as a small country and a young multi-ethnic nation. Such mutual engagement between Government and the people is an investment to grow the crucial capital we would need to tap — to be able to stay measured, balanced, afloat and intact as a people — in the face of any painful or turbulent time.

SJ — Thank you very much, Peter and Benny.

* * *

Chapter 2

Thinking about National Security

Sir David Omand

One of Sir Winston Churchill's more memorable sayings was that the further back you look, the further ahead you can see. Even if our historical perspective is foreshortened by the traumatic nature of the terrorist attacks on 9/11 we can still derive useful pointers for future national security from the experience of the last 15 years. What has that period taught us, or perhaps more accurately, what lessons could and should we have learnt by now?

Abstracting from the detail of everyday events, important as they are, I would select four linked themes for closer examination. The first theme is the importance of thinking strategically about international affairs, and a reminder of just how hard that is. The second related theme is the search for ways of strengthening the resilience of society and the critical national infrastructure upon which normal life depends. The third theme is the impact that the development of new technologies, especially the internet and the World Wide Web that it carries, is having on our security, and particularly the way that digital intelligence is guiding security activity. This leads me to conclude with a final theme, which reminds us that motivations for conflict are nevertheless deeply rooted in the constants of human nature.

Professor Sir David Omand is former director of the United Kingdom's Government Communication Headquarters (GCHQ) and currently serves as a commissioner for the Global Commission on Internet Governance.

Thinking Strategically about National Security

Traditional threats to national security from potentially hostile states have for some nations remained the most pressing national security preoccupation throughout the last 15 years, and remain the underlying justification for defensive alliances, such as NATO, and for the continuation of deterrence strategies on the part of the nuclear powers. Most advanced countries have, nevertheless, used their experience so far of the early 21st century to rethink their approach to national security strategy in the light of changing perceptions of wider threats. The common theme in the development of the 'protecting state' has been the move beyond strategy designed to protect the territorial integrity and institutions of the State, to strategy that has the direct security and safety of the public as its citizen-centric purpose.

Notable in that regard has been the way that many countries have now recognised the importance of security planning against impersonal hazards, such as extreme weather events and communicable disease, which are seen as a comparable risk to public security and safety as malign threats, especially when the long-term effects of climate change are taken into account. That train of thinking has been influential in the priority many nations have given to strengthening crisis management capabilities during the last decade, both nationally and in cooperation with other states, and to investing to gain the advantages of building greater national resilience to disruptive events.

Another strategic feature has been the rise in priority given to so-called "non-state actors", such as the members of proliferation networks and terrorist groups, and global criminal gangs capable of corrupting weak governments in many parts of the world. The concept of countries at risk of instability or collapse, and thus potentially able to provide safe havens for international terrorists groups, has also entered our strategic lexicon.

Finally, in the last few years cyber threats have emerged as a whole new category of risk, which represent a priority in national security strategies. The risks from malign actors exploiting cyberspace is now close to the top of most nations' risk register. The rapid rise in cyber crime, both by using new techniques of malware and simply the ability on the internet to conduct traditional crime at scale, is outpacing law enforcement's capability to bring those responsible to justice, leaving little alternative but to try to disrupt the criminal activity itself. Digital espionage and massive intellectual property theft have become routine. Most recently, attempts to penetrate and sabotage critical national infrastructure and to corrupt key data sets have become a major concern. Subversion, including the use of social media to spread violent extremism and hostile ideology, is testing the boundaries of free speech and legal concepts of extra-territoriality.

Advancement of specific national interests is of course the constant motivating factor in all security strategies, but a lesson drawn by many nations during the period since 9/11 has been a perceived need to 'work upstream' by applying the logic of preventive intervention to manage the risks to national security, such as the proliferation of weapons of mass destruction.

U.S. national security strategy immediately after 9/11 opened with the words "America is at war", which ushered in the military intervention in Afghanistan to overthrow the Taliban and launched the global war on terrorism. That strategic framing of the risk from al-Qaeda and its brand of violent jihadism led logically to the adoption of military, intelligence and security measures that otherwise would have been deemed inappropriate for peacetime conditions. U.S. intelligence gathering included large scale collection of digital data on domestic communications, coercive interrogation of captured al-Qaeda suspects and their long-term detention without legal process. Although some of these programs were subsequently stopped or scaled back by President Obama, the underlying legal rationale for operating against AQ (and now ISIL and its affiliated or related groups) under the law of armed conflict has continued to legitimise both military and civilian drone strike programmes against the extremists in Africa, the Middle East and South Asia. That there have been tactical successes is undeniable, but the long-term strategic impact of these methods, and the collateral damage caused, has been much less clear, as we now see with the rise of groups such as ISIL and the way that Iran and Russia have taken advantage of the situation to advance their own interests. Looking back on the period with the benefit of hindsight, the U.S. and UK intervention in Iraq that overthrew Saddam Hussein and the subsequent NATO campaigns in Afghanistan do not appear to demonstrate the strategic logic that was claimed at the time. The unfolding of events in the Syrian civil war with the rise of the so-called Islamic State and the failure to counter the use of chemical weapons by the Assad regime have further reinforced the importance of sound strategic thinking, and avoiding taking positions that nations are unable to carry through to a conclusion. On the other hand, the agreement with Iran on nuclear enrichment and capabilities is a good example of the U.S. and the EU working together, taking the long view of their common strategic interests.

The European Union took a different approach to advancing strategic interest after 9/11 that was based on that taken by the United Kingdom in its own counterterrorism strategy. The measures adopted to deal with jihadist terrorism were from the outset about risk management rather than risk elimination. The focus was reducing the threat of international terrorism to deny the terrorists that which they most sought, namely the disruption of normality through putting the public in fear as well as tempting the authorities to overreact to terrorist outrages. By following such a strategy European nations have been able largely to uphold respect for human rights, but probably at the expense of suffering more attempted terrorist attacks in the short to medium term, and living with the moral ambiguity of Europe benefiting from U.S. measures against terrorism that most Europeans themselves had foresworn.

Strengthening National Resilience

Most national security strategies now identify categories of major risk to guide security planners that include, on the one hand, those arising through malign human agencies such as terrorism or cyber sabotage and on the other hand from accidents or purely natural processes such as earthquakes and tornadoes (the former category of risk can usefully be termed threats; and the latter, hazards). In both cases planning can minimise impact and the duration of disruption, regardless of cause. The lights may go out through terrorist attack, cyber attack, industrial accident, human error or adverse weather, but the strategic imperative is to get the power back on as quickly as possible. Of course understanding causes also matters: the hazards are not consciously trying to deceive and outwit the authorities, and there is no malign agency behind them trying to analyse repsonses and learn more effective ways of threatening the public. The role of the Armed Forces in training and preparing to support the civil power in crisis has been sharpened by hard experience, for example protecting the people of New Orleans after Hurricane Katrina in 2005 and preventing the Ebola epidemic in West Africa from spreading out of control in 2014.

Much experience has been gained over the period in planning resilience, or improving the ability of a nation to withstand shocks and readjust quickly to ensure society maintains function. Many nations have been tested in two very different ways: by "sudden impact" and "rising tide" scenarios respectively. With the former, such as the huge loss of life from the 2004 Indian Ocean earthquake and tsunami or the ash cloud from the Icelandic volcanic eruption in 2010, external events burst upon governments and compell immediate responses. With rising tide situations, such as the resurgence of jihadist violence before 9/11 or the development of correlated financial risk in the derivatives markets before 2008, only over time did it become apparent that the situation was beyond normal control and emergency measures were needed. The financial crash in 2008 is also testimony to the enduring lesson of identifying the lower probability but higher impact scenarios against which some planning would be wise, in addition to taking comfort from the estimate of the most likely outcome. The key, of course, to managing such situations is to have sufficiently *early detection* of the rising trouble so the response can be organised in good time. That is different from having *early warning* of the likelihood of trouble in the first place, which might allow research into counter measures before the problem emerges.

In terms of major risks, the increasingly evident lesson in modern society is that it will be too late to wait until the adversary — terrorist or tornado — is at the gate or inside the city before taking action to prevent, protect against and prepare for the consequences of threats by building resilience. Increasingly, national security strategies are identifying the consequences of major cyber attacks and natural hazards, such as the effects of 'space weather' resulting from coronal ejections from the sun, or animal diseases jumping the species barrier, or those that are likely to flow from resource stress as the global climate changes. Such hazards also demand that governments anticipate and act now — preferably in international concert — to mitigate future consequences. Anticipation involves examining possible futures and having the imagination now to envision how circumstances might look in the future. By acting now — the act of realisation — we better take advantage of those insights. Let me illustrate with another quotation from Winston Churchill in 1935 as the threat from fascism grew:

> Want of foresight, unwillingness to act when action would be simple and effective, lack of clear thinking, confusion of counsel until the emergency comes, until self-preservation strikes its jarring gong — these are the features which constitute the endless repetition of history.

Much has been written in the last 15 years on identifying the reasons for predictive failure. Good estimates of what might happen next can be said to rely on the succesful completion of four scientific intelligence processes. First, horizon scanning to provide strategic notice of possible developments, answering questions of the 'whatever next' kind, prompting in turn scientific and social research to deepen knowledge of the possible developments and to task intelligence activity — broadly defined — to look for signs of the emergence of the risk or opportunity. Next, situational awareness of what has actually been going on, anchored in careful observation and reporting, and able to provide answers to 'what, who, where, and when' questions. Then, careful explanation of the observed situation responding to 'why and what for' questions. Armed with sound explanations that best fit the reported observations the analyst can hazard an estimate of what might happen next, and respond to the pressing 'what next, and where next' questions' posed by policy makers or security authorities.

Even where the likelihood of a risk emerging cannot be directly influenced, it will help in determining the likelihood and planning against the eventuality. The published 2015 UK Government national risk assessment, for example, distinguishes between those types of event — such as different types of terrorist attacks — whose likelihood in the next five years can be set against impact on a scale of plausibility ranging from low, medium low and so on up to high likelihood; and those events such as natural calamities and transport accidents where past evidence makes it meaningful to express the likelihood of occurrence over the next five years in probability bands. For example, of '1 in 20,000 to 1 in 2000,' then '1 in 2000 to 1 in 20' and so on up to 'greater than 1 in 2'. This approach helpfully encourages thinking about the chances of surviving the next decade *without* such an incident. Strictly, the probability that an extreme space weather event like the geomagnetic storm of March 1989 will occur tomorrow is very small; the probability it will happen on one day in the next five years becomes concerning, and over, say, the next 30 years — a plausible planning horizon for major physical infrastructure — becomes something serious to heed in planning.

The Demand and Supply of Digital Intelligence

In previous eras, personal security, in the sense of absence of fear in one's home or workplace or when travelling, might have been seen as primarily a matter for local police services. Over the last decade experience has shown how the personal security of the public has become a national policy issue because of the international ramifications. Jihadist terrorism, and the spread through the internet of the ideology of jihadist violence, does not respect borders. Reporting of events overseas on the internet such as the war in Syria can very quickly provoke domestic violence in the communities concerned and vice versa, such as the several riots in Muslim countries provoked by the 2005 publication of cartoons in a Danish newspaper held to be offensive. Internet crime by nature does not respect borders. The growth of international criminal gangs trafficking in narcotics, in people, in pornography and false identities knows no frontiers.

Insistent demands have therefore arisen over the period for more intelligence on the dictators, proliferators, terrorists, insurgents, hackers, pirates, cyber and narco criminal gangs, people traffickers and all other enemies of an open society. The demands are for timely actionable intelligence about their identities, associations, locations, movements, finances and intentions. In short, intelligence is about people as much as it is about state organisations or orders of battle of armed forces or their equipment capabilities.

By an historical coincidence, this increase in demand for information about people has coincided with rapid developments in digital communications and data storage, as well as growth in use of mobile devices (and now the Internet of Things) that enables digital information about people to be accessible. Whether Islamic State terrorists, Russian paramilitaries in eastern Ukraine, Somali pirates, Colombian and Mexican drug lords or Libyan people smugglers everyone uses the same mobile digital devices, operating over the same packet-switched high-speed networks that comprise the internet and carry the World Wide Web. These same internet-based developments also offer added potential for those who wish to hide their communications from the authorities, with an ever-increasing volume of traffic and choice of platforms and apps. End-to-end encryption and the growth in use of anonymising software is spreading, accelerated by the revelations from the material stolen by the contractor Edward Snowden from the U.S. National Security Agency and its international partners.

We are now in the digital age, and all nations are having to adapt to this coincidence in changes in the demand for intelligence on individuals, and in the potential capability of digital technology to supply it. The interaction is dynamic: new demands encourage ever more imaginative means of supply; new commercial developments in the monetisation of personal information for marketing purposes have prompted new intelligence demands that previously would not have been feasible.

A feature of the period, therefore, has been continuing international debate about the extent to which the exploitation of digital information should be constrained by law and ethical considerations of privacy and freedom of speech. The covert intelligence activities of nations such as Russia and China have not been exposed in the same way as those of the U.S. and its close allies, although it must be assumed they are every bit as intrusive in global reach. The challenge for the democracies is to achieve the intelligence mission in order to keep the public safe and secure whilst continuing to exercise full respect for privacy and other internationally accepted human rights. Public support will be needed for digital intelligence to be seen for what it is, an essential tool of national security strategy, but governed by a strategy of lawful purpose, proportionality and necessity.

Over the last five years, in particular, national security concerns have grown and there are fears that instances of cybercrime, cyber espionage, cyber sabotage and cyber subversion could increase to levels where confidence in the internet itself is damaged, and the web is no longer trusted as a safe medium for personal data or financial and commercial transactions. Most national security strategies now place cyber security high on the list of priorities, and are seeking some form of digital intelligence gathering in order to detect malware, classify it and attribute attacks to the groups or states responsible.

It is too early to know how internet connectivity between almost all of the world's population and the forecast interconnections between some 50 billion objects in the coming Internet of Things will affect global security over the next decade. That there will be an effect on the way conflict is expressed seems undeniable. The first signs of this are already apparent in the examples of asymmetric warfare seen over the last decade, with the use of advanced sensors and weapons such as remotely piloted air systems, and with hostile cyber activity by states, and the prospect of increasingly sophisatiated artificial intelligence applications. The threats to us can be expressed through State proxies or directly from potentially hostile States themselves, and can involve plausibly deniable activities of sabotage and subversion, all designed to promote national interests without triggering the traditional threshold for armed attack. We are seeing the first beginnings of such activity by Russia in the Ukraine. And the first signalling by the United States in relation to cyber attacks that the response to sabotage attempts on the critical national infrastructure might not be confined to the cyber realm.

The Future Motivations for Conflict

We cannot be sure how these trends will develop. There is, however, one constant about future threats, and that is the human nature behind them. In conclusion, we can consider categorising the spectrum of future threats based on some fundamental human motivations.

First, we must expect conflict arising from **religion, culture and identity**.

We will see continuing *struggles over religious identity and religious conviction*: examples include Sunni and Shia, Muslim and Copt in Egypt, Christian and Muslim in Northern Nigeria, Hutu and Tutsi in Rwanda and of course Muslim, Sikh and Hindu in the sub-continent.

Under this heading might also be placed *struggles over political ideology*, such as the Naxalites in northern India and Nepal. And there may be other ideological causes later in this century driving global movements, for example against capitalism and inequality, to protect the environment, or to oppose climate engineering should it ever be seriously proposed.

Struggles over cultural or tribal identity have been a feature of the last 15 years and have affected much of the Mahgreb and Mali, Tibet, the Punjab, Sri Lanka, the Basque Country, Catalonia, Corsica, Northern Ireland, some of which at least may continue to lead to outbreaks of civil disorder, and in the worst cases possibly even terrorism.

There will also be conflict arising from motivations concerning *power, hegemony, control of resources and indeed basic survival*. The experience of the last 15 years is that we should expect traditional nuclear deterrence relationships to hold. But conflict through proxies and asymmetric wars must be expected to be below the threshold for all-out war, as seen today with Hezbollah. Longstanding *struggles over control of disputed territory* must be expected to continue: examples might include Taiwan, the Senkaku Islands, Kosovo, Palestine, Gibraltar, Ceuta and Melilla, the Falkland Islands and Kashmir. *Struggles over the exploitation of natural resources* will continue with expectations of future sea-bed and mineral exploitation (such as over the Spratly Islands and the East China Sea, and the Eastern Aegean and the Arctic and the Antarctic) accentuating many disputes. Struggles for regional hegemony will continue, such as those between Saudi Arabia and Iran, and on the Korean peninsula. In this category of motivations, might be added later 21st century struggles for survival from climate change, as drought spreads and rising sea levels affect major delta regions.

Finally, there will be *conflicts over criminal gains* by organised groups corrupting state authority (examples from the last 15 years can be found in Mexico, Jamaica, Colombia, Honduras, Somalia, Guinea-Bissau and Nigeria) and with maritime piracy persisting in some areas.

The causes of conflict later in the 21st century are thus unlikely to be very different from those of previous centuries since they are rooted in the human condition; but of course the *way* these conflicts are expressed will be different, not least because of the exploitation of cyberspace. But which of these 21st century struggles become serious armed conflicts, erupting into violence by open warfare, insurgency, terrorism or just armed gangsterism, is as hard to predict today as it was in the past.

Conclusion

The goal of national security strategy is increasingly seen as the maintenance of conditions of normality, providing confidence to the public that the many major risks — threats and hazards — can be managed so normal everyday life can continue, against a backdrop of market stability, trade, innovation and the flourising of industries incuding tourism. To say that is to frame national security as a psychological construct as much as a physical one. The public must have confidence in the ability of the authorities to manage the risks. Potential adversaries must have belief that we will defend our values and our interests, based on evident security strengths and the ability to deter an adversary by denying quick or easy gains. Allies and partners must have confidence that we will stand by them when need arises, so what is said by governments and what is done by governments must match. Strategies must be backed by resources and capabilities and the public must have the evidence to merit confidence that they are part of a society that will be resilient to the shocks and surprises that the future will bring. Such thinking does not rest on an ability to predict the future or rest on an assumption that the world will become more predictable. Nations may indeed have to get used to the opposite idea, and invest in the preparations necessary to make a success of a world full of surprises that brings as many opportunities as threats and hazards.

Chapter 3

Strategic Intelligence Challenges in the 21st Century

Ilan Mizrahi

The post-9/11 world has resulted in new and complex challenges for the Intelligence sector. Global threats and the function of Intelligence were relatively clear throughout the Cold War. There were two rival superpowers, familiar local leaders were the decision makers, enemies were conspicuous and existential threats to national security, both political and military (including nuclear), were largely transparent. Even terrorism was 'simpler' as it was predominantly local and organisations employing the tactic were well known, as were the countries supporting them. Intelligence stood on three pillars: (1) The contemporary situation and forthcoming trends; (2) technology and (3) human nature. The first two were constantly in flux, while the third, major, pillar generally did not alter. Intelligence agencies were expected *vis-à-vis* such threats to expose secrets relating to type and quantity of weapons, military and operational formations and the intentions of adversaries.

The Intelligence cycle was categorical: an initial PIR (Priority Intelligence Request) was followed by targeting, collection, analysis and

---

Ilan Mizrahi is a former Head of Israel's National Security Council and former deputy head of Mossad.

then finally dissemination. The focus was on armies and terrorist organisations and not civilian populations, therefore public opinion in democratic societies was less influential on strategic decision making and Intelligence issues than it is today. As secrecy among agencies was paramount and compartmentalisation essential, dissemination and data sharing were limited, as were the number of intelligence clients (senior government officials, intelligence agencies and the military).

The world in 2015 is different. The lack of a definitive world order has resulted in a range of multi-polar players. A new cold war is emerging between central competitors using instruments of soft power, which pose unfamiliar challenges to intelligence agencies. Global and local issues are inter-connected; and the velocity of events has increased dramatically to an incredible pace. Today the world is facing a broad range of threats, from nuclear proliferation and weapons of mass destruction (WMD), to sophisticated, agile and highly motivated terrorists; as well as climate change, financial crises, popular uprisings (such as the Arab Spring), ethnic and religious conflict, the disintegration of states, and the flows of illegal immigrants which follow. As a result there is greater uncertainty and complexity which often lead to strategic surprises.

Public opinion has become more vocal and demanding through media and online social networks, and has materialised in large-scale demonstrations, such as the Arab Spring uprisings. New outlets and platforms for deliberation have facilitated greater public demand for participation in decision making, as well as additional oversight on intelligence and security agencies, which have already largely lost the public's trust. The pressure on intelligence agencies from both decision makers and the wider public to answer the question, 'what will happen?' is increasingly pressing, and inaccurate predictions based on failed intelligence or mistakes in analysis have at times had detrimental effects on credibility. Reactions to the claims made by Edward Snowden have applied further pressure. New Intelligence sector paradigms will need to be adopted in order to attempt answers to the challenges and contemporary threats.

The first quandary is whether to change the definition of National Security in light of growing internal threats, such as terrorism and in some countries, illegal immigration. Enemies are not easily identified in the current context. How for example should hostile civil society groups be managed? What type of protest act by which kind of actor can detonate a civil society movement into one of destructive violence?

This is the critical dilemma for decision makers: to define clearly strategic targets and priorities (weighing in budgets for security at the expense of other issues) especially in the Western World when it concerns domestic issues. Consider for example ISIS. When ISIS is the target, what will be the endgame? And if defeated militarily what might be the outcome?

When strategic targets are not defined clearly, it is challenging for intelligence agencies and armies to 'translate' general and ambiguous definitions to actions, particularly when changes take place rapidly, and in arenas where friend and foe are not easily distinguishable. It is essential today, more than in the past, to define national intelligence targeting policy: this means defining clear PIR, priorities, resource allocation and the coordination of national abilities and capabilities.

Technology

Advances in technology have been a game changer. While facilitating the work of intelligence agencies, potentially destructive cyber tools have also ended up in the hands of those who wish to do harm. Individuals and terrorist cells with leading-edge technological accessibility are players with pernicious power, and they are difficult to identify, deter and retaliate against. Maximum precision is needed to fight terrorism and asymmetric war, and robotics and miniaturisation will bring benefits, but again, the increasing availability of cutting-edge technologies on the open market mean that enemies may also be equipped with sophisticated devices, which will create challenges for internal security agencies fighting terrorism.

Information overload is a constant challenge and more effective data mining systems are required to assist analysts in turning data into actionable intelligence. Another key issue is the development of technologies that expose biological, chemical and nuclear signatures.

Still, it is important not to rely too heavily on technology at the expense of Humint (Human Intelligence), which is dependent on human nature and human mental ability. It is Humint that will be able to bring the vital information in fighting terrorism and asymmetric warfare.

Intelligence Collection

As mentioned above, targeting difficulties in a changing world order is the first challenge of Collection. Public opinion and decision makers demand prevention *vis-à-vis* threats of terrorism and non-conventional weapons as well as illegal migration and regional stability, which affect the potential and actual threats from foreign countries.

The information revolution supplies Intelligence with extraordinary collection capabilities but at the same time makes it harder to sort the 'chaff from the wheat', which also creates difficulties for identifying trends and targets. Osint (Open Source Intelligence) is a major source of information, yet to uncover mysteries (as opposed to secrets) covert activity is still required. However, Humint is still the central discipline as terrorist and non-conventional organisations and states operate underground.

But who is the enemy in a changing world of disintegrating nation states and changing alliances? Identifying collection targets to be covered is vital as establishing intelligence infrastructures can take years to be effective. The question thus arises as to which intelligence discipline collection efforts should focus on.

When trying to challenge domestic terrorism, and to ensure more generally the stability of the state, intelligence agencies need to cooperate and coordinate with several civilian authorities and the police. 'Community intelligence' is vital but how will intelligence agencies within the country get over their traditional reluctance to cooperate and share information?

Social media is important because of the way it seeds ideas and affects emotions and opinions. But given the scale of data that current media platforms produce and the specialised technical abilities required to collect and sort through relevant information, it will increasingly prove expedient for intelligence agencies to collaborate with the private sector and academia in order to ensure these valuable resources are effectively tapped.

The private sector is deeply involved today not only in developing and investing in technologies that contribute to national intelligence agencies, but also in the collection and assessment of information. Their technologies are supplied to any client including those with high level coding capabilities which disturb state collection, operating almost all intelligence disciplines (Humint, Cyber, Osint, Visint [Visual Intelligence]) for customers. There is no urgent need to integrate the private sector into the intelligence sector, but out-sourcing technical tasks such as social media analytics to private companies with particular expertise will be an efficient use of resources.

Revolution of Military Affairs

The Information Era has changed the face of war and intelligence. Asymmetric warfare and terrorism mean that attacking specific targets in civilian populated areas is sometimes necessary. A precision attack demands highly precise intelligence which is a challenge for intelligence. The change in military affairs also means information warfare has come into the picture: a war on the consciousness of people and wider society. But in order for information to be used effectively as a weapon, intelligence agencies are yet again called in to service and this is still another challenge.

Challenging terrorism is a major dilemma today. Both an external and internal threat, terrorist organisations are efficient in understanding our vulnerabilities and then hitting hard, similarly as ISIS has succeeded. In order to truly and deeply understand societies, terrorist groups spend years studying society, religion, culture and the internal divisions and routines of daily life in the target country. They are not necessarily dependent on supporting nation states, they do not have central command, they have a variety of financial resources and they operate in urban areas enjoying public support. In the words of Michael Herman, it is a "networks of networks".

The phenomenon of the self-made terrorist is a huge challenge. There is no solution in sight. Intelligence agencies have to identify a sole terrorist in a huge city, to drill deeper in the village, the tribe, the clan's history and way of life. In this case, Humint is a crucial discipline for identifying the individual and imminent threats, as well as making use of internal conflicts to recruit sources and conduct campaigns of psychological warfare.

It is a real challenge for Intelligence to identify, spot and win over public opinion, as well as it is a challenge to gain legitimacy to fight them.

The price of success is sometimes problematic especially when it is difficult to foresee the effect of an event. For example, Israel's success in blocking the "import" of rockets to Hamas has led to the self-production of rockets by this group. In Syria, some terrorist groups are supported by foreign countries in the face of a common enemy, but will they not turn against the supporting countries in due time?

The Private sector sells software to secure network intelligence and sells encryption tools, making it more difficult for state intelligence to collect and prevent terrorism.

Prevention is problematic, not only due to the factors mentioned above, but because it is hard to penetrate and recruit sources in deeply ideological organisations. The life expedience of a source is short, and ultimately one needs to combine several disciplines — Sigint (Signals Intelligence), Visint, investigations, vertical and horizontal coordination and cooperation and quick response.

A real dilemma exists in democratic countries where there is the challenge of balancing security and civil liberties. The balance should be decided clearly since terrorist groups exploit this dilemma in their favour. Additional Data Sharing between security agencies and law enforcement departments is needed.

Assessment

Decision makers, especially in the present circumstances will keep asking the question "What is going to happen?" This query, much more than in the past, will be almost impossible to answer, along without the next most common question, "how to we prevent surprises". Increasingly, decision makers are making demands of intelligence agencies to answer both questions. This will be almost 'mission impossible' unless one has excellent intelligence.

Here we all have a methodological dilemma — to prevent surprises and strategic changes in direction, one needs 'out-of-the-box' thinking. However, Intelligence work proceeds through consensus; if you are exceptional you might be decried. From the junior analyst to the top of the pyramid, the message will be reshaped by consensus. However, consensus entails compromise, and compromise is exactly not what 'out-of-the-box' thinking is targeting.

The connectivity, complexity and unordered domain of this chaotic, borderless and unpredictable world will make it much more problematic, and will be exacerbated further by the cognitive bias inherent to human nature. Mountains of data have produced an information overload which will lead to a diversity of issues and create problems for assessment. It will be harder to identify voices from noise, to understand trends and it will be more difficult to decide what to deliver to the decision maker, which will add difficulty to the methodological dilemma aforementioned.

Assessment is affected by the internet. The analyst turns into collector, and is in constant competition with media and private assessment companies. Although professionals may doubt the reliability and quality of their sources, their products are still disseminated widely, thereby affecting both decision makers and public opinion. Intelligence data is always incomplete, and the analyst should remain sceptical. It is indispensable for her/him to acquire a deep knowledge and understanding of divergent perspectives on politics, culture, religion and historical conflict. Common teams of collection and assessment disciplines are needed as two separate non-hierarchical teams — one for trying to identify coming trends and surprises, and the other to prepare the requisite plans to meet these challenges.

Merely sending assessments to decision makers and getting these assessments accepted is not enough; the message should be well understood and well digested. This issue is and will continue to be highly problematic, since those receiving assessments have their own direct access to information in the media and online, and through private sector products of collection and assessment. The Intelligence sector's main tasks are to present the decision maker with what is happening internally, to present probabilities for the future and to prevent surprises. The almost impossible expectation to predict what will happen in these uncertain times is a heavy burden to bear. There is no easy answer: but a special effort should still be made to recruit and train talented, daring analysts, with open access to the pyramid heads of the agency.

Structures

Facing the complexity and unpredictability of the current global order and the information overload, some players believe the answer is to establish a new organisation to coordinate all Intelligence agencies with the many agencies which already exist. These type of plans invariably fail. As Richard K Betts writes: "At the end of the day the strongest defence against mistakes will come less from any structural or procedural weakness than from the good sense, good character, and good mental habits of senior officials". Horizontal and vertical coordination is vital between agencies and within agencies, but again, good will between the players involved is the vital prerequisite. Without this assessments fail.

The real question in the present circumstances is whether the traditional division between internal and external intelligence agencies is still valid. And if so, how can cooperation and coordination between the two be strengthened? How can police, social welfare, the Ministry of Foreign Affairs and others be integrated into the intelligence community? How are unity and diversity maintained while promoting the competition and creativity necessary to deal with complex challenges? What is the golden mean between the two? Collaborative teams from several security agencies and government departments directed by the relevant leading agency might help, provided the sharing of information is carefully managed. Furthermore, within agencies, the integration of all collection divisions might be useful. Agencies facing manifold, complex security threats and hampered by lack of coordination with partners within the security framework, might need to evolve in a manner that might see one player who "sees all" aspects of collection. At the same time, given that complex security events will increasingly need quick responses where expertise is quickly brought to bear, one might envisage situations where authorities empower subcommanders to act independently, even as they act at the same time according to general guidance of the one player who "sees all".

A good example of very close cooperation is that between Intelligence and special units fighting terrorism. In Israel, this has proved successful, and shows that working closely toward assessment and conducting operations is vital among agencies. United central command with representatives from the various agencies headed by the relevant dominant agency might be yet another helpful recommendation.

Manpower

The technology revolution, including advances in cyberspace, biometrics, computer systems, calls for a highly talented, if at times, maverick young generation to be recruited into intelligence agencies. But young smart people do not generally want to work for you, nor would you want to hire all of them. Nowadays, for the young generation the appeal of high tech industries is often more alluring than the intelligence community. This benefits the private sector with new products in the domain of intelligence and security. This trend has forced intelligence agencies frequently to outsource to the private sector tasks which were traditionally in-house. The race for more technology-oriented collection risks overlooking the continued importance of the Humint discipline which is so central to intelligence work.

Conclusion

The changing world order is a major challenge for decision makers in terms of selecting clear PIRs and establishing priorities in an environment of diverse threats, from illegal migration to climate change. Negotiating shifting alliances and correctly determining friend from foe will make it harder still for intelligence agencies to operate effectively.

Technology is and will continue to be a challenge. It provides vast benefits for collection agencies and the military, and it has to be integrated into the intelligence machinery of the state. Yet this is tempered by the fact that it may fall into the wrong hands: the enemy may enjoy comparable access to sophisticated tools. Increasingly, one's enemies are equipped with advanced military and intelligence capabilities, and are using Osint and internet communication very skilfully. Furthermore, the vulnerabilities associated with rapidly developing technologies through hacking mean that ever more focus is placed on the technological side of intelligence, to the detriment of Humint which should be considered the leading discipline. Collection today means more Humint and Masint (Measurement and Signature intelligence) including biological, chemical and nuclear signatures to overcome gaps in uncovering WMDs, which may be stored or transported in underground facilities and tunnels. Humint is also essential in terms of gaining early warning in processes of radicalisation, and mitigating the unpredictable and clandestine nature of terrorist groups. Information overload means that a bold decision should be taken to decide what will be covered by Osint and what will be covered by other disciplines. The private sector is increasingly more involved in collection.

The existing tension between national security and law enforcement (especially in democratic states) is a challenge, which is growing and in need of a solution. A propitious balance must be found between respecting privacy and human rights on one hand and acquiring the requisite information to ensure the safety of citizens on the other.

The acceptance of decision makers will be more challenging, due to the complexity and uncertainty of world affairs, the availability of open source and private sector products, and the pressures of other vital domestic civilian issues. Dependence on intelligence will continue to grow dramatically. Only visionary decision makers, talented manpower (both junior and senior), professionalism and organisational culture of integrity might help the intelligence community to withstand these contemporary challenges.

Chapter 4

The Velocity of Change: Global Threats, Moore's Law and Securing the Future

David F. Heyman

Our world is not what it was 15 years ago — before 9/11, before Bali or Madrid, before H1N1 and Ebola, before Aceh and the Sumatra–Andaman earthquake, before the Stuxnet or Saudi Aramco cyber-attacks, or the Arab Spring or Russia's invasion of the Ukraine. It is not what it was, before Syria or Daesh.

And our social and economic order is not what it used to be either — before iPhones, YouTube, Twitter, Facebook or Skype; before Bluetooth, fracking, 3D printing or the sequencing of the Human Genome. Before Uber and the gig economy.

A lot can happen in 15 years. And a lot has — perhaps more so than similar epochs previously. It seems now, without notice or recognition, the greatest transformation since the Peace at Westphalia — of nation states and the international system — is upon us. There is a fundamental re-ordering of the world under way — in how we live, work and govern

David F. Heyman is a former Assistant Secretary of Policy for the United States Department of Homeland Security.

ourselves, as well as in what threatens our well-being, and in how we secure ourselves and the future.

The opening chapter of the 21st century is a mixed story. It begins following a century of extraordinary global progress — in medicine, public health, life expectancy, education, poverty reduction, standards of living, support for human rights and the spread of democratic institutions. We see across a number of these areas that advance over more than a 100 years that have made the world a better place to live.

Even in terms of political violence, after horrific destruction of life and property in the 20th century — to include two World Wars and the Holocaust, India's partition, Mao's Great Leap Forward, Stalin's purges, Pol Pot's killing fields in Cambodia, the Vietnam War, the Bosnian War and the Rwandan genocide — the world has over the past two decades greatly reduced armed conflict and political violence.

But despite such widespread gains, the past decade has also seen significant, diverse and rising global challenges: anaemic economic growth, rapid and pervasive technological change, ever more frequent and damaging cyber-attacks, mounting and intensified climate change, the rise and spread of militarised terrorism, an increase in failing states and the return of great-power politics.

These challenges significantly undermine global stability. They threaten the security of nations and could risk the peace of the world. They are also in many ways global tremors, reverberations of tectonic shifts in a world dramatically re-ordering itself. They reflect physical, technological, economic, political and even social changes that are ever more rapidly upon us. And they inform us that our institutions to secure the peace of the world have not kept pace.

A World of Change

In the United States, analyses of international security inevitably begin with 9/11 — the tragic terrorist attacks of September 11, 2001. The attacks have not only served as a point-of-departure for dramatic and sweeping security reforms in the U.S. and across the globe, but also as a point-of-reference, as country after country, in city after city have experienced their version of these attacks: Bali, Madrid, London,

Mumbai and more recently Paris, to name a few. In each case, the attacked nation proclaims that this was *their 9/11*.

But the American story of nineteen hijackers commandeering and transforming four planes into guided missiles was not just a wake-up call or warning of threats to be defended against, it was a window into the forces of change remaking the world — physical, technological, social, political and economic. It is a story that has been played out across the globe now for more than two decades — a story of planet earth in crisis, and of a dramatic restructuring of the world economic system. It is a story of the remaking of society, linked into and inseparable from cyberspace; of the diminution of borders, the power of networks and the rise of cities. And it is the story of the staggering pace in which we are experiencing change in society.

Amidst this transformation are five key forces driving change in the 21st century. They are: Planet Earth, Cyber World, Network Power, Borders and Flows and the Velocity of Change itself.

Planet Earth

To begin with, change is being driven by Planet Earth. One of the critical drivers in the 21st century is — and will be — a physical world that is convulsing, contributing to social unrest and threatening global stability. Across the globe over the past three decades we experienced ever more intensive and severe weather crises at greater and greater costs to society. Habitats are shrinking, ecosystems collapsing, the level of CO_2 in the atmosphere (and temperatures) are rising and species are dying out faster than historic rates. These physical changes, in turn, are not only weakening communities, causing death and destruction, but they are tearing at the social fabric of society by degrading food and water supplies, contributing to new health crises and uprooting and dislocating large populations.

Even if the commitments made at COP21 in Paris last December — the 2015 United Nations Climate Conference — are kept and further enhanced, and the goals are achieved, warming will continue to rise by at least another degree for the foreseeable future, or in other words, to a level twice as much as we have experienced to date. Thus, we can expect — and must prepare for — continued and perhaps greater weather effects, agricultural impacts and other related consequences of climate change, to include the associated impacts on populations that may further propagate instability and conflict.

Cyber world and network power

Second, even as COP21 may be the beginning of the end of *carbon emissions* — and a pathway for healing the significant collateral damage of the Industrial Revolution — iPhones, Wi-Fi and streaming videos, represent a new proliferation — *digital emissions* — that, with the promise of smart devices, smart cities and the Internet of Things, will both animate and confound the emerging Digital Revolution.

As the size and cost of computers and sensors over the past decade has diminished, and power increased, the utility and diffusion of information and communications technologies throughout society have exploded, enhancing operations across nearly every industry and all aspects of life, such that almost no part of society has been left untouched.[1]

Today, we can do far more, for far less cost or effort, than we could ever do before. At the click of a button, rockets are launched, power grids optimised, hospital life-support systems run, stock markets and banking transactions safeguarded, instant communications across the globe enabled, prisons are monitored, city traffic is controlled, farms can be cultivated, new cars can be assembled and missing people can be found, among other far-reaching effects.

But as is the case with all technologies, advances in ICT not only dramatically increase and empower individuals to help and heal, but also enable and augment their ability to harm as well.

When the 19 hijackers took over U.S. planes on September 11th, the re-invented high-tech cockpits of the Boeing's 757 and 767s — which were designed to reduce the number of pilots required to fly the aircraft, while increasing safety and ease of operation — were so sophisticated that they enabled the hijackers, who needed very little training or experience to guide them. Formerly, only those few individuals with the flight time, money, training and access to large complex jetliners could become professional pilots and actually fly planes. But now, almost anyone who could practice on a relatively inexpensive flight simulator, could develop the rudimentary skills required to operate the simplified controls of Boeing 757 and 767s. The advent of powerful computing capabilities had in effect put the controls of guided missile systems into the hands of novice pilots, with the click of a button.

Power derives from the ability to influence outcomes and control resources and capabilities. Advances in ICT and the creation of the internet have dramatically enhanced the power of individuals and organisations, distributing control broadly, transnationally, allowing greater social coordination and connection among previously decentralised groups, outsiders or disaffected individuals. In short, the digitalisation and networking of the world has had a levelling impact, shifting power from top-driven, large organisations, to bottom-driven smaller groups and individuals. In the 21st century, power is more about distributed resources than centralised ones. It is about information over capital. And it is about the power of networks over the power of direct control.

As such, ICT has made it possible for small actors to compete asymmetrically with larger ones. While small actors may not on their own have the resources or capabilities to contest larger powers on conventional terms, small actors nonetheless can exert influence beyond their size or means through the use of *distributed* or *network* power. Distributed/ network power refers to relatively inexpensive and accessible capabilities that can be leveraged or readily scaled for strategic effect, but that on their own, would not necessarily rise to an appreciable level.

In the business world, you see this power dynamic manifesting itself in the new digital economy where small start-ups are dramatically disrupting established industries. Companies such as Airbnb, Uber and Snapchat, for example, became multi-billion dollar sensations in less than five years, turning the hospitality, taxi and communications sectors on their heads. Companies can do this with little capital, but by piggy-backing their services on existing mobile device networks, by renting servers, data storage, and cloud computing from companies like Amazon, by using PayPal or Square to process transactions and by marketing themselves via networking giants such as Facebook or LinkedIn or other social media. Compare that to 10 or more years ago, when similar business start-ups required access to large capital investments, major financial commitments and could take years to scale to market.

The digitisation of the world and the service-isation of all manners of work, enabled by ICT and networking software, are fundamentally re-writing the social order and restructuring the world economic system.

Businesses that have embraced 21st century new power dynamics are moving away from a 200-year-old model of top-down centralised mass production and distribution, to a distributed model of bottom-up peer-to-peer sharing and on-demand delivery; from a concentration of capital in the hands of a few, to creation of wealth through catalysis of self-organising markets of the many.

In international affairs (leaving aside the revolution in military affairs in the 1990s which in many ways pioneered the use of distributed or network power), we also see this type of power dynamics emerging, where ICT advances have enabled small actors to challenge larger powers and the existing order. Specifically, ICT and social networking are being employed in three principal ways: (1) as a *force-multiplier* to amplify individual voices and capabilities to influence and achieve political effects; (2) as an *enabler* of global terrorism to extend groups' reach and facilitate operations and (3) as a *vehicle* for activists, criminals, spies, terrorists and war-fighters to achieve harmful, even kinetic effects (e.g., deface a website, steal credit card numbers, steal sensitive information or destroy infrastructure).

As a *force-multiplier*, the sophisticated networking, social media and data analytics technologies that helped target enough citizens to elect Barack Obama to be President in 2008 are also being utilised by activists around the globe to organise protests, highlight injustices and government crackdowns and sway public opinion. These efforts not only have led to historic demonstrations against governments (e.g., civil unrest in Moldova in 2009, the 2009 Green Revolution in Iran), but also to the dramatic overthrow of entrenched authoritarian regimes in Tunisia, Egypt and elsewhere, throughout the Arab Spring.

As an *enabler* of global terrorism, internet technology makes it easy for individuals to find like-minded but perhaps geographically distributed peers, and communicate with them in real-time, with relative anonymity, even secrecy, across borders. As recently as a decade ago terrorism required substantial face-to-face interaction: recruitment, radicalisation, indoctrination, planning, training for and financing attacks all included some level of physical interaction with others and with the potential targets.

Today, terrorists and terrorist-wannabees can harness the power of the internet and other digital technologies, and access tremendous capabilities for very little cost. They can use social media to create a brand image, market themselves and recruit followers, as Daesh has done in Syria and Iraq. Instead of travelling to training camps in Pakistan, Afghanistan, Syria or elsewhere, terrorists can download, store and hide bomb-building and related training materials on tiny flash drives, concealed by encryption or simply access the material on password-protected chat rooms online, as the Tsarnaev brothers did prior to the Boston Marathon bombing. Terrorists can even use digital technologies to manage their operations, as was evident in Mumbai in 2008 and Paris in 2015.[2,3]

Finally, because so much of daily life is now connected to the internet — businesses, manufacturing, city services, banking, transportation and all sorts of critical infrastructure — the internet serves as an ever more attractive and accessible *vehicle* for malicious actors to infiltrate, attack, hold hostage, steal and even destroy valuable assets across the globe. Not surprising, cyber threats, over the past decade, have significantly increased, expanding markedly and globally, in frequency, scale, sophistication and severity. Just in the past two years we have seen the largest credit card breach in history, the largest computer worm in history and the largest denial of service attack in history — affecting hundreds and hundreds of million victims.

Borders and flows

A third force re-ordering the world is the changing nature of borders and dramatic growth of global flows.

Since the Peace at Westphalia in 1648, the concept of sovereignty, that the modern state derives from, established two key principles: first territoriality, which is the concept of defining and establishing *borders*, and second, the principle of citizenship, which is the notion of granting exclusive rights to those within those established borders, and prohibiting those outside from participating in bureaucratic state matters. To ensure these rights, sovereign states assume a public authority, a government or a ruler, that is both preeminent and autonomous to other institutions. This idea of sovereignty has been the backbone of modern international affairs: the notion that every state has the right of self-governance over its people and territory serves as the foundation of international security.

Over the past 50 years, however, the rise of global flows — the movement of people, goods and services, capital and technology around the globe — and of non-state actors has diluted this premise. First, following World War II, large multinational corporations grew up out of new markets and the efforts to rebuild in Europe and Japan. Second, extensive technological advances in transportation and communications in the 1970s and 1980s — in jet aviation, containerised cargo, coaxial and fibre optic cables and computing — reduced the costs of trade and travel, and extended the reach of large organisations. Third, regional and global economic integration, to include the founding of the European Economic Community, GATT, ASEAN, WTO, NAFTA, MERCOSUR and a multitude of trading agreements, brought down trade barriers and further reduced costs. And fourth, after the sweeping political liberalisation that followed the collapse of the Soviet Union, markets were further expanded.

Today, the global movement of people, goods, services and finance has reached previously unimagined levels. Total global flows of goods and services reached $26 trillion in 2012, or 36 percent of global GDP, 1.5 times the level in 1990.[4] More people live and work in countries they were not born in; more capital flows, communications, trade, exchanges and business transpire between states than ever before. Flows of people, money and communications have also all reached their highest levels ever. As such, global flows are now vital to all aspects of a state's economy — fostering innovation, fuelling businesses, extending supply networks, fostering education and other exchanges, creating markets and driving growth. One in three goods today crosses national borders and more than one-third of financial investments are international transactions.[5] By 2025, global flows could reach $54 trillion to $85 trillion, more than double or triple their current scale.[6,7]

In short, over the past few decades, global flows have become not just a luxury, but rather a functional part of nation states. As a result, nation states can no longer be fully delimited by borders with clear interiors and exteriors.

The velocity of change

Finally, what perhaps is far less appreciated and may be much more pernicious than any of the particular challenges we face is the rate of change in which we experience global security challenges in society today. Put simply: the velocity of change may be increasing beyond our ability to adapt and overcome rising threats.

Change is a vector: it has direction from one thing to another, and magnitude in terms of speed or quantity. If change is slow or incremental, it may be imperceptible, like a gradual hill on a road barely inching upwards over miles and miles. Throughout the vast majority of human history, change in society has in fact progressed relatively slowly. Only in recent times — over the past 200 years has the velocity of change increased appreciably, with attendant dangers.

The curve of human evolution over time, for example, is a long linear graph with a rapid asymptotic acceleration at the very, very end, like the tip of a wing turning sharply upward to the sky. It represents billions of years for single-celled organisms to become animals, hundreds of millions of years later for the first humans to walk the earth and millions of years more before modern humans evolved, around 10,000 years ago. Changes may be dramatically accelerated in the near future as advances in computing and genetic engineering are contemplated to enhance and rapidly advance human capabilities.

The graph of human population demographics and socioeconomic development looks very much the same as one for human evolution: over a period of thousands of years, up until the middle of the 18th century, there were very small rates of population growth, economic expansion and social development. In 1788, James Watt's invention of an improved steam engine helped usher in the industrial revolution, and with it, another rapid, exponential growth in human civilisation, which has seen remarkable growth since then. It is not a coincidence that socioeconomic changes spurred on by the industrial revolution have also contributed to parallel exponential fluctuations in Earth's ecological and environmental well-being, as economies grew in conjunction with carbon emissions and environmental changes. Graphs of global environmental change mirror these, showing glacial changes up until about 200 years ago, and a sharp rise over the past few decades.

Technological change mirrors and indeed increasingly drives these changes. The diffusion of ICT throughout every aspect of life has made communication and information processing and analysis ubiquitous, and ushered in the information age. It has also changed (and is changing) the nature and balance of power across society and international affairs. The penetration of and pervasiveness of computing and information technologies in our lives is moving faster than ever with the rise of connected devices, networks, smart cities and the Internet of Things. As computers are integrated into and begin to mediate *every* aspect of our lives, our lives, in turn, begin to change at the rate of computation. Taking Moore's law into account, which demonstrated regular exponential growth in the number of transistors on a microcircuit, and a doubling of performance of computers every 18–24 months, the velocity of change across all matters of society is about to accelerate even and ever more. The timelines for some global challenges such as climate change are more or less known. But the proliferation of digital emissions and associated cyber threats is in some ways of far greater concern, as they may manifest global consequences, not over a period of centuries, but at the speed of light.

A World of Difference

In short, we are witnessing, almost imperceptibly, but also, as described, with great tumult and speed, a shifting away from an older, known world order — a world formed out of the ashes of two World Wars and from the many associated post-war multilateral organisations, where structures of government, rules of the road, norms of state behaviour and expectations of international actors were largely understood and unchanging.

The new world is in fact still an emergent one, built on new power dynamics of bottom-up and distributed linkages, fused to the internet and our global trade and travel systems, where structures, norms and expectations have yet to be defined, where change *is* the norm, and where extensive and pervasive networks of actors from all corners of the world, walks of life and stations in society, can cohere as needed, as desired, on-demand.

Twenty-five years ago, the collapse of the Soviet Union coincided with tremendous and pervasive change around the world — political and economic liberalisation, which in parallel with extraordinary technological changes, have fundamentally altered global security, commerce, politics and trade. The resulting globalisation brought about a new and high degree of international interconnectedness, and extensive expansion of global flows that have afforded great economic benefits. It also introduced new vulnerabilities and opportunities for international criminals, terrorists and even state actors, within growing networks of connected cyber and physical infrastructure, to include our international trade and travel systems. These vulnerabilities became apparent post-9/11, but have been even more evident over the past decade, with the proliferation of international terrorism and cyber-attacks, the virtual collapse of weak states and the rise of new bio threats.

New Threats

What is clear among so much change is that the principal national security concern for most countries has shifted: from large, centralised, geo-strategic threats — invading armies, strategic nuclear weapons and the Cold War — to more localised threats, economic interests and sectarian violence. Most recently, threats have increasingly arisen consequent to new power dynamics driving change in the 21st century: threats are smaller, distributed and mobile, but can coalesce or scale, leading to achieve large, devastating effects. These security concerns are increasingly borderless and fluid like floods, seeping across state lines and inflicting more damage where infrastructures and state actions are weakest. They include, most notably, terrorism, bio-hazards and cyber-attacks, but also severe-weather-related crises.[8]

Bio

In the world of bio-threats, over the past two decades, rapid urbanisation and associated changes in land use and agriculture in countries where disease is endemic or potentially endemic has contributed to the emergence of a number of potential pandemic-causing diseases (e.g., SARS, H1N1 and Ebola). When combined with the extensive increases in trade and travel that are the hallmarks of globalisation, it makes possible for these new and emerging infectious diseases to rapidly spread around the world.

In March of 2009, for example, a four-year-old boy in eastern Mexico's La Gloria village contracted H1N1 or swine flu, and six weeks later, the disease had spread to Spain, Israel, New Zealand, Austria, Germany, the United Kingdom and Switzerland, causing the World Health Organization to raise their influenza pandemic alert to its highest level. Similarly, in 2014, we saw an Ebola disease outbreak — which historically does not spread beyond the local outbreak community — impact 10 countries, causing over 11,000 deaths and approximately US$1.6–25 billion in economic losses.[9,10]

Cyber

Cyber threats, too, over the past decade, have increased and spread markedly and globally, in frequency, scale, sophistication and severity.[11] To appreciate the pervasiveness of this new threat, a 2010 industry report found that 65 percent of adults worldwide had been a victim of a cyber-crime.[12] In the United States, the volume of malicious software on American networks has more than tripled over the past five years. Virtually every national security threat and crime that the FBI now faces is cyber-based or facilitated.[13] We see a similar pattern in the UK where cybercrime is the second most common crime.[14] The range and number of cyber threat actors, methods of attack and who are being targeted as victims are also expanding, affecting everyone — in government, in the private sector, in private lives and around the globe.[15]

The 2009 Cornficker worm cyber-attack was an example of how *widespread* cyber-attacks can be; it infected millions and millions of computers in nearly every country in the world, and cost up to an estimated $US9.1 billion.[16] By contrast, the 2012 Saudi Aramco attacks, which erased data on three-quarters of Aramco's corporate PCs; the 2010 Stuxnet attack that sabotaged Iranian centrifuges; and the 2014 Sony attacks that temporarily shut down the company all showed how destructive discrete *targeted* attacks could be.

Extreme-weather

We have in recent decades experienced ever more severe (and borderless) weather disasters, at greater and greater costs to society. Of all major disasters during this period, 90 percent of them were a result of weather-related events; they caused nearly $2 trillion in damage, 606,000 lives to be lost and over 4.1 billion people to be injured or displaced. They spanned the globe[17] and broke long-standing records: 13 of the 14 warmest years on record occurred in the 21st century; 7 of the top 10 costliest natural disasters and hundreds of other record-setting extreme weather events have occurred since 2001.[18,19]

Extreme weather also can produce significant global strife. The 2003 European heatwave, as an example, caused over 30,000 deaths across 8 countries, and over 13 billion euros in estimated damages.[20] In 2007–2008, food shortages caused world food prices to soar, pushing hundreds of millions of people into poverty, and causing protests in 61 countries, of which 23 turned violent.[21] Similarly, between 2006 and 2010, Syria experienced the most severe drought ever recorded in an area known as the greater Fertile Crescent. It was a drought that was exacerbated both by climate change, and poor management by the Assad regime, to include ignoring severe overcrowding, poor infrastructure, deep unemployment and rampant crime. The drought ended up perpetuating three problems: it caused massive agricultural failures and livestock mortality; it intensified existing water and food shortages; and led to the internal displacement of nearly two million rural inhabitants who sought refuge in urban areas, which were already under stress. This, in turn, put pressure on Syria's major cities where the displaced relocated to, and contributed to social unrest that precipitated the civil war.[22]

Terrorism

Lastly, terrorists, criminal groups and other non-state actors, in particular, have been able to harness the forces of globalisation and associated changes in technology, using international trade and travel systems, the internet, access to weapons and horizontal network structures in ways that are difficult to trace and disrupt. These groups, while distributed globally, are able to insinuate themselves locally, by inspiring, recruiting, planning and even operating over the internet and through social media. Moreover, they have been able to infiltrate weak states, such as Libya, Nigeria, Afghanistan and Yemen; smuggle in illicit goods and weapons; and establish cells to challenge state authority. As an example, during the 2011

Libyan uprising, military weapons were looted from state armouries, acquired by terrorist groups in the Sahel (al-Qaeda in the Islamic Maghreb, or AQIM), and subsequently transferred to other terrorist groups including Boko Haram. Boko Haram, in turn, was able to smuggle those weapons across porous Nigerian borders and deploy them to mount ever more deadly attacks in Nigeria.

The Islamic State (a.k.a., Daesh or ISIL), which started as an insurgency in Iraq in 2003, spread in Iraq in 2006, to Syria in 2013, and now has established operations in Libya, Egypt, Saudi Arabia, Yemen, Algeria, Afghanistan, Pakistan, Nigeria and the North Caucasus.[23] In Syria and Iraq, Daesh has been able to grab and hold land, collect taxes, and operate effectively as a governing authority over a self-proclaimed caliphate.

The unrest in the Middle East, particularly within terrorist safe havens established in weak states, has inspired and facilitated other low-level but persistent lone-wolf or small group terrorist attacks on nearly every continent; it has contributed to the virtual collapse of a number of states in the region; and, along with violence in sub-Saharan Africa caused the highest number of people displaced by conflict and violence around the world in generations.[24] The conflict in Syria has morphed from a civil war, to sectarian violence and, now to a world at war, by any other name: well-over 65 nations today are afflicted by or involved in Syrian refugee resettlement or Syria-related warfare.

Security Frozen in Time

In spite of these significant and growing new threats, the fundamental security architecture of governments has remained locked into institutions developed during the 1970s and 1980s or earlier — one exception being homeland security and parts of the counterterrorism community. In the face of these new threats, traditional national security institutions such as conventional military forces are less useful because the enemy is not an invading army; to the contrary, the use of thousands of soldiers or even strategic nuclear deterrence, is in many ways a feckless defence against electrons, microbes and suicidal individuals with guns. Furthermore, technical assistance, such as what helped Eastern Europe emerge from Communism, is not as relevant to troubled countries such as Egypt,

Nigeria, Yemen, Iraq or Libya. These are countries increasingly unable to secure their borders, prevent the illicit movements of people and goods and collect customs revenues, which has led many of them to the edge of state failure. And yet, border security gets minimal attention at best, and certainly far less attention than the purchase of aircraft, tanks or the training of military forces.

More useful for many of these countries would be the ability to identify, investigate and interdict illicit or dangerous traffic across and within their borders, particularly people and weapons, but also malicious code and, perhaps even microorganisms. Before a terrorist group can take and hold territory, for example, they must establish ties, safe houses, training camps and build up arsenals. Good border security tied to good law enforcement would give weak or vulnerable countries the ability to deal with domestic problems without added, imported hazards.

New Thinking

Accordingly, the security architecture required to deter, prevent, protect against and respond to 21st century threats needs to be fundamentally rethought. The confluence of society's reliance on expanding global flows, on cross-border infrastructures and on the emerging Internet of Things on the one hand, and the rise of small highly mobile threats that can scale with potentially devastating consequences on the other, requires us to define a new framework for international security that will permit and accelerate economic development, while also safeguarding society.

Given that power in the 21st century increasingly derives from networks that act as force multipliers, nation states must adopt and harness this new dynamic as much for security as for economic development. Governments must be better able to find and thwart small dangerous signals that can threaten global stability and national security — electrons carrying malicious code, viruses carrying deadly diseases, terrorists planning vicious attacks, even wasteful carbon-based energy.

To accomplish this requires a number of fundamental shifts in thinking.

First, governments need to change from a traditional national security predisposition for and historical reliance principally on armed forces and overseas intelligence, to a new approach that includes and leverages customs, borders, and immigration capabilities as well as information sharing and big data analytics, among others — capabilities more closely associated with homeland security than traditional national security.

Second, governments need to embrace 21st century power dynamics and transform current security architectures from an emphasis on top-driven, centralised institutions, to more distributed, bottom-driven and networked organisations. They must go glocal: that is, partner locally, but also connect globally.

Third, as conflict moves from the physical to the digital world, governments need to establish equivalent norms and rules of the road around global cyberspace. The Geneva Conventions have governed rules of war for over 150 years; indeed, a similar convention for cyber space is warranted.

And last, given how unlikely and infeasible it is to stop all threats — terrorists may get through, cyber-attacks could succeed, and severe weather storms will happen — national security must not only rely on prevention strategies, but also embrace *resilience* as a strategic asset. Communities that build resilience not only improve security, but by mitigating consequences, they also can achieve a level of deterrence, by denying would be attackers their intended goals.

As we look to find solutions to new global security challenges, one of the best models for this is homeland security. Unfortunately, even the mention of homeland security today oftentimes elicits allergic reactions. After over a decade in operation, amidst all its growing pains and despite programmatic successes, homeland security unfortunately conjures up images of the Transportation Security Authority (TSA) doing enhanced pat-downs, NSA[25] and intrusions of privacy, or even border security and illegal immigration. So for many, considering homeland security as a model for new thinking in global security may be anathema.

But even with challenges in implementation, the concept is right. Homeland security is an evolutionary improvement in national security.

National security was a post-World War II innovation that conjoined two largely separate government domains — foreign affairs and military policy — under a single rubric and integrated National Security Council. Homeland security adds a third pillar — domestic security — to these domains. In doing so, homeland security creates a bridge for national security, linking foreign and domestic affairs, local communities and international security, and war-fighting and law enforcement. In a world of increasing hybridicity,[26] where there are fewer and fewer clear lines between foreign and domestic, between military and criminal acts, or between one border and the next, homeland security advances a model relying on hybrid security as a means to thwart hybrid or asymmetric threats.

As such, it is a powerful new tool built to find a needle in a haystack, a small signal in global flows. To accomplish this, homeland security brings 21st century power to 20th century national security architectures. It does so in three compelling ways.

First, in terms of organisation, while national security is historically strategic, centralised and top-driven, homeland security is transactional, decentralised, and bottom-driven. National security is about state action; homeland security is about the actions of local communities, businesses and individuals.

Second, in terms of culture, while the national security culture grew out of the military and intelligence communities, homeland security is more about law enforcement and emergency management. In national security there is a culture of secrecy and a need to protect the nation's most sensitive information. In homeland security there's an expectation of transparency. The ability to find the needle in the haystack is made possible through information sharing: homeland security is about moving from a need to know posture, to a duty to share and connect dots, while protecting privacy and civil liberties.

Third, in terms of management, while national security is mobilised through a unity of command, in homeland security, operations are accomplished via a unity of effort. In effect, everyone must row in the same direction, but no one entity has the power to compel all others.

In practice, U.S. homeland security has successfully employed this 21st century security architecture against aforementioned new and emerging threats. This has been accomplished through the creation of a number of multi-layered, many-faceted and multinational efforts — in counterterrorism, transportation and border security, cybersecurity and by building national resilience. In *counterterrorism*, for example, bottom-up programs such as the National Suspicious Activity Reporting (SAR) and See Something, Say Something™ initiatives, link individuals and cops on the street to state and local government intelligence fusion centres to provide national law enforcement with behaviours and indicators related to terrorism, crime and other threats. It was this program that helped thwart Faisal Shahzad from successfully bombing Times Square in May 2010.

In *borders*, a number of information sharing and analysis tools and programs — C-TPAT,[27] CSI,[28] ACAS[29] and ATS,[30] among others — have enhanced awareness of people, material, cargo and containers making the journey to the United States. Through these efforts, homeland security authorities have been able to assess whether these entities pose a risk, and have been able to divert thousands of malicious actors and dangerous material from ever coming to America.

For *resilience*, homeland security programs working with individuals, businesses, communities and other government agencies, have advanced greater understanding of and preparedness for the impacts of a changing climate; promoted resilient infrastructure investments; bolstered disaster response information sharing and collaboration; and facilitated business continuity planning, among others.

And separately, to better manage *carbon emissions*, city managers are beginning to take advantage of the rise of connected devices and the Internet of Things. These new tools are enabling cities to install and network embedded sensors and controls across transportation systems, buildings, electric grids and other civil infrastructure to save energy, and build smarter, safer, more resilient and more sustainable cities.

New Governance

The difficulty for state governments today is that as the velocity of change accelerates, the ability of large, centralised national governments to adapt to highly mobile, hard to detect threats is also becoming harder.

This is where homeland security can play a greater role.

The tools to adapt — agility and mobility — are more likely found in smaller, more nimble entities, closer to the source of the problem. Radicalisation to violence, energy consumption, and disease infections, for example, all take place at the local level, on the streets, in the buildings, homes, and hospitals of cities. Even botnets and hacks begin at a lower level — exploiting weak security practices or vulnerabilities on a single computer or network.

As threat vectors devolve into small, distributed actors, acts, or actions, policies and programs to secure societies must also devolve — to cities, to private companies, and to individuals.

What has changed in the world is that in the 21st century security is a global public good. We are only as strong as the weakest link. As such, there can be no free-riders. Security is a shared responsibility — even and especially for individuals. As the sayings go, everyone has a role to play: "if you see something, say something" (*counterterrorism*); "72 is on you" (*severe-weather disasters*); "cough into your elbow" (*biothreats*); and "think before you click" (*cybersecurity*). These small acts — when effectively linked to local law enforcement, public health, emergency management, and private enterprise and ultimately national governments, in turn working with counterparts around the globe — can scale to powerful protection for society.

Conclusion

Our world is indeed not what it was 15 years ago. The sweeping changes ushering in the 21st century neither reflect business as usual, nor an established order. To the contrary, turmoil across so many spheres hints at a world in transition, a pivotal and historic time between two eras.

In the years ahead, we can well expect continued and increasing tumult, as entrenched establishments become unhinged, and change increases ever faster. This will drive new — and expand existing — security challenges we face. Our ability to adapt to and manage change, and secure the future, will increasingly rest on our ability to harness the power of networks, information, digital technology and globalisation, but also to safeguard against threats seeking to exploit the same.

That means nation states must fundamentally re-think national security. They must continue to prepare for and deter large war, but a principal focus of national security must also emphasise smaller, scalable threats — natural and deliberate. As threats to society devolve, our security architecture to face them must also devolve. A bottom-driven networked security architecture is the hallmark of homeland security, and should be considered side-by-side military and intelligence capacity building for strengthening the capabilities of other states, to advance their homeland security interests and our own. In short, national security must be better tied to local communities and individuals, but also networked globally, as homeland security can do.

In particular, we must fortify border and law enforcement capabilities in vulnerable nations, to prevent the establishment of safe havens by malicious actors. We must secure and ensure the resilience of global networks and global connectedness, as much as we do territory. And we must put in place an effective and lawful governance regime for cyberspace, as we have done for physical space. Most important, we must recognise that everyone and every organisation has a role to play.

And in the actions of each of us, we can secure the world for all of us.

Endnotes

1. For example, in 2015 there were over 3.2 billion internet users and 7 billion mobile cellular subscriptions worldwide, up from fewer than 400 million users and 1 billion subscribers in 2000. See: *ICT Facts and Figures: The World in 2015.* http://www.itu.int/en/ITU-D/Statistics/Documents/facts/ICTFactsFigures2015.pdf (Retrieved 20 November 2015). For trends in e-commerce, e-government, education and other ICT penetration, see also International Telecommunication Union, *Measuring the Information Society Report 2014.* http://www.itu.int/en/ITU-D/Statistics/Documents/publications/mis2014/MIS2014_without_Annex_4.pdf (Retrieved 9 January 2016).

2. For additional information, see Lachow, I., & Richardson, C. (2007). Terrorist Use of the Internet: The Real Story, *Joint Force Quarterly*, 45, 100–103. http://ndupress.ndu.edu/portals/68/Documents/jfq/jfq-45.pdf. See also: *The Use of the Internet for Terrorist Purposes.* (2012). Vienna: United Nations Office on Drugs and Crime, in Collaboration with UN Counterterrorism Implementation Task Force and also Behr, I., Reding, A., Edwards, C., & Ribbon, L. (2013). *Radicalisation in the Digital Era: The Use of the Internet in 15 Cases of Terrorism and Extremism.*the use of distributeden an enormous spike in hactivism, cybercrimes, and attacks on critical infrastructure. physicalchange th

3. As an example, see: Wax, E. (2008). Mumbai Attackers Made Sophisticated Use of Technology. *Washington Post Foreign Service.* http://www.washingtonpost.com/wp-dyn/content/article/2008/12/02/AR2008120203519.html.

4. James, M., Jacques, B., Susan, L., Olivia, N., David, P., Sebastian, J., & Sree, R. (2014). *Global Flows in a Digital Age: How Trade, Finance, People, and Data Connect the World Economy.* McKinsey Global Institute. http://www.mckinsey.com/insights/globalization/global_flows_in_a_digital_age (Retrieved 6 January 2016).

5. *Ibid.*

6. *Ibid.*

7. Among factors contributing to further growth: more people are living outside their country of birth than ever before: 50 percent more than in 1990; the number of people holding multiple passports is increasing; the number of regional and bilateral trade agreements (RTAs) between countries, which reduce trade barriers, and which has quadrupled since 1990, will continue to grow, including when it is operational, the Trans-Pacific Partnership. According to the World Bank, trade between RTA partners now makes up 40 percent of global trade. See World Bank. http://www.worldbank.org/content/dam/Worldbank/GEP/GEParchives/GEP2005/GEP2005Chap2.pdf.

8. This does not exclude great power and large actor struggles, which continue to dominate national security concerns, but are not new. Iranian expansion of missile capabilities may threaten Europe; Chinese new aircraft carriers, anti-satellite technologies, and actions in the South China Seas; and Russian aggression in the Ukraine, and elsewhere, are among rising concerns that will continue to require nation states to maintain strong national defences, intelligence and even unconventional capabilities, to include cyber defence.

9. See U.S. CDC 2014 Ebola Outbreak in West Africa. http://www.cdc.gov/vhf/ebola/outbreaks/2014-west-africa/index.html.

10. Ebola: Most African Countries Avoid Major Economic Loss but Impact on Guinea, Liberia, Sierra Leone Remains Crippling. (2015). Washington, DC: World Bank Group.

11. ISTR20: Internet Security Threat Report Vol. 20. (2015). Symantec. See also Clapper, J. Statement for the Record Worldwide Cyber Threats House Permanent Select Committee on Intelligence. Washington, DC: Director of National Intelligence.

12. The Norton Cybercrime Report: The Human Impact 2010. http://www.symantec.com/about/news/release/article.jsp?prid=20100908_01 (Retrieved 21 November 2015).

13. Comey, J. (2015). Statement before the Senate Committee on Homeland Security and Governmental Affairs. Washington, DC https://www.fbi.gov/news/testimony/threats-to-the-homeland.

14. Improving Crime Statistics in England and Wales. (2015). In Crime Statistics, Year Ending June 2015. Office of National Statistics.

15. *Ibid.*, p. 2.

16. http://www.zdnet.com/article/confickers-estimated-economic-cost-9-1-billion/.

17. The Human Cost of Weather-related Disasters 1995–2015. (2015). United Nations Office for Disaster Risk Reduction (UNISDR), Centre for Research on the Epidemiology of Disasters Institute of Health and Society.

18. World Meteorological Organization, Press Release No. 985, 24 March 2014. https://www.wmo.int/pages/mediacentre/press_releases/pr_985_en.html (Retrieved 6 January 2015). See also figure below, *Global Ranked Land and Ocean Temperatures for Last Fifty Years*, from WMO Statement on the Status of Climate in 2013, https://drive.google.com/file/d/0BwdvoC9AeWjUeEV1cnZ6QURVaEE/edit (Retrieved 6 January 2015).

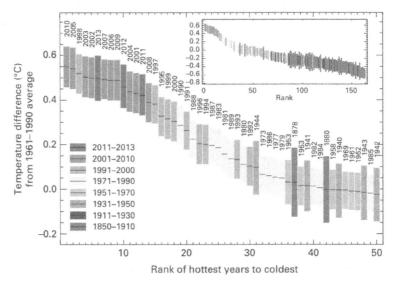

19. Examples include: Korea's worst flooding since 1959 (2002); a record-breaking heat wave in Europe, causing tens of thousands of deaths (2003); the worst drought in Brazil in 60 years (2005); the worst flooding in the UK in 60 years (2007); Pakistan's worst floods in history, affecting 84 of 121 districts and more than 20 million people; the warmest month ever in Moscow since the beginning of modern meteorological records, among

others. For more, see *Weather Extremes in a Changing Climate*: *Hindsight on Foresight*. (2011). World Meteorological Organization. https://www.wmo.int/pages/mediacentre/news/documents/1075_en.pdf (Retrieved 6 January 2015). as wellfrom the carbon to the digital economy...century.environment.rsenal.nvolved.. The hybrdization olution.

20. Impacts of summer 2003 heat wave in Europe. (2004). Environment Alert Bulletin. http://www.unisdr.org/files/1145_ewheatwave.en.pdf.
21. Examples include: Korea's worst flooding since 1959 (2002); a record-breaking heat wave in Europe, causing tens of thousands of deaths (2003); the worst drought in Brazil in sixty years (2005); the worst flooding in the UK in sixty years (2007); Pakistan's worst floods in history, affecting 84 of 121 districts and more than 20 million people; the warmest month ever in Moscow since the beginning of modern meteorological records, among others. For more, see World Meteorological Organization, "Weather Extremes in a Changing Climate: Hindsight on Foresight." No. 1075. Copyright 2011. ISBN: 978 92 63 11075 6.
22. Colin P. K., Shahrzad M., Mark A. C., Richard S., & Yochanan, K. (2015). Climate Change in the Fertile Crescent and Implications of the Recent Syrian Drought, *Proceedings of the National Academy of Sciences of the United States of America*, 112(11), 3241–3246.
23. Islamic State moves in on al-Qaeda turf — *BBC News* (15 June 2015). http://www.bbc.com/news/world-31064300 (Retrieved 30 November 2015).
24. According to the *UNHCR Mid-Year Trends 2015*, "the total number of refugees has increased significantly and consistently over the past four years. Starting from 10.4 million at the end of 2011, the number increased to 10.5 million in 2012, to 11.7 million in 2013, and finally to 14.4 million by the end of 2014. By mid-2015, it had reached an estimated 15.1 million, its highest level in 20 years. Within three and a half years, then, the global refugee population grew by 4.7 million persons — some 45 per cent." The report goes on to say that "the main contributing factor to this trend has been the war in the Syrian Arab Republic...but the outbreak of armed conflicts or deterioration of ongoing ones in Afghanistan, Burundi, the Democratic Republic of the Congo, Mali, Somalia, South Sudan, and Ukraine, among others, have [also] contributed to prevailing trends".
25. NSA stands for the National Security Agency. NSA is a member of the U.S. intelligence community. It is responsible for signals intelligence.
26. I define **hybridicity** to refer to a state of being whereby two different or discreet entities simultaneously exist as one.

27. C-TPAT stands for Customs-Trade Partnership Against Terrorism. In this program there are over 10,000 companies who have established an agreement to work with U.S. CBP to protect the supply chain, identify security gaps, and implement specific security measures and best practices. Through Mutual Recognition Arrangements with 10 countries and the European Union, CBP links with other international industry partnership programs to create a unified and sustainable security posture that can assist in securing and facilitating global cargo trade.

28. The Container Security Initiative (CSI) target and prescreen maritime containers to ensure all containers that pose a potential risk for terrorism are identified and inspected at foreign ports before they are placed on vessels destined for the United States.

29. The Air Cargo Advance Screening program targets and prescreens air cargo that may pose a risk for terrorism.

30. The Automated Targeting System (ATS) performs risk assessments on information pertaining to international travelers and import and export shipments attempting to enter or leave the United States.

Part II
Resilience

Chapter 5

The Role of Community Resilience in Advancing Security

Stephen E. Flynn

In the aftermath of the November 13, 2015 Paris attacks, *New Yorker* staff writer Adam Gopnik, wrote that "terrorist nihilism is an inevitable and recurring product of modernity . . . Terrorism will not end".[1] Gopnik's sobering observation was seemingly confirmed just three weeks later when on December 2, 2015, the community of San Bernardino, California tragically endured an attack on a training session and holiday gathering of local public health officials. The husband and wife attackers, Syed Rizwan Farook and Tashfeen Malik, had no criminal record and had never been identified by law enforcement and intelligence officials as potential terrorists.

For many public officials and security professionals, acknowledging that acts of terror cannot always be prevented is a difficult pill to swallow. Following the attacks on New York and Washington on September 11, 2001, U.S. political leaders vowed "to take the battle to the enemy" and declared, "the only defense is offense". Security agency heads would frequently assert, "We have to be right 100 percent of the time while terrorists have to

Stephen E. Flynn is a Professor of Political Science and Director of the Center for Resilience Studies at Northeastern University, and bestselling author of *America the Vulnerable* and *The Edge of Disaster: Rebuilding a Resilient Nation*.

be right only once". Such statements were meant to convey unbridled commitment to detecting, intercepting and defeating terrorists.

One unintended consequence of muscular avowals to do whatever it takes to prevent acts of terrorism is that it fuels unrealistic public expectations. When terrorist attacks inevitably occur, leaders end up looking like they have oversold their counter-terrorism efforts. The resultant loss in public trust ends up creating fertile political ground for demagogues and pressure to enact new draconian, costly and often self-defeating protective measures.

Another consequence of a myopic focus on preventing every act of terrorism is that it weakens support for adequately investing in preparations to respond to and recover from attacks when they occur. Critics can portray such investments as coming at the expense of greater vigilance and characterise them as an act of resignation. However, a lack of preparedness almost guarantees that terrorists will get a bigger "bang for their buck" in terms of the disruption and societal overreaction they will generate if they carry out a successful attack. Such success, in turn, translates into further fuelling the motivation for adversaries to carry out future attacks.

Too often missing from counter-terrorism strategies is an appreciation of the potential role that community resilience can play as a deterrent. Bolstering resilience involves developing the means to better withstand, nimbly respond to, recover and learn from, and adapt to disruptive events.[2] A community that is resilient will require an adversary to possess significant capabilities to generate the kind of disruption that makes terrorism an appealing weapon. Should terrorists have to marshal greater capabilities, they elevate the risk that their activities will be detected and intercepted. As a result, resilient communities end up making less attractive targets.

When it comes to combatting terrorism, it turns out that offense is not the only defence. Community resilience mitigates the consequences of a terrorist attack should one occur, while at the same time undermining an adversary's intent to carry out these attacks in the first place.

Terrorism and Three Illustrations of Community Resilience

One of the likely reasons that community resilience has been underappreciated is that when attacks occur, the headlines focus almost exclusively on the destruction wrought and the lives lost. The media then turns its attention to investigating who was responsible and identifying what vulnerabilities the attackers were able to exploit. Lost in the shuffle are often the important stories of how the targeted communities dealt with these attacks. This is unfortunate since it is these overlooked stories that can provide valuable lessons on how terrorists can be deprived of much of the terror and societal disruption they aspire to generate.

Boatlift and the attacks of 9/11

The image of the toppling of the World Trade Centre Towers in New York City on September 11, 2001, is etched into the world's collective memory. But almost entirely overlooked was another drama that played out in lower Manhattan literally as the towers were coming down. Mariners from all around New York harbour came together that day in a spontaneous armada to help organise and carry out what turned out to be the largest sea evacuation in history.

The story of the 9/11 boatlift began with many of the people in and around the World Trade Centre fleeing south to escape the fires and debris as the Twin Towers were struck by American Airlines Flight 11 and United Airlines Flight 175. Once they reached the tip of Manhattan, they were trapped. After the towers had collapsed, they could not go back north which meant that their only way out would be by boat. U.S. Coast Guard Lieutenant Michael Day was on scene aboard the Pilot Boat *New York*. He sent out a radio call for "All available boats", directing any vessel that wanted to assist with the evacuation of lower Manhattan to report to nearby Governors Island. Within minutes hundreds of tugboats, ferries, tourboats and private boats had set out to help. Over the course of the next nine hours, these vessels rescued nearly 500,000 civilians. By comparison, the sea evacuation at Dunkirk during World War II led to the rescue of 338,000 British and French soldiers over the course of nine days.[3]

The rescue of the British Expeditionary Force and soldiers of the French army at Dunkirk inspired Winston Churchill's historic "We shall never surrender" speech. On June 4, 1940 in an address before Parliament, Churchill acknowledged that the Dunkirk evacuation was in response to a devastating military setback. Nonetheless, he celebrated the resilience of the British people who he declared would "ride out the storm of war and outlive the menace of tyranny".[4]

But no such acknowledgement of the resilience of the New York maritime community found its way into the public discourse in the aftermath of 9/11. Indeed, it was not until a full decade later before the story was finally told in a short documentary produced and written by this author and narrated by the actor, Tom Hanks.[5]

While on its face, the organisation and execution of the 9/11 boatlift was spontaneous and unplanned, in fact it had been shaped to a substantial degree by well-established attitudes and capabilities within the maritime community. First, mariners possess a centuries-old tradition of rendering assistance to those in distress. This evolved out of both the inherent danger of transiting the high seas as well as the practical limits of what governments were able to do with respect to safeguarding the passengers and crews of vessels flying under their flag. Second, mariners are well-practiced in coming together as small teams and operating in concert in the face of both routine and novel situations. Third, vessels interact with each other in accordance with a well-established set of norms and practices codified in the "Navigation Rules and Regulations Handbook".[6] These include rules of the road and guidance for ship-to-ship communication. Finally, professional mariners place special value on preparedness for emergencies to include regular training and exercises. As a result, operators of hundreds of vessels were willing and able to nimbly respond to needs of nearly one-half million New Yorkers. In short, the resilience of this community contributed significantly to mitigating the disruption and suffering that al-Qaeda aimed to achieve on 9/11.

Boston Strong and the 2013 Marathon Bombing

On the afternoon of April 15, 2013, two improvised explosive devices (IED) were detonated near the finish line of the Boston Marathon. The IEDs sprayed metal shards, ball bearings and nails, severing limbs and causing massive injuries to the nearby onlookers. Three of the victims died and over 260 suffered injuries that required urgent hospital care.

The attack represented the most significant terrorist event on U.S. soil since September 11, 2001. It was carried out by two brothers, Tamerian and

Dzhokhar Tsarnaev, who were self-radicalised and unconnected to outside terrorist groups. Once the Tsarnaev brothers were identified as suspects, the hunt to capture them commanded extraordinary media attention. The resultant focus on the law enforcement response to the bombings came to overshadow early reporting on the exceptional medical and community response. Still, the resilience of Bostonians, captured by the expression "Boston Strong", became an important part of the Marathon Bombing story.

As with the case of New York mariners on 9/11, the Boston medical response had deep roots in formal and informal preparedness. The marathon organisers had arranged for a medical tent and a large number of ambulances and other vehicles to be located near the finish line which could be used to transport injured or dehydrated runners. It turned out that a number of the bystanders as well as runners were doctors, nurses, emergency medical technicians and military combat veterans who were trained in trauma medicine, including the treatment of blast injuries. Further, as a result of training experiences where arriving police cars ended up blocking exit routes, officials knew to issue frequent broadcasts to keep the roadways clear so that ambulances could take the injured from the site. As a result, within 22 minutes all victims with serious injuries were in or on their way to nearby hospitals.

Because of frequent training and exercises, Boston hospitals were well prepared to handle mass casualty events. The city has eight Level 1 trauma centres and a coordination centre had been activated for the Marathon to oversee the distribution of patients to prevent too many victims arriving at any given emergency room. There was also a bit of good fortune. Since the explosions had gone off just prior to the 3 pm hospital staff shift, there were twice the personnel on hand to manage the victims. Additionally, since the marathon took place on a holiday, no elective surgery had been scheduled that day, so that all operation rooms were available to handle the arriving casualties.

Within one major trauma centre, "micro-sites" were created to allow doctors and nurses to focus on an individual patient with minimal distraction by the emergency care that was being provided by other teams on other victims. Extraordinarily, particularly given the severity of many of the injuries, there was not a single fatality among all the bombing victims who reached a hospital alive.[7]

In addition to the exceptional work by hundreds of medical personnel, the general community also selflessly responded to the incident. At the finish line, dozens of volunteers ignored the risk of follow-on explosions and dove in to help provide care for the victims. Other members of the community supported the investigation by sending their photos and videos. Many families played host to runners who were stranded in the aftermath of the race.[8] The day after the bombing, "One Fund Boston", a charity to support the bombing victims was established. It collected and distributed $61 million dollars to 230 victims and survivors in 75 days.[9]

The "Boston Strong" story demonstrates the importance of preparedness when it comes to mitigating the casualties associated with a terrorist attack. It also highlights the importance of creating conditions where the general community is both encouraged and empowered to volunteer their skills and resources to respond to these events. Too often public safety officials resist inviting and accepting assistance from non-professionals. What they must do instead is actively plan for spontaneous acts of kindness and identify in advance ways to fully harness volunteers to augment their efforts. Given the ubiquity of social media tools, there is a growing array of new opportunities for engaging the public in disaster response and recovery.

In a statement from the White House on the evening following the Marathon bombings, President Barack Obama observed that:

> Boston is a tough and resilient town. So are its people. I'm supremely confident that Bostonians will pull together, take care of each other, and move forward as one proud city. And as they do, the American people will be with them every single step of the way.[10]

Boston's investment in preparedness for a mass casualty event clearly saved many lives. The speed of the investigation, which was undertaken with overwhelming support from the community, helped to reduce public apprehension about the risk of follow-on attacks. Finally, the determination by Bostonians to return to their normal routines served as a source of inspiration for others, much like World War II Londoners did by showing their grit in the face of aerial bombings during the Blitz.

If the Marathon bombers envisioned that their attacks would help demoralise the American public, in fact they achieved the opposite result. What they ended up exposing was the resilience of the Boston community. In the hours after the attack, "Boston Strong" appeared as a highly popular hashtag on Twitter. According to the city's leading newspaper, it quickly became "a handy shorthand for defiance, solidarity and caring. In its ubiquity, 'Boston Strong' presents a united front in the face of threat".[11]

The November 2015 Paris attacks

On the evening of November 13, 2015, three terrorist teams launched six attacks in Paris and Saint-Denis, a northern suburb. The teams were armed with assault rifles and suicide vests. 130 people were killed and over 300 more suffered injuries.[12]

As with Boston, Paris activated a massive medical response that drew on years of comprehensive planning and training. The city's emergency medical services were mobilised and a crisis unit was stood up at the Assistance Publique–Hopitaux de Paris (APHP). The Director of APHP ordered the activation of the city's "White Plan", which had been developed two decades before to mobilise the capabilities of medical staff at 40 hospitals with 200 operating rooms across the metro-Paris region. In addition, a psychological support unit was set up with psychiatrists, psychologists, nurses and volunteers. As a result, there was never a shortage of personnel to attend to the hundreds of victims who arrived for emergency care.

Many of these medical professionals had worked together in response to the January 2015 attacks against *Charlie Hebdo*. Most had also participated in training exercises and had been involved with updating emergency plans in the preceding months. Their training protocols had drawn on experiences in Israel, Spain, England and most recently Boston. Fortuitously, the emergency medical services and Paris fire brigade had participated in an exercise simulating a response to multiple shootings on the very day of the Paris attacks.

While the focus in the Boston Marathon bombings was to send victims as quickly as possible to the nearby hospitals in order to receive physician care, the Paris medical response involved deploying units into the field to perform triage and to provide prehospital care. On the evening of November 13, 2015, medical workers were sent to eight emergency sites to work alongside police and rescue workers. Each team had 15 individuals to answer the calls, and five physicians. Mobile units composed of a physician, nurse and driver were deployed to provide initial treatment for victims and to take them to the most appropriate trauma centre or nearest hospital. Other units were held in reserve to avoid saturating the first crisis site and to respond to new emergency situations.

In hospitals that typically staff two operating rooms, the activation of the "White Plan" mobilised sufficient staffing to support up to ten operating rooms per hospital for treating injured patients. A rapid triage was organised at the entry of the emergency department. Training conducted over several months facilitated the ability to provide fast-track service for victims who suffered from bullet wounds. Each hospital maintained two trauma leaders who oversaw the entire cohort of injured patients. Within 24 hours, emergency surgeries for all the victims were completed. There were only four deaths among the 302 injured patients, including two who died upon arrival at the hospital.[13]

Outside of the hospitals, Parisians responded much as Bostonians had two years prior. Immediately after the shootings and explosions, signs and hashtags appeared saying "même pas peur" — "you don't scare me".[14] The night after terrorism gunmen sprayed his bakery with bullets, Mezian Ahmed, a Parisian baker was open for business. And the old and young people of Paris defiantly returned to the open-air cafés.[15]

Summary Lessons from Three Resilient Communities

We live in an age where there will always be individuals and groups with extreme causes. Some of them will succeed in gaining access to deadly weapons. Quite simply, it will not be possible to always detect and intercept those who are intent on carrying out acts of terrorism. Since terrorist attacks cannot always be prevented, we must increasingly align our approach to one akin to how we deal with natural disasters and disease outbreaks. Communities must invest time and resources in preparing to withstand, respond to and bounce back from these attacks. What is required is a serious commitment to conducting planning and training for when things go wrong, because at some point, they will go wrong. Concurrently, public safety professionals must engage in aggressive outreach to the general public.

Individually and collectively, the 9/11 Boatlift, the "Boston Strong" response to the 2013 marathon bombings, and the 2015 Paris attacks response highlight the benefits of bolstering resilience at a metro-regional scale. During and after a crisis is not the time to develop institutional and personal relationships. Instead neighbourhood groups, response organisations, security agencies, emergency planners, hospitals and public health organisations need to forge an understanding of their respective capabilities and needs well in advance of a major disaster. These relationships should be forged by developing common systems and shared protocols, conducting table-top and field exercises, and evaluating what went right and what went wrong during actual events. The goal should be to make coordination and collaboration within and across a community a natural act.

In addition to actively working to bolster community resilience, leaders should ensure that demonstrations of resilience are widely recognised and celebrated. Resilience is the antidote to the fear that terrorist organisations aspire to generate. Faced with the loss of the World Trade Centre towers, the New York maritime community demonstrated how people can come together and devise novel solutions to complex problems under even the most trying circumstances. In the aftermath of the Marathon bombing, Bostonians demonstrated competence, compassion and defiance. And after the tragic November 2015 shootings in Paris, medical professionals and everyday Parisians showed how the City of Lights can illuminate the best of humanity even when subjected to its darkest shadows.

When Adam Gopnik asserted that terrorism will never end, he also argued that "terrorism cannot triumph". He is right. Terrorism will always be an act of futility and desperation as long as communities and countries are resilient.

Endnotes

1. Gopnik, A. (2015). "Open Letter to a Friend in Paris." *The New Yorker.* http://www.newyorker.com/culture/cultural-comment/open-letter-to-a-friend-in-parishttp://www.newyorker.com/culture/cultural-comment/open-letter-to-a-friend-in-paris. (Retrieved 1 March 2016).

2. This definition of resilience is derived from "Critical Infrastructure Security and Resilience," Presidential Decision Directive-21, The White House. (2013). https://www.whitehouse.gov/the-press-office/2013/02/12/presidential-policy-directive-critical-infrastructure-security-and-resil. (Retrieved 1 March 2016)

3. BOATLIFT: An Untold Story of 9/11 Resilience. (2011). Stephen Flynn writer and executive producer Sean Burke; narrated by Tom Hanks; directed by Eddie Rosenstein, EyePop Productions. https://www.youtube.com/watch?v=MDOrzF7B2Kg (Retrieved 1 March 2016)

4. Winston Churchill. (1940). "We Shall Fight on the Beaches," Address to the House of Commons. http://www.winstonchurchill.org/resources/speeches/128-we-shall-fight-on-the-beaches. (Retrieved 1 March 2016)

5. BOATLIFT: An Untold Story of 9/11 Resilience. *Ibid.* (Retrieved 3 January 2016)

6. Navigation Rules and Regulations Handbook. (2014). Washington, DC: U.S. Coast Guard. http://navcen.uscg.gov/pdf/navRules/CG_NRHB_20150929.pdf. (Retrieved 3 January 2016)

7. Herman B. "Dutch" Leonard, Christine M. Cole, Arnold M. Howitt, and Phillip B. Heymann. (2014). Why was Boston Strong? Cambridge: Harvard Kennedy School Program on Crisis Leadership, pp. 7–9.

8. *Ibid.*, p. 14.

9. About One Fund. https://secure.onefundboston.org/pages/about. (Retrieved 3 January 2016)

10. President Obama Speaks on the Explosions in Boston. (2013). Washington: The White House. https://www.whitehouse.gov/blog/2013/04/15/president-obama-speaks-explosions-boston. (Retrieved 3 January 2016)

11. Zimmer, B. (2013). "'Boston Strong,' the Phrase that Rallied the City," *The Boston Globe.* http://www.bostonglobe.com/ideas/2013/05/11/boston-strong-phrase-that-rallied-city/uNPFaI8Mv4QxsWqpjXBOQO/story.html. (Retrieved 1 March 2016)

12. Marcus, M. B. (2013). "Injuries from Paris Attacks Will Take Long to Heal." *CBS News.* http://www.cbsnews.com/news/injuries-from-paris-attacks-will-take-long-to-heal/. (Retrieved 1 March 2016)

13. Hirsch, M., Carli, P., Nizard, R., Riou, B., Baroudjian, B., Baubet, T., Chhor, B., Chollet-Xemard, C., Dantchev, N., Fleury, N., Fontaine, J., Yordanov, Y., Raphael, M., Burtz, C. P., & Lafont, A. (2015). "The Medical Response to Multisite Terrorist Attacks in Paris." *The Lancet.* pp. 1-4. http://www.sciencedirect.com/science/article/pii/S0140673615010636. (Retrieved 1 March 2016)

14. Gopnik, *Ibid.*

15. Siegel, R., (2015). "One Week after Paris Attacks, Life Continues in the Place De La Republique." *NPR All Things Considered.* http://www.npr.org/2015/11/20/456831528/one-week-after-paris-attacks-life-continues-in-the-place-de-la-r-publique. (Retrieved 1 March 2016)

Chapter 6

Social Resilience and the Troubles in Northern Ireland

John, Lord Alderdice

Everywhere we are faced with the challenge of understanding and countering violent extremism. Academics and politicians tend to think intellectually about the rationale for people becoming disenchanted and security agencies try to contain unrest through security measures that make creating trouble a difficult and personally costly matter. But the religious and political agendas to which violent activists adhere, like so many of the things that really impact on our lives as individuals and communities, are matters of 'feeling' more than of 'thinking' and motivate people to take huge risks with themselves and their welfare. We can give rationalistic explanations for the involvement of young people in terrorism, but they hold these views and act on them with a passion that is not merely rational. They are 'devoted' actors rather than 'rational' actors. After many years of exploring these matters I am not convinced that it is fundamentalist religious or political beliefs in themselves that lead to radicalisation and terrorism. In Ireland the terrorists, despite self-identifying

John, Lord Alderdice is a Liberal Democrat member of the House of Lords, Senior Research Fellow and Director of the Centre for the Resolution of Intractable Conflict at Harris Manchester College, Oxford and Chairman of the Centre for Democracy and Peace Building in Belfast.

as Protestants and Catholics, were generally not in church on Sundays, and similarly most young Islamist radicals who undertake terrorist actions have a scanty acquaintance with Muslim theology. They are driven by passion and rage about what they see as humiliation of their people and injustice in their world and their religion is a badge of identity. If our communities are to find resilience in facing violent extremism, we need to seriously address the emotional roots of the problems felt by the communities of those who attack us, as well as understand the emotional responses of our own wider community.

In addition to thinking about why terrorists act as they do, we also need to consider how they organise and engage. The IRA, and now much more powerfully and globally, Islamist terrorists, have recognised the resilience of networks when pitted against the hierarchical structures and bureaucracies of our societies. They operate through resilient networks, whether mediated by the internet or through friends or family connections, while our political, governmental and security agencies for the most part remain bureaucratic, hierarchical and slow to react. We need to understand these differences and change our approach if we are to help our societies to develop resilience in the face of these challenges.

The principles outlined in this chapter have emerged through the experience of living and working in Northern Ireland but I have also explored quite extensively how they may be applied in other troubled communities. I think these principles, as distinct from the structures and details, are applicable in many places.

From 1989 until 1998, throughout the development of the Irish Peace Process, I was the Leader of the cross-community political party called Alliance. During the implementation of the Good Friday Agreement until 2004, I was the first Speaker of the Northern Ireland Assembly. For six years after my retirement as Speaker I dealt with the unresolved problems of weapons and security normalisation as one of the four members of the Independent Monitoring Commission (an international body established by the British, Irish and U.S. Governments). And now, though the violence is largely in the past and a power-sharing government has been in place for many years, as the Chairman of the Centre for Democracy and Peace Building — a non-partisan civil society organisation I have established in Belfast — I am addressing the problems of enduring communal identities which drive our remaining divisions. These differing roles allowed me to observe from different angles those things which contributed to resilience or the lack of it in the community.

Every society is different and I do not wish to present the Northern Ireland experience as one which others should apply as a simple 'read-across'. Rather an understanding of our problems and the way we have dealt with them may suggest some principles of human engagement in large groups, principles that may have relevance elsewhere. What then can one say about the general principles of moving from *de facto* civil war to the building of a civil society?

Paradoxically, to deepen our understanding of general principles we must examine the particular historical and emotional drivers of a number of situations. I have often told about the man confronted during the Troubles in a difficult part of Belfast, and asked whether he was a Protestant Muslim or a Catholic Muslim. Like many amusing stories it shows insight. Those who know nothing of these faiths still instinctively appreciate that religious faith may be used as a badge of identity and this man was in danger of attack because of the feelings of hatred of the other group shown by the young men who challenged him. They were not aroused by a rational debate about the complex doctrinal divergence which developed between Protestantism and Roman Catholicism since Martin Luther nailed his theses to the door of the Castle Church in Wittenburg in 1520. While Protestant loyalists may well be able to quote the dates and celebrate some 17th century battles between the Dutch Protestant Prince William of Orange taking the British throne from the Catholic, King James, they have little appreciation of the complex historical background of the time. Dr Ian Paisley, the firebrand preacher who led them, was very committed to his brand of fundamentalist Protestant theology and understood the historical issues, but he was eventually able to go into power-sharing government as the First Minister of Northern Ireland with a Deputy First Minister, Martin McGuinness, a Catholic Nationalist who had been a leader of the Provisional IRA, a Republican, and his sworn enemy. Neither of them had changed their beliefs, and Dr Paisley did not become a secularist, but they found a way of living and working together despite their disagreements, largely consigning IRA terrorism and the loyalist paramilitary violence to history. In other words, it was not as simple as that holding their beliefs provoked them to violent action since they were able to maintain their beliefs and yet move away from violence.

For hundreds of years Irish Nationalists and Republicans (mostly but not exclusively Roman Catholics) used violence to try to expel the British from Ireland. After the partition of Ireland in 1921 when most of the island gained independence, the six north-eastern counties remained within the United Kingdom because a substantial majority of the population who were Unionist and mostly Protestant wanted it so. In every decade after the partition, there were armed insurrections by Catholic Republicans who wanted independence. In the 1960s the civil rights marches in Northern Ireland were violently attacked by Dr Paisley and his loyalist followers, not because they were part of a worldwide civil rights movement but as a recurrence of historic republican subversion.

The initial government response was a police crack-down. When the situation deteriorated with massive numbers of shootings and bombings, executive detention without trial was introduced. This was disastrous, not only because it was ineptly carried out, but the sense of moral outrage it induced acted as a recruiting sergeant for violent republicanism and led to an almost total loss of community cooperation in working class communities on both sides of the divide, but especially in Catholic areas. For the next quarter of a century intelligence gathering became extremely difficult and community policing impossible. This itself was in fact a form of community resilience in the face of a security engagement by the government, but it was a resilience that produced a negative outcome. Eventually the British Government realised it had made a disastrous policy mistake but its cessation of executive detention did not reverse the situation. While demonstrably fair judicial action, stringent equality legislation (particularly in regard to employment), a genuine resolution of all the complaints of discrimination in voting rights and housing and massive efforts at economic development of areas of social need all helped to some extent to stabilise the situation, they did not resolve it. The terrorism continued with various changes of tactics and sophistication on all sides. It became a chronic stalemate — neither the British Army nor the IRA could be defeated by the other and neither could win.

There were many political initiatives throughout the 1970s and 1980s based on the idea that the exclusion of the more extreme elements might facilitate negotiations by moderate elements on both sides, but these efforts were always undermined from the outside by the extremists. Eventually in the late 1980s, and more particularly in the 1990s, we began to explore the possibility of engagement with more extreme and even violent elements and slowly and painfully created a process of inclusive engagement. This took years to achieve, and meantime the terrorist attacks continued.

It was not until 1994 that the Provisional IRA (the main violent republican organisation) called a cessation of violence, and after that Sinn Fein — their political representatives — were admitted to the Talks Process. Even then another four years of difficult, complex and painful negotiations were needed before the 1998 Belfast Agreement was achieved, and we have continued with a decades-long implementation program.

I have been struck by some similarities in various parts of the world which have experienced terrorist campaigns (2009)[1]. In Latin America, India, Pakistan, Nepal, the Balkans and the Middle East, those with whom I have talked, including some extreme Islamists, all have the same emotions and the same way of thinking and talking about their problems, even though their history, religion and politics are very different. They tend to elevate transcendent values, (not just religious ones, but things like "respect for my culture" and "justice for my people") above socio-economic drivers, and they find their identity being fused with that of their group, rather than maintaining the sense of a complex and individualistic identity. These ways of thinking characterised by sacred values and fusion with the group identity have been well explored by Scott Atran (2013)[2] and Harvey Whitehouse (2014)[3] in a series of important research projects.

These groups may also adopt the tactic of asymmetric warfare that we call terrorism. It tends to be used by disparate and even opposing groups because they recognise the resilience of networks when pitted against hierarchical structures and bureaucracies. The development of the internet was just such a recognition of the resilience of networks, but our political, governmental and security agencies remain hierarchical sitting ducks for the terrorists — much like the British Army with their bright red uniforms during the American War of Independence. Networks operate in a completely different way and to different rules — leadership within these networks depends not on position but on the capacity to inspire. Discipline is very difficult, and hysterical reactions, often as a result of an outburst of rage, are hard to contain. Nevertheless, it has been necessary in Northern Ireland to learn it is not power and force, but engagement, inclusion and the building of relationships that gives the possibility of finding a different way of conducting our differences.

I have already mentioned the long-term process of talks which led to the power-sharing arrangements of government in Northern Ireland. This has been necessary in other areas, notably in the most contentious area of policing. Although it would have been inconceivable not so long ago, Sinn Fein is now giving support to a reformed police service and former IRA members are participating, not as uniformed officers, but in the community oversight bodies for policing. It is not enough to have central direction. There must be community engagement, so every Northern Ireland community now has a District Policing Partnership where former opponents can work together to provide a community policing service.

If such community engagement and resilience is such a good idea, why is it not adopted? There are two groups of factors that work against it.

The first is the deliberate exclusion of a large section of one community from aspects of public life, including shouldering authority and responsibility for community decisions. This discrimination against non-unionist and Catholic people had an entirely deleterious on the health of civic society in Northern Ireland. While the terrorist campaign was entirely unjustified, deliberately excluding people from the civic life of Northern Ireland played a significant part in creating the conditions in which terrorism emerged.

Terrorism is neither the result of poverty nor social and economic disadvantage. Those are important issues and their redress is a moral imperative. However, there is poverty in many places without terrorism. What is the root of terrorism? I recall a leading member of a paramilitary organisation, also a political figure, describing how as a teenager he really wanted to be a motor mechanic. He went along to his local garage and asked for a job, but was refused. He tried to press his interest but the owner made clear he did not employ Catholics. He described a deep sense of humiliation and a bitter sense of anger at the unfairness. None of us likes to be humiliated. It is profoundly emotionally toxic. If you humiliate someone they will probably neither forget nor forgive you, and if they meet you many years later, the first and lasting thing they will remember about you is how they felt when you humiliated them.

That senior participant in the inter-party negotiations then said "You know, I sometimes think to myself, if I'd got that job as a motor mechanic would I ever have got involved in the things I got involved with afterwards?" This was a man who had been a very powerful figure in one of the most deadly and successful terrorist organisations in the world at the time. I was left with the lasting picture in my mind of some fellow who runs a little garage in Northern Ireland, who, if he had given this particular 16 year old a job, might have prevented many deaths and injuries. Two things strike me from that story. Firstly, the impact we as individuals have in our everyday interactions whose outcome we can never predict. Secondly, on a societal level, the impact of exclusion, disrespect, and humiliation on the future well-being of society. Creating a truly <u>civil</u> society means building it on respect for all its citizens rather than by exclusion, disregard or humiliation. What were the steps to move away from conflict and towards a more inclusive society?

The first key step was the preparedness to meet and talk with those who had been involved in violence. For a long time, the general view (which originally I shared) was that those on the extremes, especially those engaged in violence, could not and should not be part of any talks or negotiations. However, every other attempt failed and so we became eventually and gradually more open to engagement. The participants did not start by <u>feeling</u> respect for each other, but they did start to behave respectfully towards one another, and when people in the community saw their political representatives and their political aspirations being treated with respect and their own human rights being respected, things began to change.

One of the few things the parties could agree in the very early days of the Inter-Party Talks was that we all wanted to see protections for human rights. Everyone could see they had much to gain from this. I have never yet met a politician who said, "I don't much care whether the rights of my people are respected". Once one demands respect for the rights of one's own people it becomes difficult to state one's disregard for the rights of others. No one at the Talks wanted their own rights disregarded, and achieving agreement clearly meant that everyone's rights must be protected.

If purposely excluding Catholic Nationalists was one element in damaging societal resilience, a second key factor was the way a whole generation moved away from elected politics as a contribution to society. They did not turn to violence, but they opted out of politics. When in the late 1960s things broke down into violence and increasing chaos, the British Government stepped in to prorogue the Northern Ireland Parliament in 1972, taking effective political authority back to London.

All that was left was very modest local government powers. There were responsibilities for parks and cemeteries and rubbish disposal, but housing, roads and social services had earlier been removed from Local Government. When the Parliament was prorogued, agriculture, health and social security, transport, policing, the environment and the economy, were all removed as well. For the next 25 years, elected politicians in Northern Ireland had neither power nor responsibility. The Lord Mayor of Belfast could not get a streetlight fixed without making a request to a civil servant responsible to a government minister from London.

As a result, people lost interest in what politics could deliver. Businessmen, professionals, academics and people in the voluntary and community sectors all left elected, representative, democratic politics. There was no power; the violence meant that holding political power could be dangerous at times; and few people had a vision for finding a way out. Able people who wanted to contribute to society took up government appointments to statutory bodies, or became involved in community activities and NGOs of the kind you will find in any healthy society with an active civic life. The difference is that in most other democracies these organisations take their place alongside electoral politics, rather than displacing or replacing them.

The British Government was keen to maintain stability and some independent validity for its governance of the community, so increasingly government spending was dispensed through the organisations described above. Some Boards were set up by the government with community appointees, but with fewer elected representatives being appointed. NGOs became very powerful and those who were appointed to them had a good deal of control, but they did not have to make too many difficult decisions because the government was prepared to pump very large amounts of money into Northern Ireland to maintain some order — even when public spending was being cut back in the rest of the United Kingdom under Prime Minister Margaret Thatcher. The budget for Northern Ireland at that time, not including security, was about nine billion pounds sterling for a population of one and a half million people. The tax revenue from Northern Ireland was about half that, so approximately £4.5 billion was given in an annual grant from the British Exchequer to a community of 1.5 million people. That substantial subvention made possible the flourishing of the NGO sector but they became the *bête noire* of many elected politicians, because while elected representatives had absolutely no power, they still had to go out and knock on doors, deliver leaflets and get abused by their constituents for things they did not have the power to change. The appointees were actually able to make important decisions without elected accountability and this denuded and diminished elected politics.

Does it matter if people choose not to get involved in elected politics? While the community and NGO sector is an increasingly crucial component of democracy, democratic societies need democratic structures and that means some kind of system whereby people choose who they want to represent them. Without the process of knocking on doors, attending public meetings, holding constituency surgeries and most importantly putting oneself forward for election, people on the ground do not see politicians as representing them.

Government needs to be able to take difficult decisions, like balancing the demands of firefighters and the health of the wider economy. Who should get paid more — firefighters or nurses? These decisions are not simple economic questions. Without good people who are prepared to put themselves forward for election, there will be poor decisions and the whole community will all suffer.

So not only is the health and resilience of a community adversely affected by excluding some groups, it is also harmed when good people opt out. This is not just a problem for communities in conflict, but for many western communities.

Let me summarise. Where a section of the community feels humiliated and disrespected and experiences a powerful and pervasive sense of unfairness, there is a reduction in the positive social resilience that can hold the community together.

When groups have the toxic emotional experiences of humiliation, injustice and existential threat they no longer operate on the basis of best individual self-interest. Instead they become 'devoted actors' judging their actions on 'sacred values'. Their identity also becomes 'fused' with that of their group.

Social resilience is not only weakened by the practices of discrimination and exclusion but also by a conviction in the community that one has nothing to gain by contributing through engagement in elected politics and sharing in communal responsibility.

The resulting loss of local responsibility leads to less responsible politics, and loss of civil commitment is the start of the dangerous road to an uncivil society.

Building respectful behaviour between different sections of the community, valuing elected politicians and all sections of the society and sharing the responsibility and the rewards of governing the community among the public, private and voluntary sectors can make those communities 'somewhere that everyone can feel at home'. Such a positive identification contributes greatly to such societies being able to bounce back under stress.

Endnotes

1. Alderdice, J. T. (2009). Sacred Values: Psychological and Anthropological Perspectives on Fairness, Fundamentalism and Terrorism, *Annals of the New York Academy of Sciences,* 1167, 158–173.
2. Atran, S., & Ginges, J. (2013). Religious and Sacred Imperatives in Human Conflict, *Science,* 336, 855–857.
3. Whitehouse, H., & Lanman, J. A. (2014). The Ties that Bind Us: Ritual, Fusion, and Identification, *Current Anthropology,* 55(6), 674–695.

Chapter 7

Resilience and National Security: "Everyone Has a Plan 'Til They Get Punched in the Mouth"*

Norman Vasu

Introduction

Resilience is a concept with an embarrassment of definitions and conceptions spanning many different domains. Over the years, the term has gained great currency with its semantic domain expanding from its initial employment in the field of physics and ecology, to biology, psychology and finally to social studies. This semantic expansion of the term from the hard to the social sciences and humanities is unsurprising as it may be representative of an attempt to redress the dominant methodology of the experimental sciences where complex systems are treated as if they are simple mechanical equipment open to analysis by examining their constituent parts in controlled laboratory conditions.[1]

In the reporting of world news, the term became *du jour* to describe the stoic-ness of a community confronted with a crisis. Indeed, many were keen to emphasise how London is a "resilient city" and the

_____

* Mike Tyson's reply when asked about his strategy to fight Evander Holyfield.

Norman Vasu is Senior Fellow and Deputy Head of CENS, as well as head of CENS' Social Resilience Programme.

"resilience of the British people" in order to describe a society's ability to return to normal life post-crisis.[2] Post-7/7, the ubiquity of the term is inescapable. For example, owing to their stoic response to terrorism in various cities, Mumbaikars to Parisians have been described as resilient while New Orleans, by overcoming Katrina, has been dubbed a resilient city.

With its etymological roots in the Latin *resilire* — meaning to jump back or recoil and more commonly employed in physics to describe the ability of materials to return to their original shape or position after being exposed to external pressures — resilience does appear to be the accurate word when describing a community's positive response to a crisis.

Obviously, the term is naturally appealing to those on the ramparts of national security owing to the generally fair belief that society cannot be protected from all threats — be they man-made or natural.[3] After all, if one cannot prevent everything, it is best one prepares for the failure to do so. Resilience then offers the goal and hope of a rapid recovery after the unavoidable occurs.

While the proliferation of the term's employment arguably demonstrates the concept's utility, the wide range of understandings and application of the term makes conceiving of a framework for national security based on resilience difficult at best.

This chapter explores in three broad parts the meaning of the term and discusses its applicability when thinking about national security. Firstly, it draws a distinction between resistance and resilience — two concepts often confusingly coupled together. It argues resistance is the attempt to prevent a crisis while resilience is the ability to overcome a crisis after it occurs. The second part of the chapter shows that there are two forms of resilience *vis-à-vis* national security. While resilience can be conservative — that is, the preservation of the status quo — it can also be dynamic — that is, an adaptive resilience that embraces change for society's betterment after a crisis. This section argues that for resilience to manifest and be of value, a dynamic resilience should be embraced. The chapter concludes by showing how the term resilience offers its greatest utility when thinking about inconceivable threats.

Difference between Resistance and Resilience

Prior to proposing a viable strategy to manage the ever-evolving threatscape faced by the modern state, a few questions should be considered. Firstly, what is the nature of the threat/s involved? The answer to this question determines the appropriateness of applying the concept of resilience. Is the threat something that can be prevented, eliminated or avoided? Or is the threat something where little mitigation, elimination or avoidance can be achieved?

Arguably, there is a sharp distinction between these two capacities. Actions to mitigate preventable threats perhaps should not fall under the concept of resilience — such action may be instead understood as resistance. Actions taken to overcome unpreventable threats may then perhaps be better classified as shoring up resilience. Resistance involves putting into place preventative measures which keep a particular danger away from society. Resistance is largely static in nature and is appropriate in circumstances where threats are known and measured preventative steps can be adopted. Examples include using fire resistant building materials in areas where there is a high risk of fires and implementing screening checks on airline passengers for explosives to prevent a bomb threat.[4]

Efforts to be resilient are usually taken when attempts to resist a threat are unsuccessful.[5] This may include situations where resistance has been ineffective (e.g., levees built to keep flood waters are breached), measures put in place are not fit for purpose (e.g., building flood retaining walls that are unable to contain a tsunami), or when there is a high opportunity cost for resistance (e.g., building a wall around a city for protection prevents people from escaping in the event of a fire). Within such a distinction between resistance and resilience, resilience — the capacity to both absorb disturbances and undergo change in order to maintain the core elements of a system — is something that is initiated when the unpreventable occurs.[6] Hence, the concept does not necessarily ensure the status quo is maintained after a disturbance or a disaster — there may be a need to adapt and alter to secure the core functions, structure and identity of society. It is an approach that does not emphasise short-term stability but rather long-term survivability.[7]

Both resistance and resilience entail different capabilities. It is therefore important to consider both carefully in light of the context of its application to specific threats.

Two Forms of Resilience

When resistance fails, that is, when the unpreventable occurs, two forms of resilience may be considered — conservative resilience and dynamic resilience.[8]

The first, the resilience of conservatism or engineering resilience, involves systems with properties able to return to a pre-determined specification or design or able to function within specifications in the wake of a disturbance. An example of this type of resilience can be seen in computer systems designed to return to or function under pre-determined specifications; its resilience is therefore measured in how quickly a system can return to a functioning state or the number of conditions under which it will still continue functioning. Expressed in another manner, this conservative form of resilience is driven by a desire to return exactly back to the way things were.

The second form of resilience is dynamic and has been referred to as ecological or adaptive resilience. As the term suggests, the concept has its roots in ecology as opposed to engineering. This type of resilience is basically suited for systems that experience frequent surprises and it takes into account the increasing levels of complexity and uncertainty which dominate today's societies. It therefore works under the assumption that the option for returning to a pre-determined state or condition may not be possible or even desirable. The focus of ecological resilience is therefore on attributes of persistence and adaptability. Expressed in another manner, this dynamic form of resilience is comfortable with adaptation in order to ensure survivability where life will carry on but it will do so through change.

While conservative resilience works for certain types of systems and risks (e.g., binary or linear systems such as computers or the rigidity of metal), it appears that dynamic resilience is better suited for complex social systems[9] and to manage unknown threats. A major criticism of conservative resilience is the fact that it does not capture the complexity and dynamism of social systems such as the modern state. For example, when faced with the challenge of environmental change, a traditionally agricultural community can opt to employ conservative resilience — the preservation of an agricultural lifestyle whatever the cost — or it may choose to approach it in a dynamic manner — agriculture is no longer viable and new ways of life have to be explored. Undertaking strategies focusing on returning to a pre-determined outcome may lead to a misjudgement of not only the complexity involved but the system's ability to adapt and evolve along with disturbance. Instead, when dealing with a social system, dynamic resilience may provide a better framework for taking into account the complexity involved as well as the uncertainty surrounding the occurrences and effects of a disturbance. It is this understanding of resilience that is being formulated as a possible approach in dealing with unknown threats in national security and disaster management.[10]

Resilience Against the Unknown

There is increasing interest in the concept of resilience in dealing with national security threats that are either unknown or difficult to predict.[11] This is arguably where the concept has the most utility; while known threats can be devastating, there are opportunities — following the discussion above — to prepare for them.[12] This is not possible when preparing for unknown threats, which heightens the need to consider dynamic resilience. Recent catastrophes such as the earthquake, tsunami and nuclear disaster that struck Japan in 2011 underscore the importance of being able to persist in the face of extreme circumstances and to adapt to a new reality. What are the attributes of societies that are resilient in the face of unexpected threats? Available research suggests resilient communities are those with robust levels of resources and adaptive capacity.[13]

Resources in this context are defined as "objects, conditions, characteristics, and energies that people value".[14] What is valued depends on tangible and intangible assets held to be important in the context of a particular society; this can include tangibles such as food and water supplies, to more intangible assets such as educational levels, economic wealth and social cohesion. Such resources should be identified beforehand as being crucial to enable the society concerned to absorb the effects of a disaster. Robustness here is understood as the ability of a certain resource to continue functioning under a broad range of conditions. Evaluating the robustness of these resources involve assessing: (a) the performance of a particular resource in accomplishing its function; (b) the available diversity of resources and (c) ensuring that there is available redundancy of a particular resource.

As such, governments may want to consider a resilience stock-take based on the above criteria. For Singapore, the various ministries can plan to come up with standardised evaluations of resources identified as crucial for sustaining the country should a disaster strike. However, ensuring the robustness of key resources may not be a cost-effective exercise by today's commercial standards, when resources can be used in a more productive manner. For example, maintaining redundancies may entail storing aside basic assets, which is an expensive and commercially unviable thing to do. Hence, it is important to keep in mind that trade-offs will have to be negotiated between competitiveness and robustness; to strike a compromise that does not maximise one to the detriment of the other.

Adaptive capacity on the other hand involves a society's capacity to utilise its collective memory, experiences and learning in a manner facilitating innovation and reorganisation where necessary, in order to adapt to changing conditions and to maintain its core functions, structure and identity. Included in this is the ability to communicate and share experiences as well as to self-organise in the absence of specific directions. Reference to resilience in this case must take into consideration the fact that it is a community-level capacity; as such, there is a need to ensure that a large part of society is similarly committed and can work together in a concerted effort. One tangible manner in which this can be achieved is by continually communicating security concerns with the wider public. By including the wider public in discussions on national security matters, ownership of problems and the finding of solutions are taken out of the hands of elites and democratised.[15]

Research notes that while a community with high levels of resources and adaptability can be said to be resilient, this is perhaps a luxury few can afford.[16] Instead, a community that has high levels of robust resources or alternatively high levels of adaptability can afford to have lesser levels of one of the other. A balance needs to be struck taking into consideration the particular situation of the society concerned. This is an important point bearing in mind resources are finite and decisions will have to be made on what should be prioritised.

Conclusion

In conclusion, it is important to consider the role resilience plays and how it fits into a country's overall national security structure. This includes considering the optimal mix of resistance and resilience strategies to adopt. Also crucial is the rationalisation of what can be accomplished, whether what is needed is resilience to return to a pre-determined specification or to provide for ways to deal with the unknown.

As uncertainty becomes more pervasive in an increasingly complex global environment, a framework supporting the persistence and adaptability of a system — a dynamic resilience — can provide society with the capacity to respond to disasters in a manner that best ensures their chances of survival. Perhaps that is the most prudent approach to surviving a punch to the mouth.

The author would like to thank Yeap Su Yin and Yolanda Chin for their comments on the chapter.

Endnotes

1. For an Example of the Diverse Ways in which "Complex Systems" have be Understood and Analysed — Ranging from Chemistry, Biology, Evolution and Physics, *Science*, 284(5411).
2. Len Duvall, Chair of the Metropolitan Police Authority, 8 July 2005. http://policeauthority.org/metropolitan/publications/statements/050708/index.html (Retrieved 2 March 2016) and "This is What One Dreads....", *Daily Mirror*, 9 July 2005. http://www.mirror.co.uk/news/uk-news/this-is-what-one-dreads-549657 (Retrieved 2 March 2016) A particularly illustrative example of the resilience exhibited was the creation of a website which proudly stated 'We're not afraid'. More importantly, despite fears of a strong backlash in the form of racially motivated attacks on Britain's Muslim minority population that would strike at the heart of multicultural Britain, the initial spike in incidences post-event was only short-lived. Figures published by the Crown Prosecution Service showed that while there had indeed been a rise in attacks

against Muslims and Asians a major backlash could not be witnessed and the social structure of Britain remained largely intact. According to Director of Public Prosecutions Ken MacDonald, "The fears of a large rise in offences appear to be unfounded [...] Although there were more cases in July 2005 than for any other month, the rise did not continue into August and overall in 2005–2006 there was an increase of nine cases compared to the previous year". Dodd, V. (2005). Calls for Calm as Fear of Severe Backlash Grows, *The Guardian* (13 July) and Backlash against Muslims after 7/7 Exaggerated, *Reuters* (4 December 2006).

3. For example, consider the nausea-inducing overly employed quote about terrorists only having to be lucky once while security agencies have to be lucky all the time.

4. Longstaff, P. H., Armstrong, N. J., & Perrin, K. (2010). Building Resilient Communities: Tools for Assessment. White Paper, Institute for National Security and Counterterrorism, Syracuse University.

5. It must be noted that this does not involve a binary, one or the other option. One can have steps put in place to resist threats as well as develop measures that would ensure resilience should the threat occur.

6. This understanding of the concept of resilience is taken from the definition provided by Resilience Alliance (RA). RA has defined resilience as "the capacity of a system to absorb disturbance, undergo change, and still retain essentially the same function, structure, identity and feedbacks". The definition can be found at http://www.resalliance.org/resilience (Retrieved 27 December 2015).

7. Longstaff, P. H., Armstrong, N. J., & Perrin, K. (2010). Building Resilient Communities: Tools for Assessment. White Paper, Institute for National Security and Counterterrorism, Syracuse University.

8. *Ibid.*

9. Systems which are complex are usually made up of numerous constitutive elements which are linked and have intricate levels of dependencies. Furthermore, unlike simple systems where two plus two always equals four, complex systems are usually characterised as nonlinear systems where lines of cause and effect are not clearly evident. As a result, the influence and reaction of each constitutive element over the entire system is highly unpredictable. Examples of complex systems include the global weather pattern, ecological systems and social systems. For a more in depth discussion of social resilience within complex social systems, see Vasu, N., Grace in Times of Friction: The Complexity of Social Resilience. RSIS Commentary 72/2007, S. Rajaratnam School of International Studies, 11 July 2007.

10. Longstaff, P. H. (2005). Security, Resilience, and Communication in Unpredictable Environments Such as Terrorism, Natural Disasters, and Complex Technology. Program on Information Resources Policy, Center for Information Policy Research and Harvard University. Also, refer to Manyena, S. B. (2006). The Concept of Resilience Revisited, *Disasters*, 30(4), 433–450.

11. Allenby and Fink argue that the enhancement of resilience "is a rational strategy when the probability and specifics of a particular challenge are difficult to define". See Allenby, B., & Fink, J. (2005). Toward Inherently Secure and Resilient Societies, *Science*, 309(5737), 1034–1036. Further, the Crisis and Risk Network (CRN), Center for Security Studies, Zurich notes that with the "integration of its resilience concept and policy into the broader approach to civil protection and risk management, Switzerland is in line with those countries that regard resilience as the only suitable alternative to the unrealistic goal of providing an entirely secure environment for their inhabitants". See CRN Report, "Examining Resilience: A concept to improve societal security and technical safety". Center for Security Studies, ETH Zurich, 2009.

12. In the Singaporean context, an argument can be made that Singapore resists known threats to national security very well while it is the unknown threats requiring resilience that may pose the greatest challenge. See, Vasu, N., & Loo, B. (2010). Total Defence for National Security: An Assessment. In Terence, C. (ed.). *Management of Success: Singapore Revisited*, Singapore: Institute of Southeast Asian Studies.

13. This is based on the research by Patricia Longstaff *et al.* on a framework for assessing community resilience. The research focuses on the importance of resource robustness and adaptive capacity as key building blocks in maintaining community resilience. See Longstaff, P. H., Armstrong, N. J., Perrin, K., Parker, W. M., & Hidek, M. A. (2010). Building Resilient Communities: A Preliminary Framework for Assessment, *Homeland Security Affairs*, VI(3).

14. This is based on the research by Longstaff, Armstrong, Perrin, Parker and Hidek on a framework for assessing community resilience. The research focuses on the importance of resource robustness and adaptive capacity as key building blocks in maintaining community resilience. See Longstaff, P. H., Armstrong, N. J., Perrin, K., Parker, W. M., & Hidek, M. A. (2010)., "Building Resilient Communities: A Preliminary Framework for Assessment", Homeland Security Affairs, Volume VI, (No. 3). (September 2010).

15. For a more thorough discussion of this point, see for example Vasu, N., & Loo, B. (2010). Total Defence for National Security: An Assessment. In

Terence, C. (ed.). *Management of Success: Singapore Revisited*, Singapore: Institute of Southeast Asian Studies.

16. Longstaff, P. H., Armstrong, N. J., Perrin, K., Parker, W. M., & Hidek, M. A. (2010). Building Resilient Communities: A Preliminary Framework for Assessment, *Homeland Security Affairs*, VI(3).

Part III

Radicalisation and Extremism

Chapter 8

On Radicalisation

Marc Sageman

It is an honour to write a paper for the 10th anniversary of the Centre of Excellence for National Security and I wish to thank the centre for its kind hospitality during my time there. Much has been written about terrorism in the past decade and the concept of radicalisation has emerged as the key to understanding it. Before 2005, very few people wrote about radicalisation. They wrote about terrorists and joining a terrorist organisation, but since the tragedy of July 7, 2005, they realised that many of them, like the London bombers, were ordinary young people who turned to violence. Before that event, people comforted themselves that terrorism was something foreign, imported to one's country, but the London bombers shattered this illusion. Since then, radicalisation has become an obsession. However, despite a growing literature on the concept, our understanding of the term has reached a state of stagnation.[1] This chapter summarises our current understanding of this concept.

We need to understand that the word "radicalisation" means two different things. One is the acquisition of extreme ideas, cognitive radicalisation and the other is the turn to violence, behavioural radicalisation, allegedly based on these extreme ideas. The two are related but quite distinct: many

Marc Sageman is a former operations officer at the United States Central Intelligence Agency and author of books *Understanding Terror Networks* and *Leaderless Jihad*.

people have so-called extremist ideas but very few turn to violence, either domestically or as a foreign fighter wannabe. Here, I am concerned only with behavioural radicalisation, the use of violence rather than the far more common talk about violence. Talk does not necessarily lead to action. Only very few people talking about violence go on to use violence: it has a very low base rate, which must be accounted for in our understanding of radicalisation.

In this chapter, I divide theories of radicalisation into three major perspectives: lay theories, perpetrators' theories and expert theories. Each of these perspectives makes assumptions that are unexamined and are uncritically accepted. My aim is to critically evaluate them.

Lay Explanations

The essence of the first perspective, lay theories of radicalisation, is to view terrorists as outsiders, who do not belong to one's group. This reduces them to simple individual stereotypes, driven by simple internal factors such as personality or ideology, and neglects contextual factors. In social psychology, this common tendency is called the fundamental error of attribution.[2] This perspective takes the politics out of terrorism and reduces it to personal predisposition. Two common explanations in this perspective are that terrorists either are criminals or suffer from mental illness. However, the empirical literature in the field shows that terrorists come from a variety of backgrounds and the vast majority of them have no criminal history. As to mental illness, after several decades of research, a consensus has emerged that terrorists do not suffer from any major mental illness, and the search for a terrorist personality has given way to the elaboration of the process of becoming a terrorist.[3] A third explanation within this perspective is that terrorists are simply guided by wrong ideas. This explanation emphasises the role of ideology as an explanation for the perpetrator's behaviour.[4] Its proponents point to the hateful discourse of self-appointed "preachers of hate" and internet proselytisers and stress their importance in the process of "radicalisation". More recently, these proponents of the crucial role of ideology in behavioural radicalisation have adopted a new politically correct phrase, taking attention away from Islam. Now, governments are concerned about countering violent extremism, or CVE for short.

This popular ideological explanation for radicalisation heralds the internet as a very important factor in the increase in young Muslims volunteering to join forces with various Islamist groups in Syria or Iraq. There is no doubt that ideology — or the "narrative" in the present lexicon of counter-terrorism — is an important part of any explanation in the turn to political violence. This explanation suggests that the "narrative" on the internet finds a fertile ground in "vulnerable," "naïve," "at risk," "predisposed" individuals, who fall prey to it. Indeed, alarmists view Daesh as actively engaging in a huge propaganda campaign targeting these vulnerable people to recruit them in its ranks. The image is one of a very technologically savvy enemy organised in a top-down manner and engaging in a virtual fight for the souls of "vulnerable" people.[5]

There are multiple problems with this explanation. Mere exposure to wrong ideas can explain neither their adoption nor their power to lead people to turn to such self-harmful behaviour as political violence. Very few people exposed to the jihadist message ever choose to go abroad to fight. This very low base rate of radicalisation as a result of exposure was usually explained away by postulating some sort of coercive face-to-face indoctrination of naïve individuals. But such coercion is difficult to achieve on the internet as users can just log off and move on with their lives. This eventually leads to a tautological argument that only people susceptive to the "narrative" are radicalised and points to their radicalisation as an indicator of their susceptibility.

Therefore, the ideological explanation must be linked to some theory of social influence that explains why only a very few adopt this ideology while the vast majority rejects it. One such explanation could simply be normal socialisation through parents or school. Presumably, the narrative reinforces parents' socialisation and motivates people to turn to violence. But most terrorists did not grow up with their violent ideas (except those persecuted minorities in their own homes, like the Palestinians): indeed, such ideas are usually adopted over the strong resistance of their parents and school teachers. A different type of socialisation is indoctrination, where experienced believers teach newcomers about the ideology. However, most lay people find this ideology inherently incredible and believe that this process is far more coercive than benign learning and somehow forces newcomers to adopt the new ideas. This sort of brainwashing is presumed to involve control of rewards and punishments, compelling recruits to adopt the new ideas. However, such coercive methods are difficult to carry out on the internet.

Another possible type of influence is suggestion: particularly vulnerable people fall under the spell of magnetic people, like a process of hypnosis. This version implies that naïve and probably ignorant young people come under the suggestion of charismatic leaders, who transform them into "true believers."[6] After 9/11, the assumption was that sinister al-Qaeda agents lurking in the shadows of mosques spotted naïve Muslims based on some personal vulnerability ("at risk") and turned them over to recruiters, who indoctrinated them into joining the organisation. These spotters/recruiters allegedly formed an organised worldwide "network" of terrorists, ready to take advantage of naïve Muslims and convince them to go to al-Qaeda training camps, where their brainwashing was completed.[7] However, after over a decade of intense search in the United States, no spotter/recruiter has been discovered — except for FBI undercover officers or *agents provocateurs*.[8]

The internet has given a new life to this explanation. The view now is that sophisticated virtual recruiters surf the internet, mostly on Facebook or other social media, to spot these vulnerable young Muslims and indoctrinate them online. But a closer understanding of the way people use the internet refutes this general online passivity. People on the internet are not passive victims but are quite active in their desire to communicate with others. They turn on their computer, log on to their social media, Facebook page or jihadi websites and try to reach out to similar others. They try to make sense of their world, construct meaning from available models, actively shape their lives and make choices accordingly. Indeed, internet users self-select to the various ideological sites they like. Nor are these sites consistent in their ideological message. Many strands of ideology co-exist on each forum, monitored by an administrator, who sets the tone and keeps out detractors. Some overall assumptions may unify them, such as the West is at war with Islam and jihad is an individual duty not a collective one, but there are many wide disagreements about strategies and tactics.

It appears that there is an increase in lone wolf domestic terrorists,[9] which seems to coincide with the spread of the internet. They represent a particular challenge to the idea of indoctrination as there is little or no interaction with similar others. How is the rise of the internet related to the rise of lone wolves? None of the above explanations seems to account for it.

A final lay explanation of the turn to political violence abandons the quest to discover internal predispositions and adopts a strictly behavioural view of terrorists. This view postulates that people are rational actors, behaving in a utilitarian fashion seeking to maximise benefits and avoid costs. Their behaviour is the observable result of their cost/benefit calculations according to a predetermined set of preferences.[10] This is the rational choice theory, whose simple assumptions allow scientists to precisely calculate probabilities of choices and predict behaviour. This view provides a simple explanation for the adoption of a new ideology. This process is neither filling a gap of naïve ignorance nor suggestion, but the result of an indoctrination that selectively rewards its acceptance (through the provision of love and inclusion in a desirable group) and punishes its rejection (through ostracism or retribution). Such selective rewards and punishments lose some of their strength over the internet. Indeed, lone wolves present a challenge to this perspective. Since they are, by definition, loners, there are no others to reward or punish them into believing wrong ideas or the "narrative". Suicide terrorism also presents a very difficult problem for this perspective. A person willing to kill himself for a cause is definitely not maximising his self-interest without distorting the notion of self-interest beyond recognition. This violates the assumptions of rational choice theory. Such a person can certainly act rationally, but not within the utilitarian meaning of this perspective.[11]

Suicide terrorists also present a more general set of difficulties for the ideas-driven behaviour thesis. What kind of ideas have the strength to convince individuals to kill themselves? While some self-appointed lay experts on Islam argue that the answer lies in Islam itself, this is not credible. Over a billion people believe in Islam and only a few hundred people have committed suicide in a terrorist act. Furthermore, many non-Muslims have also carried out suicide terrorism. So looking for the answer in Islam does not explain why the overwhelming majority of Muslims (a ratio of over a million to one) do not commit such heinous acts and why non-Muslims carry them out. The answer must lie beyond the ideas themselves and forces these advocates to revert to a psychological explanation.

Perpetrators' Explanations

When terrorists are asked about their use of violence, they blame it on grievances. However, this answer quickly fails to satisfy because of the same low base rate problem: a huge number of people share the same grievances but only a very few turn to violence. When probed deeper, they blame circumstances. This is the other side of the previously mentioned fundamental error of attribution. People tend to attribute another person's negative behaviour to internal predisposition, often his belief system — an attribution bias. However, they tend to attribute this same negative behaviour in themselves to compelling circumstances — the actor–observer bias. I suspect that this tendency can also be extended to social groups, implying that members identifying with their own group believe their in-group members' actions are forced upon them by circumstances while those of out-group members are due to internal predispositions.

This explanation that blames circumstances captures the sense of doubt and insecurity that people experience when acting in the midst of history and have to choose between uncertain alternatives. Pundits, who have not participated in these events, often use a simplistic linear post hoc determinism for them in contrast with participants' narratives, which show the difficulty they have in detecting the significant aspects of these events from the sea of background minutia. The participants' sense of confusion about their behaviour is palpable, given the uncertain consequences of the options open to them at the time.[12] The certainty and linearity of pundits can come only retrospectively, when the complexity of circumstances can be reduced to an abstraction of what we know post hoc to have been the significant factors, blissfully ignoring that the actors have trouble detecting this true signal from all the noise at the time. Instead, pundits focus on the person to explain behaviour. Our language has developed a causal vocabulary of how mental states, especially emotions, lead to certain behaviour, but there is no equivalent lexicon for how situations lead to specific behaviour, with the exception of threats, which are experienced as fears. People follow this tendency of pundits to ignore circumstances and terrorists' own understanding of how their situations influenced them in carrying out their violent actions. Before the reader dismisses this type of explanation as merely a perpetrator's exculpatory justification for his or her crimes, he should consider that three quarters of a century of social psychological experiments support the terrorists' insight that circumstances influence behaviour more than internal predisposition.

Focusing on political actors' subjectivity and the meaning they attribute to their action necessarily privileges this situational explanation. Circumstances seem to exert strong pressure on people to behave in a certain way. This explanation lumps together grievances, static circumstances and the dynamics of events. The static dimension captures the structural elements of the context, or what Marxists used to call the conjuncture, and includes the opportunity structure of using violence.[13] It brings a dynamic element to the analysis, as events unfold in a certain way. In trying to apprehend this evolution, an explanation must provide an account of the chain of events as a path-dependent concept of how people experience historical events. It is path-dependent because some irreversible events, like homicide, engage people along a path that affects the order of their decisions. This means that any account of radicalisation must follow a rigorous chronology of the significant events that affect actors' understanding of their world. Their resulting action becomes a precedent that becomes incorporated in their repertoire of actions and easily comes into their mind.[14] The cognitive availability of recent events means that people react to them rather than to long past events that are probably forgotten. Too many studies of terrorism collapse time, which leads to erroneous causal attribution of behaviour to long forgotten events, such as childhood "traumas" or slights to family honour that the child allegedly and obsessively remembers and seeks to avenge. Such pathological long-term childhood obsessions are rarely the cause of political violence. Empirically, the few cases of murderous obsessions, often fascination with one's target, were generated in adulthood. In other words, the incorporation of a violent act into one's easily available cognitive repertoire changes things: crossing the threshold of violence changes a group and makes later group violence more likely.

Nevertheless, this explanation with its connotation of strong environmental pressure for a certain behaviour is not, by itself, an adequate explanation, for it falls again victim to the low base rate problem, which is the iron requirement of specificity of any adequate explanation. These large structural factors affect millions of people, but only a very few turn to political violence. So, this explanation is not specific enough to lead to a full understanding of the process of radicalisation. Circumstances are interpreted by the actors and this interpretation is important. An explanation based on circumstances brings us back to subjective factors of the individual trying to make sense of his world and himself in this world. The focus on how political actors conceived of themselves, their friends and their context does not mean that they understand this process of radicalisation. The whole field of social psychology and now that of cognitive sciences in general show that people are often not aware of why they act the way they do. They often give post hoc justifications to interviewers that seem to provide an explanation for their past behaviour. However, when compared to the rigorous environment of the laboratory, many of these justifications seem not to be the actual reason for their behaviour.

The internet, which challenges authorities' hegemonic attempts to impose their perspective on a public, may foster radicalisation in this perspective. The internet is a source of information, describing the circumstances terrorists are reacting to and the opportunity to make sense of them through discussions with their peers. It expands their opportunity to access relevant information and, as a process of self-selection, it may also nurture and reinforce a strong atypical view of the world, which increases the gap between their understanding of a situation and that of the rest of society. Terrorists rely on their own websites that focus on certain events while society relies on its media, which also prioritises events to report and describes them according to its own assumptions about the world. Each group condemns the other as biased, because each views and interprets the same event from its own perspective. The internet may exacerbate this mutual incomprehension between terrorists and society.

Expert Explanations

There is a third set of explanations for this process of radicalisation, which ideally attempts to transcend lay or terrorist explanations. However, social scientists are part of society and cannot shed all their biases when analysing terrorist behaviours. They usually end up providing a more sophisticated elaboration of the lay perspective — or worse, adopt a government's counter-terrorist bias when dealing with terrorists. However, some scientists try to transcend this bias and understand this process of radicalisation. I have divided these types of explanations into individual, group and sociological explanations.

Individual explanations

Consistent with the fundamental error of attribution, most expert explanations of radicalisation fall into the individual set. Jerrold Post is one of the prominent advocates of this perspective. He came up with three explanations. The first one is simply that terrorists carry out the mission of their parents, like Palestinian terrorists. He poetically summarised the essence of this argument: "When one has been nursed on the mother's milk of hatred and bitterness, the need for vengeance is bred in the bone".[15] A second explanation is exactly the reverse, namely a rebellion against the generation of their parents, like the 1970s Leftist revolutionaries.[16] Thus, in Post's dichotomous world, parents have a strong positive or negative influence on their children's potential for political violence. However, most empirical studies of terrorists show that parents' impact on them is not as important as their peers' influence, which is very different from that of their parents. Indeed, even Post recognised that parental influence did not seem to matter with the 9/11 terrorists. Here he abandoned their parents and argued that they became "true believers" by subordinating their individuality to the group, uncritically accepting the directives of a "destructive charismatic leader", which became a "moral and ... sacred obligation".[17] Here Post seems to revert to Le Bon's suggestibility argument that charismatic leaders transformed suggestible young people into fanatic killers and suicide bombers. But empirical studies have failed to discover any such zombies, with little or no free will.[18]

Ariel Merari is one of the rare scholars who has interviewed failed suicide bombers. He compared four Palestinian bombers who tried to kill themselves but failed because of a malfunction of the bomb itself with 11 would-be bombers, who aborted their mission at the last minute. He found that all 4 of the true suicide bombers had a dependent/avoidant "personality" as opposed to 6 of the 11 controls, who aborted their mission.[19] The small numbers involved prevent us from generalising this finding to a larger population and can only be used as anecdotal evidence at this point.

Other psychologists have suggested that the primary motivation in the turn to political violence was a quest for personal significance.[20] A historian even called this desire for self-glorification the Herostratos syndrome after the man who burned down the Temple of Artemis in Ancient Greece just to achieve fame.[21] There is indeed some element of self-glorification in the turn to political violence. Most terrorists feel they are part of a vanguard. They feel they matter in the larger scheme of things. But these feelings are private, for they are willing to sacrifice themselves anonymously, knowing that their significant act might not bring them glory. My own interviews with terrorists show that when their narcissism became too blatant, their comrades moved away from them. Selfish motives are frowned upon among terrorists.

Wiktorowicz postulated some sort of "cognitive opening" as the core dynamic for radicalisation and readiness to adopt extremist ideas.[22] However, his poorly defined concept just seems to be a lay understanding that exposure to a dramatic event may quickly change the beliefs of a person. There is little specificity in his concept, as it is easy to find some sort of vague cognitive "opening" — whatever that means — in retrospective self-reports, especially when the interviewer is eager to find one. The internet can play a critical role in this abrupt change of ideas by providing images that may shock the viewer to such an extent as to motivate him or her to do something. Videos of victimised people with whom one shares a sense of social identity may trigger this "cognitive opening" as can be gathered in many empirical accounts of terrorists.[23] But this vague notion may be more accurately described as identification with the victims.

Finally, Bandura postulated that terrorism required a prior moral disengagement which involved blaming and dehumanising the victims.[24] But such disengagement may be a natural and normal consequence of the process of self-categorisation and reduction of out-group members to stereotypes.[25]

Group explanations

Half a century ago, Solomon Asch and Stanley Milgram conducted classical experiments on conformity[26] and obedience to authority[27] respectively, showing how people easily fell under the influence of a small group and were even willing to kill subjects when urged to do so by scientific authority. Philip Zimbardo showed the power of roles in transforming randomly chosen young men into sadistic prison guards or emotionally broken prisoners.[28] These experiments show the power of situations to dramatically affect behaviour without actors even being aware of the subtle experimental manipulations of their environment.[29] Building on these findings, Borum[30] and Moghaddam[31] each tried to synthesise relevant psychological literature into very different linear mechanisms of radicalisation. But these plausible theories suffer from a lack of empirical support.[32]

McCauley and Moskalenko[33] proposed an intriguing set of five individual and four group mechanisms in a context of "jujitsu politics", which constitute this process of radicalisation. The five individual mechanisms — personal grievance, slippery slope, love, risk and status, and unfreezing — are normal psychological processes. What they call unfreezing is simply changing one's mind — unfreezing one's old ideas, developing new ideas and refreezing these new ideas. In a sense, unfreezing is similar to Wiktorowicz's cognitive opening, without the drama for this change of mind. The four group processes — group grievance, polarisation, competition and isolation — are also fairly normal. The notion of "jujitsu politics", that the terrorists are in an escalating competition with the state is an important insight upon which they unfortunately do not elaborate. The weakness of their argument is that their various mechanisms are ad hoc, based on anecdotal and selective confirmatory evidence.[34] Furthermore, McCauley and Moskalenko are careful to state that none of their mechanisms either alone or in combination is either necessary or sufficient to bring about violence.[35] In other words, they do not know how significant or even relevant each of their mechanisms is. Since they are ubiquitous psychological mechanisms, their detection may not mean anything for radicalisation. Nor do we know how prevalent the mechanisms are in the process of turning violent. Indeed, this process may very well occur without any of their identified mechanisms. This severely limits the usefulness of their list.

Sociological explanations

Half a century ago, Ted Gurr postulated that relative deprivation leads to frustration, which leads to aggression and rebellion.[36] He supported his theory with large cross-country correlations. However, many of the people who become terrorists are the children of the elite of their respective countries and did not experience relative deprivation in any meaningful sense of the term.[37] The source of their frustration, if any, was not relative deprivation, and this was not the cause of their violence. This finding limits the usefulness of Gurr's theory as a mechanism of radicalisation. As Gurr's theory was elaborated before the emergence of the internet, it plays no role in this theory. Indeed, it may actually undermine his argument. Through the internet, many young people seem to be attracted to struggles in far distant lands. Relative deprivation in their own country could not have motivated them in adopting a foreign cause.

Khosrokhavar uses classical Weberian methodology to understand radicalisation by constructing six ideal types of terrorists based on their membership in groups of various sizes and on responsiveness to local or foreign appeal. However, despite the title of his book, *Radicalisation*, he does not provide any description of their respective process of turning to violence.[38]

A very active area of sociological research is the field of contentious politics, using insights derived from social movements.[39] Using a unique database that had a meaningful control group, McAdam reconstructed the process of mobilisation or recruitment into high risk activism.[40] However, his subjects were militantly non-violent and his process therefore cannot explain the turn to political violence. Nevertheless, based on the insights of social movement theory, Alimi, Demetriou and Bosi tried to elaborate the process of violent radicalisation.[41] Unfortunately, these authors confine themselves to the various social mechanisms of how formal social movement organisations turn to violence and neglect the fact that the vast majority of instances of political violence or terrorism are acts of individuals or small groups, who do not belong to any such formal organisation. They are certainly part of an imagined political protest community but are not members of any formal organisation. Theirs is a radicalisation without organisation. Furthermore, their explanation is often not consistent with the chronology of events and seems too impersonal for it does not capture their intense experience of turning to political violence. They must breathe life back into their narrative and recapture the fact that radicalisation is deeply enmeshed with real blood, which is one of the reasons why this process is so fascinating.

An important insight has emerged out of the intelligence community, faced with the fact that terrorist attacks are extremely rare and law enforcement agencies complain that they are drowning in an ocean of false alarms overwhelming their resources to identify and track down real threats. Their major request is for help to get around this low base rate problem and distinguish the very few true positives that will turn to violence from the vast majority of false positives. These false alarms are young people who brag and pretend that they are tough and dangerous, especially on the internet, but, in fact, just talk, talk, talk — and do nothing. The study of the disparity between the great numbers of wannabes and the rarity of actual violent acts has generated a consensus in government agencies around a two-step model of the turn to violence. According to it, the first step is joining a political protest community, which the government calls radicalisation; and the second is the actual turn to violence, which it calls mobilisation (to action). This label creates confusion within academia, which, following social movement theory, calls the act of joining a political protest community mobilisation. The government's hope is that true positives give off detectable signature words and behaviors that predict their turn to violence. So far, to my knowledge, no government agency has reached a consensus about these indicators and/or tested their specificity.[42]

A new realisation in social movement research is the importance of identity in the turn to political violence. Blending self-categorisation and social movement perspective, van Stekelenburg and Klandermans argue that there is no radicalisation without identification. By identification, they mean a politicised collective identity in contrast to a government or society.[43] This adoption of the notion of identity based on self-categorisation theory rather than individual clinical psychology corrects misconceptions of insightful theories of radicalisation based on individual identity,[44] which of course cannot explain collective identity except as a pathological process. Likewise, social or collective identity of terrorists is the accurate description of what Pisoiu conceptualises as an occupation in her recent insightful book.[45]

Conclusion: A Synthesis

Combining the self-categorisation and social movement perspectives, we can draw some conclusions about the process of radicalisation.

First, for any political protest, there needs to be an activation of a politicised social identity in contrast to a rival out-group as Stekelenburg and Klandermans argued. This self-categorisation is contextual[46] and can be based on ideology, ethnicity, occupation… It creates an imagined community and reduces out-group members into stereotypes.

Second, as noted by McCauley, Moskalenko, Sommier and della Porta,[47] the process of radicalisation takes place in the context of an escalation of conflict between political challengers and the state or society. There is good empirical evidence for such an escalation to a major terrorist attack.[48] Within this escalation, there is a cumulative radicalisation of discourse, in which many people mistake the extremist speech (ideology) for the turn to violence since the words are so violent. However, there is a huge gap between words and deeds and this virulence of discourse is mirrored in the speech from champions of the state or society.

Third, this escalation of conflict may turn to violence under two common conditions: political dissenters' disillusionment with peaceful political process and moral outrage at state aggression against their group. Under such threats against their imagined community, some political protestors volunteer to become soldiers protecting their community. This is a second self-categorisation into a martial social identity, which leads to political violence, for violence is simply what soldiers do. All politically violent individuals whom I interviewed and who admitted their alleged crimes viewed themselves as soldiers for their respective comrades and cause. This second self-categorisation explains the lone wolf phenomenon as they think of themselves as soldiers defending their imagined community by themselves. The process is the same for one person as it is for several people who act together. This process also implies that the number of politically violent people is much smaller than the number of members in their imagined political protest community, explaining the low base rate problem. It also implies that the number of terrorists is not stable but strongly dependent on the actions of the state, which indeed may inadvertently encourage more and more people to turn to violence according to their misguided policies. Radicalisation can only be understood within this conflict between the state and challengers.[49]

Bibliography

Aaronson, T. (2013). *The Terror Factory: Inside the FBI's Manufactured War on Terrorism*, Brooklyn, New York: Ig Publishing.

Abou e. F. K. (2005). *The Great Theft: Wrestling Islam From the Extremists*, New York: HarperCollins.

Alimi, E., Demetriou, C., & Bosi, L. (2015). *The Dynamics of Radicalization: A Relational and Comparative Perspective*, New York: Oxford University Press.

American Psychiatric Association. (2013). *Diagnostic and Statistical Manual of Mental Disorders*, Fifth Edition, Washington D.C.: American Psychiatric Publishing.

Arquilla, J., & Ronfeldt, D. (eds.). (2001). *Networks and Netwars: The Future of Terror, Crime, and Militancy*, Santa Monica, California: RAND.

Asch, S. (1956). Studies of Independence and Conformity: A Minority of One Against a Unanimous Majority, *Psychological Monographs: General and Applied*, 70(9), 1–70.

Bandura, A. (1990). *Mechanisms of Moral Disengagement*. In Reich, (ed.). 1990, pp. 161 – 191.

Bastié, E. (2014). Omar Omsen, propagandiste du cyberjihad, *Le Figaro*. http://www.lefigaro.fr/actualite-france/2014/12/02/01016-20141202ARTFIG00374-omar-omsen-propagandiste-du-cyber-djihad.php.

Bloom, M. (2005). *Dying to Kill: The Allure of Suicide Terror*, New York: Columbia University Press.

Borowitz, A. (2005). *Terrorism for Self-Glorification: The Herostratos Syndrome*, Kent, Ohio: Kent State University Press.

Borum, R. (2004). *Psychology of Terrorism*, Tampa, Florida: University of South Florida.

Clarke, R., & Newman, G. (2006). *Outsmarting the Terrorists*, Westport, Connecticutt: Preager Security International.

Carrie R. W. (2002). Mobilizing Islam: Religion, Activism and Political Change in Egypt, New York: Columbia University Press.

Crenshaw, M. (ed.). (1995). Terrorism in Context, University Park, Pennsylvania: The Pennsylvania State University Press.

Deborah, W. (2006). *The Internet in the Middle East: Global Expectations and Local Imaginations in Kuwait*, Albany: State University of New York Press.

Della D. P. (2013). *Clandestine Political Violence*, New York: Cambridge University Press.

de Tocqueville, A. (1986). *De la Démocratie en Amérique; Souvenirs; L'Ancien Régime et la Révolution Paris*: Bouquins, Robert L. S. A.

Enyo (2009). *Anatomie d'un Désastre: l'Occident, l'islam et la guerre au XXIe siècle*, Paris: Éditions Denoël.

Fawaz, G. (2005). *The Far Enemy: Why Jihad Went Global*, Cambridge: Cambridge University Press.

François, B. (2005). *L'islamisme à l'heure d'Al-Qaida*, Paris: Éditions La Découverte.

Gambetta, D. (ed.). (2005). Making Sense of Suicide Missions, Oxford: Oxford University Press.

Gabriel, W. (2006). *Terror on the Internet: The New Arena, the New Challenges*, Washington, D.C.: United States Institute of Peace Press

Gunaratna, R. (2002). *Inside al Qaeda: Global Network of Terror*, New York: Columbia University Press.

Gurr, T. (1970). *Why Men Rebel*, Princeton: Princeton University Press.

Habeck, M. (2006). *Knowing the Enemy: Jihadist Ideology and the War on Terror*, New Haven: Yale University Press.

Hafez, M. (2003). *Why Muslims Rebel: Repression and Resistance in the Islamic World*, London: Lynne Rienner Publishers.

Hafez, M. (2007). *Suicide Bombers in Iraq: The Strategy and Ideology of Martyrdom*, Washington, D.C.: United States Institute of Peace Press.

Hoffer, E. (1963). *The True Believer: Thoughts on the Nature of Mass Movements*, New York: Time Incorporated, Time Reading Program Special Edition.

Hoffman, B. (2008). The Myth of Grass-Root Terrorism, *Foreign Affairs*, 87(3), 133–138.

Hogg, M., & Reid, S. (2006). Social Identity, Self-Categorization, and the Communication of Group Norms, Communication Theory, 16, 7–30.

Homeland Security Policy Institute & Critical Incident Analysis Group (2007). *NETworked Radicalization: A Counter-Strategy*. http://www.gwumc.edu/hspi/policy/NETworkedRadicalization.pdf.

Horgan, J. (2005). *The Psychology of Terrorism*, Abingdon, England: Routledge.

Jocelyne, C. (2004). *L'Islam à l'épreuve de l'Occident*, Paris: Éditions La Découverte.

John, E. (1999). *The Islamic Threat: Myth or Reality?*, New York: Oxford University Press.

John, E. (2002). *Unholy War: Terror in the Name of Islam*, New York: Oxford University Press.

Kahneman, D. (2011). *Thinking, Fast and Slow*, New York: Farrar, Straus and Giroux.

Kahneman, D., Slovic, P., & Tversky, A. (eds.). (1982). *Judgments under Uncertainty: Heuristics and Biases*, Cambridge, England: Cambridge University Press.

Kepel, G. (2002). *Jihad: The Trail of Political Islam*, Cambridge, Massachusetts: Harvard University Press.

Kepel, G. (2004). *Fitna: Guerre au coeur de l'islam*, Paris: Éditions Gallimard.

Khosrokhavar, F. (1997). *L'islam des jeunes*, Paris: Flammarion.

Khosrokhavar, F. (2002). *Les Nouveaux martyrs d'Allah*, Paris: Flammarion.

Khosrokhavar, F. (2014). *Radicalisation*, Paris: Éditions de la maison des sciences de l'homme.

King, M., & Taylor, D. (2011). The Radicalization of Homegrown Jihadists: A Review of Theoretical Models and Social Psychological Evidence, *Terrorism and Political Violence*, 23(4), 602–622.

Kruglanski, A., Chen, X., Dechesne, M., Fishman, S., & Orehek, E. (2009). Fully Committed: Suicide Bombers' Motivation and the Quest for Personal Significance, *Political Psychology*, 30(3), 331–357.

Lankford, A. (2013). *The Myth of Martyrdom: What Really Drives Suicide Bombers, Rampage Shooters, and Other Self-Destructive Killers*, New York: Palgrave Macmillan.

Le Bon, G. (1895/1998). Psychologie des foules, Paris: Quadrige, Presses Universitaires de France.

Martens, A., Sainudiin, R., Sibley, C., Schimel, J. & Webber, D. (2014). Terrorist Attacks Escalate in Frequency and Fatalities Preceding Highly Lethal Attacks, *PLoS ONE*, 9(4).

McAdam, D. (1986). Recruitment to High-Risk Activism: The Case of Freedom Summer, *The American Journal of Sociology*, 92(1) (July 1986), 64–90.

McAdam, D. (1988). *Freedom Summer*, New York: Oxford University Press.

McAdam, D., Tarrow, S., & Tilly, C. (2001). *Dynamics of Contention*, Cambridge: Cambridge University Press.

McCauley, C., & Moskalenko, S. (2011). *Friction: How Radicalization Happens to Them and Us*, New York: Oxford University Press.

Merari, A. (2010). *Driven to Death: Psychological and Social Aspects of Suicide Terrorism*, New York: Oxford University Press.

Michael, C. (2000). *Commanding Right and Forbidding Wrong in Islamic Thought*, Cambridge, U.K.: Cambridge University Press.

Michael, G. (2012). *Lone Wolf Terror and the Rise of Leaderless Resistance*, Nashville, Tennessee: Vanderbilt University Press.

Milgram, S. (1974). *Obedience to Authority: An Experimental View*, New York: Harper Torchbooks.

Moghaddam, F. (2005). The Staircase to Terrorism: A Psychological Exploration, *American Psychologist*, 60(2), 161–169.

Moghaddam, F. (2006). *From the Terrorists' Point of View: What They Experience and Why They Come to Destroy*, Westport, Connecticut: Preager Security International.

Morozov, E. (2011). *The Net Delusion: The Dark Side of Internet Freedom*, New York: Public Affairs.

Nesser, P. (2012). Individual Jihadist Operations in Europe: Patterns and Challenges, *CTC Sentinel*, 5(1), 15–18.

Pantucci, R. (2011). *A Typology of Lone Wolves: Preliminary Analysis of Lone Islamist Terrorists*, The International Centre for the Study of Radicalisation and Political Violence (ICSR), King's College London.

Pape, R. (2005). *Dying to Win: The Strategic Logic of Suicide Terrorism*, New York: Random House.

Patricia, C. (2004). *God's Rule: Government and Islam, Six Centuries of Medieval Islamic Political Thought*, New York: Columbia University Press.

Pedahzur, A. (2005). *Suicide Terrorism*, Cambridge, England: Polity Press.

Perry, S., & Hasisi, B. (2015). Rational Choice Rewards and the Jihadist Suicide Bomber, *Terrorism and Political Violence*, 27, 29–52.

Philip, Z. (2007). *The Lucifer Effect: Understanding How Good People Turn Evil*, New York: Random House.

Pisoiu, D. (2012). *Islamist Radicalisation in Europe: An Occupational Change process*, New York: Routledge.

Post, J. (2007). *The Mind of the Terrorist: The Psychology of Terrorism from the IRA to al-Qaeda*, New York: Palgrave Macmillan.

Quintan, W. (ed.). (2004). *Islamic Activism: A Social Movement Theory Approach*, Bloomington, Indiana: Indiana University Press.

Quintan, W. (2005). *Radical Islam Rising: Muslim Extremism in the West*, Oxford: Rowman & Littlefield Publishers, Inc.

Raymond, B. (2003). *Islam without Fear: Egypt and the New Islamists*, Cambridge, Massachusetts: Harvard University Press.

Regina v. Omar Khyam *et al.* Central Criminal Court, Old Bailey, March 21, 2006 to April 30, 2007.

Reich, W. (ed.). *Origins of Terrorism: Psychologies, Ideologies, Theologies, States of Mind*, Washington, D.C.: The Woodrow Wilson Center Press.

Richard, B. (2004). *Jihad: From Qur'an to bin Laden*, Houndmills, Hampshire: Palgrave Macmillan.

Ross, L., & Nisbett, R. (1991). *The Person and the Situation: Perspectives of Social Psychology*, New York: McGraw-Hill.

Roy, O. (2004). *Globalized Islam: The Search for a New Ummah*, New York: Columbia University Press.

Sageman, M. (2004). *Understanding Terror Networks*, Philadelphia: University of Pennsylvania Press.

Sageman, M. (2008). *Leaderless Jihad: Terror Networks in the Twenty-First Century*, Philadelphia: University of Pennsylvania Press.

Sageman, M. (2014). The Stagnation in Terrorism Research, *Terrorism and Political Violence*, 26(4), 565–580.

Sageman, M. (2015) (in press), *The Turn to Political Violence*, New York: Basic Books.

Semelin, J. (2007). *Purify and Destroy: The Political Uses of Massacre and Genocide*, New York: Columbia University Press.

Silke, A. (ed.). (2003). *Terrorists, Victims and Society: Psychological Perspectives on Terrorism and its Consequences*, Chichester, England: John Wiley & Sons, Ltd.

Silber, M., & Bhatt, A. (2007). *Radicalization in the West: The Homegrown Threat*, New York: The New York Police Department Intelligence Division. http://www.nypdshield.org/public/SiteFiles/documents/NYPD_Report-Radicalization_in_the_West.pdf.

Simon, J. (2013). *Lone Wolf Terrorism: Understanding the Growing Threat, Amherst*, New York: Prometheus Books.

Sommier, I. (2008). *La violence politique et son deuil: L'après 68 en France et en Italie*, Rennes: Presses Universitaires de Rennes.

Taylor, M. (1988). *The Terrorist*, London: Brassey's Defense Publishers.

Turner, J., Hogg, M., Oakes, P., Reicher, S., & Wetherell, M. (1987). *Rediscovering the Social Group: A Self-Categorization Theory*, Oxford: Blackwell Publishing.

Stekelenburg, V. J. (2014). Going All the Way: Politicizing, Polarizing, and Radicalizing Identity Offline and Online, *Sociology Compass*, 8(5), 540–555.

Stekelenburg, V. J., & Klandermans, B. (2007). Individuals in Movements: A Social Psychology of Contention. In Klandermans, B., & Conny. (eds.). *Handbook of Social Movements Across Disciplines*, New York: Springer Science + Business Media, LLC, pp. 157–204.

Endnotes

1. Sageman, M. (2014). The Stagnation in Terrorism Research, *Terrorism and Political Violence*, 26(4), 565–580.
2. See Ross, L., & Nisbett, R. (1991). *The Person and the Situation: Perspectives of Social Psychology*, New York: McGraw-Hill, pp. 119–144.
3. See Taylor, M. (1988). *The Terrorist*, London: Brassey's Defense Publishers.; Reich, W. (ed.). (1990). *Origins of Terrorism: Psychologies, Ideologies, Theologies, States of Mind*, Washington D.C.: The Woodrow Wilson Center Press.; Crenshaw, M. (1995). (ed.). *Terrorism in Context*, University Park, Pennsylvania: The Pennsylvania State Press.; Silke, A. (ed.). (2003). *Terrorists, Victims and Society: Psychological Perspectives on Terrorism and its Consequences*, Chichester, England: John Wiley & Sons, Ltd.; Horgan, J. (2005). *The Psychology of Terrorism*, Abingdon, England: Routledge, pp. 47–106.; Sageman, M. (2004). *Understanding Terror Networks*, Philadelphia: University of Philadelphia Press, pp. 83–91 for a summary and critique of the terrorist personality approach. However, there is still a tradition dating back to the 1880s of mental health professionals and amateur psychologists making claims about terrorists, even though they have never actually examined one. They still believe that terrorists suffer from some sort of mental disorder on the basis of very selective anecdotal evidence. See Lankford, A. (2013). *The Myth of Martyrdom: What Really Drives Suicide Bombers, Rampage Shooters, and Other Self-Destructive Killers*, New York: Palgrave Macmillan. This is the latest example.
4. See Enyo (2009). *Anotomie d'un Désastre: l'Occident, l'Islam et la guerre au XXIe siècle*, Paris: Éditions Denoël and Habeck, M. (2006). *Knowing the Enemy: Why Jihad Went Global*, Cambridge: Cambridge University Press, as examples of such literature. This "blame it on Islam" argument has been soundly refuted by a consensus of true scholars of political Islam. See Abou e. F. (2005). Raymond, B. (2003); Richard, B. (2004); François, B. (2005); Jocelyne, C. (2004); Michael, C. (2000); Patricia, C. (2004); John, E. (1999) & (2002); Fawaz, G. (2005); Mohammed, H. (2003); Gilles, K. (2002) & (2004); Farhad, K. (1997) & (2002); Olivier, R. (2004); Carrie, W. (2002); and Quintan, W. (ed.). (2004).
5. This is the premise of many "counter-radicalisation" programs such as the Quilliam Foundation in Britain or the *Centre de Prévention contre les Dérives Sectaires liées à l'Islam* in France.
6. Hoffer, E. (1963). *The True Believer: Thoughts on the Nature of Mass Movements*, New York: Time Incorporated, Time Reading Program Special Edition, popularized the expression "true believer" in the early 1950s in an

attempt to explain Nazism and Communism and other mass movements. This was the explanation for political violence in the late nineteenth century, based on the ideas of Gustave Le Bon, 1895/1998, who argued that people in a crowd regressed to a more primitive state, making them susceptible to suggestion by charismatic leaders.

7. This is the view promoted by Gunaratna, R. (2002). *Inside al Qaeda: Global Network of Terror*, New York: Columbia University Press, but see also Post, J. (2007). *The Mind of the Terrorist: The Psychology of Terrorism from the IRA to al-Qaeda*, New York: Palgrave Macmillan, pp. 204–205. This was also the view from law enforcement, see Silber, M., & Bhatt, A. (2007). *Radicalization in the West: The Homegrown Threat*, New York: The New York Police Department Intelligence Division.

8. See Aaronson, T. (2013). *The Terror Factory: Inside the FBI's Manufactured War on Terrorism*, Brooklyn, New York: Ig Publishing.

9. Michael, G. (2012). *Lone Wolf Terror and the Rise of Leaderless Resistance*, Nashville, Tennessee: Vanderbilt University Press.; Nesser, P. (2012). Individual Jihadist Operations in Europe: Patterns and Challenges, *CTC Sentinel*, 5(1), 15–18.; Pantucci, R. (2011). *A Typology of Lone Wolves: Preliminary Analysis of Lone Islamist Terrorists*, The International Centre for the Study of Radicalisation and Political Violence (ICSR), King's College London.; Simon, J. (2013). *Lone Wolf Terrorism: Understanding the Growing Threat*, Amherst, New York: Prometheus Books.

10. See Clarke, R., & Newman, G. (2006). *Outsmarting the Terrorists* (Westport, Connecticut: Preager Security International.

11. Perry, S., & Hasisi, B. (2015). Rational Choice Rewards and the Jihadist Suicide Bomber, *Terrorism and Political Violence*, 27, 29–52, who use Umar Farooq Abdul Mutallab as an illustration fail to convince due to a bizarre disconnect between the evidence they present and their theoretical arguments. They also use an exclusive Palestinian sample to generate their theory, which reverts back to a partial "blame it on Islam" argument that completely ignores the unique Palestinian situation and its anti-Zionism.

12. de Tocqueville, A. (1835). *De la Démocratie en Amérique*; *Souvenirs*; *L'Ancien Régime et la Révolution* in Robert L. S. A. (ed.) Paris: Bouquins, pp. 761–762, in his *Souvenirs* experienced the same contrast between those who write about history and those who live it.

13. This is what social psychologists call the demands characteristics of a situation and Max Taylor calls affordance.

14. This is the concept of availability heuristics. See Kahneman, D., Slovic, P., & Tversky, A. (eds.). (1982). *Judgments under Uncertainty: Heuristics and Biases*, Cambridge, England: Cambridge University Press, pp. 163–208 and

Kahneman, (2011). *Thinking, Fast and Slow*, New York: Farrar, Straus and Giroux, pp. 129–145.

15. Post, J. (2007). *The Mind of the Terrorist: The Psychology of Terrorism from the IRA to al-Qaeda*, New York: Palgrave Macmillan, p. 37.

16. *Ibid.*, pp. 101–158.

17. *Ibid.*, p. 193. Apparently, Post seems to believe that this subordination of an individual to the group is a pathological process. As Turner, J., Hogg, M., Oakes, P., Reicher, S., & Wetherell, M. (1987). *Rediscovering the Social Group: A Self-Categorization Theory*, Oxford: Blackwell Publishing, demonstrate with self-categorisation theory this is actually a common, normal and natural phenomenon.

18. See Bloom, M. (2005). *Dying to Kill: The Allure of Suicide Terror*, New York: Columbia University Press,; Gambetta, D. (ed.). (2005). *Making Sense of Suicide Missions*, Oxford: Oxford University Press, Hafez, M. (2007). *Suicide Bombers in Iraq: The Strategy and Ideology of Martyrdom*, Washington, D.C.: United States Institute of Peace Press.; Merari, A. (2010). *Driven to Death: Psychological and Social Aspects of Suicide Terrorism*, New York: Oxford University Press.; Pape, R. (2005). *Dying to Win: The Strategic Logic of Suicide Terrorism*, New York: Random House.; Pedahzur, A. (2005). *Suicide Terrorism*, Cambridge, England: Polity Press.

19. Merari. (2010). Unfortunately, the findings from an instrument like the Rorschach Inkblot Test does not translate into the definition of what is meant by dependent/avoidant personality, pp. 142–145.; see American Psychiatric Association. (2013). *Diagnostic and Statistical Manual of Mental Disorders,* Fifth Edition, Washington D.C.: American Psychiatric Publishing, p. 647. Indeed, the narrative evidence Merari provided for his four cases of true suicide bombers shows that they displayed persistent initiative to convince their respective terrorist organisation to take them on as suicide bombers. Such initiative is inconsistent with the behavior of people with a dependent or avoidant personality disorder.

20. See Kruglanski, A., Chen, X., Dechesne, M., Fishman, S., & Orehek, E. (2009). Fully Committed: Suicide Bombers' Motivation and the Quest for Personal Significance, *Political Psychology*, 30(3), 331–357.

21. Borowitz, A. (2005). *Terrorism for Self-Glorification: The Herostratos Syndrome*, Kent, Ohio: Kent State University Press.

22. Wiktorowicz, Q. (2005). *Radical Islam Rising: Muslim Extremism in the West*, Oxford: Rowman & Littlefield Publishers, Inc. pp. 85–98.

23. See for instance Sageman, M. (2008). *Leaderless Jihad: Terror Networks in the Twenty-First Century,* Philadelphia: University of Pennsylvania Press,

pp. 3–11, pp. 52–57. These examples show that the viewing of the atrocities in Bosnia and the killing of a Palestinian boy caused the respective future terrorists to experience intense moral outrage that changed their perspective of the world and motivated them to do something about it.

24. Bandura, A. (1990). Mechanisms of Moral Disengagement. In Reich, (ed.). *Origins of Terrorism: Psychologies, Ideologies, Theologies, States of Mind*, Washington, D.C.: The Woodrow Wilson Center Press, pp. 161–191.

25. Hogg, M., & Reid, S. (2006). Social Identity, Self-Categorization, and the Communication of Group Norms, *Communication Theory*, 16, 7–30.

26. Asch, S. (1956). Studies of Independence and Conformity: A Minority of One Against a Unanimous Majority, *Psychological Monographs: General and Applied*, 70(9), 1.

27. Milgram, S. (1974). *Obedience to Authority: An Experimental View*, New York: Harper Torchbooks.

28. Zimbardo, P. (2007). *The Lucifer Effect: Understanding How Good People Turn Evil*, New York: Random House.

29. See Ross, L., & Nisbett, R. (1991) *The Person and the Situation: Perspectives of Social Psychology*, New York: McGraw-Hill.

30. See Borum, R. (2004). *Psychology of Terrorism*, Tampa, Florida: University of South Florida; a non-peered reviewed pamphlet.

31. Moghaddam, F. (2005). The Staircase to Terrorism: A Psychological Exploration, *American Psychologist*, 60(2), 161–169; and Moghaddam, F. (2006). *From the Terrorists' Point of View: What They Experience and Why They Come to Destroy*, Westport, Connecticut: Preager Security International.

32. See King, M., & Taylor, D. (2011). The Radicalization of Homegrown Jihadists: A Review of Theoretical Models and Social Psychological Evidence, *Terrorism and Political Violence*, 23(4), 602–622.

33. McCauley, C., & Moskalenko, S. (2011). *Friction: How Radicalization Happens to Them and Us*, New York: Oxford University Press.

34. *Ibid.* Two other social factors that they listed, hatred and martyrdom, are not mechanisms.

35. *Ibid.*, p. 214.

36. Gurr, T. (1970). *Why Men Rebel*, Princeton: Princeton University Press.

37. For instance, the 1880s Russian People's Will members and 1960s Weathermen. Some members of the current wave of global neo-jihadi terrorists are also children of the elite of their respective countries.

38. Khosrokhavar, F. (2014). *Radicalisation*, Paris: Éditions de la maison des sciences de l'homme.

39. McAdam, D., Tarrow, S., & Tilly, C. (2001). *Dynamics of Contention*, Cambridge: Cambridge University Press.

40. McAdam, D. (1986). Recruitment to High-Risk Activism: The Case of Freedom Summer, *The American Journal of Sociology*, 92(1) (July 1986), 64–90; and McAdam, D. (1988). *Freedom Summer*, New York: Oxford University Press.

41. Alimi, E., Demetriou, C., & Bosi, L. (2015). *The Dynamics of Radicalization: A Relational and Comparative Perspective*, New York: Oxford University Press.

42. At a recent conference, a government contractor claimed to have constructed a reliable screening tool on the basis of these alleged signature behaviours. However, when questioned, the presenter did not understand the basic notions of sensitivity and specificity required to test the accuracy of these instruments. Given the very low probability of terrorist attacks, these instruments will be completely counter-productive, generating far more false positives than would otherwise come to the attention to law enforcement agencies. Moreover, they would cause real harm to innocent people suspected of and perhaps detained on suspicion being terrorists. Again this illustrates the low base rate problem plaguing counter-terrorism.

43. Stekelenburg, V. J., & Klandermans, B. (2007). Individuals in Movements: A Social Psychology of Contention. In Klandermans B., & Conny, R, (eds.). *Handbook of Social Movements Across Disciplines*, New York: Springer Science + Business Media, LLC: 157–204; and Stekelenburg, V. J. (2014). Going All the Way: Politicizing, Polarizing, and Radicalizing Identity Offline and Online, *Sociology Compass*, 8(5), 540–555.

44. See for example, Sommier, I. (2008). *La violence politique et son deuil: L'après 68 en France et en Italie,* Rennes: Presses Universitaires de Rennes.; or Semelin, J. (2007). *Purify and Destroy: The Political Uses of Massacre and Genocide*, New York: Columbia University Press.

45. Pisoiu, D. (2012). *Islamist Radicalisation in Europe*: *An occupational change process*, New York: Routledge.

46. This therefore incorporates the insights of the perpetrators' explanations.

47. Della, D. P. (2013). *Clandestine Political Violence*, New York: Cambridge University Press.

48. Martens, A., Sainudiin, R., Sibley, C., Schimel, J. & Webber, D. (2014). Terrorist Attacks Escalate in Frequency and Fatalities Preceding Highly Lethal Attacks, *PLoS ONE*, 9(4).

49. This skeletal schema is elaborated in my newest book (Sageman, 2016) and supported with primary sources from multiple campaigns of political violence.

Chapter 9

'Radicalisation': The Transformation of Modern Understanding of Terrorist Origins, Psychology and Motivation

Andrew Silke and Katherine Brown

Post 9/11, understanding how people become terrorists has come to be discussed in terms of "radicalisation". Today, radicalisation is typically seen to refer to a complex and dynamic process which results in individuals coming to embrace a violent ideology in support of a political or religious cause. Without doubt, the issue of radicalisation has become a core fixture of contemporary efforts to understand and combat terrorism. Yet, clearly, terrorism has an extraordinarily long history and what is called radicalisation today, in the past was referred to do much more mundanely as "becoming" a terrorist, "joining" a terrorist group or of being "recruited".[1] No one talked of the IRA being radicalised, or Shining Path, or Black September or the Red Brigades. Though all of these older groups certainly were by our modern understanding.

Andrew Silke is Head of Criminology and Director of Terrorism Studies at the University of East London;
Katherine Brown is a lecturer of Islamic Studies in the Department of Theology and Religion at the University of Birmingham.

Ultimately, the emergence of the term "radicalisation" to describe this process of deepening involvement in radical violent causes and activism is a very recent phenomenon. It effectively began in the aftermath of 9/11, when a shift started to move away from talking about people "becoming" terrorists, "joining" terrorist groups or being "recruited". As an alternative, the term "radicalisation" first started to appear in documents discussing how people became involved with terrorist causes or movements in 2002, but by 2007 it had effectively taken over policy and research discourse on this subject. Exactly what "radicalisation" meant, however, was open to some interpretation.[2] Compared to the previous terminology, it was certainly a more exotic term which presumably described a more exotic process.

It did not help that, like terrorism itself, radicalisation as a term arrived already mired with some political baggage, and was quickly shackled with even more, all of which has hindered, rather than helped its scientific development. One of the most straightforward of the recent scientific definitions of radicalisation, for example, comes from Horgan and Braddock, who defined it as: "the social and psychological process of incrementally experienced commitment to extremist political or religious ideology".[3] Taken at face value, such a perspective offers plenty of scope to develop our understanding, but as Peter Neumann highlighted, the politicisation of the term created a multitude of obstacles:

> Unfortunately the concept of radicalisation, as used in many government-linked quarters, suffers from politicisation, is fuzzy, applied one-sidedly (only non-state actors are assumed to radicalise, not governments), often lacks a clear benchmark (adherence to democratic principles and the rule of law, abstaining from the use of violence for political ends), and is linked too readily with terrorism (broadly defined) as outcome. Its broader application to political activism of individuals and movements in societies where social development is blocked by non-democratic extremist regimes is problematical.

Terrorism as a term has also been mired with similar difficulties in how it has been defined, though this has not restricted the enormous growth in terrorism studies in recent years, or research on a bewildering range of topics linked to the area.[5] Similarly, the development of theoretical models and research on radicalisation has been enormous in recent years, and the focus of this chapter is to attempt to review some of the major developments in our understanding of radicalisation and the significant issues connected to the phenomenon.

Theoretical Models of Radicalisation

The past decade has been an exceptionally vibrant period for the development of models of radicalisation.[6] New research has fuelled a plethora of theories around what factors and processes drive radicalisation, and provided a range of sometimes very different perspectives on the issue. There is not enough space in this chapter to review all of these models, but we can focus attention on some of the major ones, bearing in mind that it is likely that new models will continue to emerge and many of the current ones will be refined further.

Moghaddam's staircase model of radicalisation

Fathali Moghaddam's staircase model was one of the first detailed models and since its publication in 2005 it has become one of the most influential of the theoretical models.[7] In a recent review it was identified as among the 100 most cited articles on terrorism.[8] The model presents radicalisation as a phased process, involving six stages in total. Figure 1 provides an outline of the model.

There are six stages in total and each stage is represented by a different step in the staircase. The higher you progress in the model, the fewer the number of people who reach each level, and the step metaphor is designed to reflect that progress through the different phases is not automatic or inevitable. The ground level of the model starts with perceptions of discontent and a desire by individuals to improve their situation. If they are unsuccessful in doing this, feelings of frustration and anger developed towards any individual's beliefs are responsible for these setbacks. Moral disengagement from standard social norms occurs as the individual increasingly begins to adopt the moral framework of the terrorist group or cause. This deepens as the individual progresses up the staircase, to the

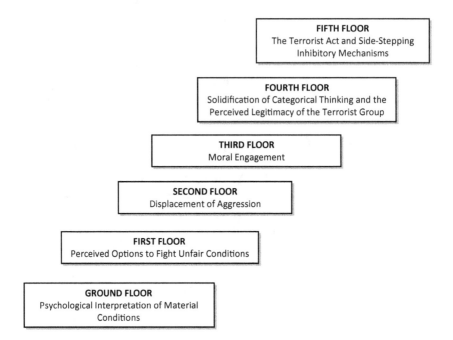

Figure 1:   Moghaddam's staircase model of radicalisation

point where in the final stage they are incorporated within the terrorist movement and are willing to carry out acts of violence on behalf of the cause.

McCauley and Moskalenko's 12 mechanism model

Published in 2008, the McCauley and Moskalenko model argues that radicalisation can happen at three different levels: individual, group and mass.[9] Within this framework, each level might best be considered as comprising a set of different pathways leading to radicalisation, and 12 different mechanisms as to how this can happen are described. Table 1 outlines the model and the mechanisms.

At the level of the individual, radicalisation is caused primarily by grievances, either experienced directly or by the group the individual identifies with. Group and mass radicalisation can be the result of competition and conflict with other groups or states. With the model, radicalisation is

Table 1:   McCauley and Moskalenko's 12 mechanism model

Level of radicalization	Mechanism
Individual	1. Personal victimization
	2. Political grievance
	3. Joining a radical group — the slippery slope
	4. Joining a radical group — the power of love
	5. Extremity shift in like-minded groups
Group	6. Extreme cohesion under isolation and threat
	7. Competition for the same base of support
	8. Competition with state power — condensation
	9. Within group competition — fissioning
Mass	10. Jujitsu politics
	11. Hate
	12. Martyrdom

defined as a "change in beliefs, feelings, and behaviors in directions that increasingly justify intergroup violence and demand sacrifice in defense of the ingroup."[10]

Importantly the model stresses the reactive nature of radicalisation. For 10 out of the 12 mechanisms, radicalisation is occurring in response to events and forces in the environment, and particularly, threats to the individual and group. The model overall stresses the importance of environmental context in understanding how and why radicalisation happens. A further important element is that ideology is not a key causal factor of radicalisation in this model. Indeed, in the original article describing the model, ideology is not mentioned at all. It does receive attention in later accounts, but overall within this framework, ideology is not the key driving force. As McCauley and Moskalenko noted in 2010, radicalisation can occur without an ideology:

> There are many paths to radicalisation that do not involve ideology. Some join a radical group for thrills and status, some for love, some for connection and comradeship. Personal and group grievances can move individuals toward violence, with ideology serving only to rationalise the violence.[11]

A final noteworthy element of the model is McCauley and Moskalenko's conclusion that "Radicalization emerges in a relationship of intergroup competition and conflict in which *both sides* are radicalized" [emphasis added]. Thus, it is not just terrorists who are radicalised, but also those who are fighting against them. Radicalisation, then, is not a process that only produces terrorists, but rather affects all sides in violent conflicts.

Kruglanski et al.'s quest for significance model of radicalisation

A more recent model on radicalisation has been offered by Kruglanski *et al.*, which looks as if it will become a quite influential theory.[12] The model effectively emerged from research studies exploring the role of significance quest in terrorist motivation. Studies in the area suggest that the move towards an extremist ideology is for many a way of dealing with perceived inadequacy and failure in their own lives, and of attempting to increase their own self-esteem and sense of significance.[13] How the model works is outlined in Fig. 2.

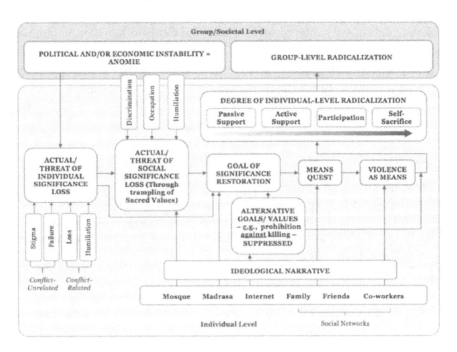

Figure 2:   Kruglanski *et al.*'s quest for significance model of radicalisation

Unlike McCauley and Moskalenko's model, ideology plays a much more central role in this framework. For Kruglanski *et al.* there are three major elements in the radicalisation process: (1) an individual motivation for personal significance (often a reaction to perceived failures, threats and setbacks in life); (2) an ideology which identifies appropriate ways to achieve personal significance and then (3) social processes which bring the individual into contact with this ideology.

There is empirical support for some elements of the model. For example, a loss or drop in personal significance is likely to cause a "collectivistic shift" in an individual's sense of identity.[14] This effectively means that the individual's identity shifts towards a more group-based identity, with greater priority and meaning given to the group's norms and values. Studies suggest that this is further linked with both a greater willingness to sacrifice and to support violence on behalf of the group and its values.[15]

Key Factors Associated with the Radicalisation Process

While there may be considerable variation in emphases, inevitably the various models of radicalisation also have significant overlaps. Where there is general agreement between them is usually around the view that radicalisation is a complex and dynamic process which results in individuals coming to embrace a violent ideology in support of a political or religious cause. The process is not inevitable nor does it follow a single route. Instead, most of the models highlight that there are multiple pathways to violent extremism and that the process of getting there can often be an erratic experience capable of going in a variety of directions.

As even the brief review of theoretical models in the previous section illustrates, there is no single root cause of radicalisation. Indeed, more than 200 different factors have been identified by research which could play a role in the radicalisation process.[16] Not all of these factors feature in every case, and there is often very considerable variation. Ultimately, radicalisation is not simply the sum of different factors, but rather that the different factors seem to play a role at different stages in the process.[17] Key events can motivate individuals to radicalise further or to de-radicalise, and overall radicalisation is best seen as a complex, nonlinear and dynamic process.

The general trend in research findings though is that radicalisation is the result of the interaction of both personal factors (e.g., individual susceptibility) and environmental factors (e.g., social relationships, community attitudes).[18] Studies have also highlighted that static and dynamic factors both play significant roles in radicalisation. Static elements include, for example, demographic factors such that young people aged 15–24 are most at risk, and males are usually more affected than females.[19] Dynamic factors can include social relationships, which in most cases are probably one of the key elements in the radicalisation process. Camaraderie, social support and a sense of belonging can all be powerful incentives for becoming and staying involved with a radical group.[20]

In his analysis of the life histories of hundreds of jihadi terrorists, Edwin Bakker found that these individuals tended to become involved in terrorism through networks of friends or relatives and that generally there were no formal ties with terrorist networks.[21] More recent research suggests that in up to 20 percent of cases family members played a key role in introducing and initiating an individual to an extremist movement. In contrast, friends played the key role in almost 50 percent of cases.[22]

Psychological vulnerability can also play a significant role, though this should not be confused with mental illness or serious psychological problems, which overall are present in relatively few cases of serious radicalisation.[23] The presence of an extremist ideology is a further factor, though the key element here is probably how an individual latches onto the ideology and incorporates elements of it within their own identity. The transformation of the individual's identity is an important dimension, rather than, for example, nuances within the ideology. Indeed, radicalised individuals can often have a surprisingly simplistic and shallow understanding of the ideology.[24]

In the following section we will explore in more detail a selection of these different factors which have been linked with the radicalisation process.

Psychological Vulnerability to Radicalisation

The issue of psychological vulnerability to radicalisation has attracted growing attention, though there is variation in how this is interpreted and assessed.[25] A range of psychological factors have been identified as important to radicalisation including: issues of grievance, perceived injustice, identity, anger, revenge and a quest for significance. Certainly, most extremists believe at the time of their offending that their actions are morally justified, and various psychological processes (such as deindividuation, mortality salience, moral disengagement and risky shift) appear to play an important role in facilitating their involvement.[26] We can now consider some of these issues in more detail.

Quest for significance

Quest for significance has already been discussed in relation to Kruglanski *et al.*'s model of radicalisation.[27] One of the key findings in this regard is that perceived success in life appears to be a factor in radicalisation. Individuals who perceive themselves as less successful identify more with their religion or nationality. Kruglanski *et al.* explained this in terms of a collectivistic shift. Of concern here are studies which show that people who see their identity primarily in these terms are more likely to express support for extremist violence. Other research shows that feelings of shame or insignificance correlate with support for extremism and political violence.[28] Linked to this, recent research in the UK has found that Muslim individuals with symptoms of mild depression were more likely to express support for terrorism and political protest.[29]

Thus, the gravitation towards an extremist ideology is for many a way of dealing with perceived inadequacy and failure in their own lives, and of attempting to increase their own self-esteem and sense of significance.

Identity

How someone sees their identity appears to be an important factor.[30] People who see their identity as individuals first, are less likely to support or feel positive about an extremist ideology. In contrast, people who have a collectivistic identity (i.e. they see their identity first in terms of their religion or nation) are more supportive of extremist violence. Past life events can play an important role in an individual's sense of identity. Studies show that there is a strong relationship between self-reported life failure (or lack of success), and greater identification as a member of a collective (nation or religion). Those who experience a loss of significance are more likely to then adopt collective ideologies that will provide them with significance. Once someone has adopted a group-centred identity, studies show they are more likely to engage in activity in support of that group.

Self-esteem

Linked with the quest for significance, many theories have assumed that individuals with lower levels of self-esteem can be more vulnerable to radicalisation.[31] In this framework, the extremist ideology can offer people a way to enhance their self-esteem. Recent research results, however, suggest a more complex picture with self-esteem effects. Low self-esteem is associated with increased vulnerability to radicalisation, but so too is high self-esteem. Findings show that individuals with moderate levels of self-esteem seemed to be the most resilient to violent radicalisation.[32]

Added to this, is the related finding from other research studies that people at early stages of radicalisation can show low self-esteem, but individuals at later stages (who have been heavily radicalised) actually report high self-esteem (a result of embracing the ideology and the message that the individual is an active member of a valued in-group).[33]

Mortality salience

When people are exposed to death-related thoughts or imagery this results in what psychologists refer to as a 'mortality salience' effect. Psychological research has shown that even very subtle cues relating to death can create a mortality salience effect — even when the cues are not consciously recognised by the person involved.[34]

Mortality salience has a number of psychological effects. After exposure to such images people will usually feel an increasing pride in and identification with their country, religion, gender, race, etc. They experience exaggerated tendencies to stereotype and reject those who are different from themselves. The group you belong to is even better than it was before, even more worthy of your support. Your rivals though are diminished and less deserving of sympathy or compassion. People feel greater hostility toward those who are perceived as different-others or as a threat.

These changes in attitude and perceptions are also linked to changes in behaviour. Some of these are relatively subtle, such as sitting closer to a person who shares your own culture, while moving further away from foreigners. Others are starker, including increased physical aggression toward anyone critical of cherished beliefs.

Crucially, mortality salience has also been found to lead to an increase in support for extremism when it is linked to group identity. For example, one study found that under mortality salience conditions white Americans expressed more sympathy and support for other Whites who expressed racist views. In the Middle East, researchers found that Muslim students under mortality salience conditions expressed more support and sympathy for suicide bombers, and also expressed a greater willingness to carry out suicide attacks themselves.[35]

The more that important cultural icons and beliefs (e.g., in the context of militant jihadi terrorism, reference to the Quran, the Prophet Mohammed and other vital aspects of Islam) are involved, the more pronounced the effect is likely to be. Mortality salience leads to an increased attachment and protectiveness towards such beliefs and also produces increased hostility and aggression toward others who appear to be denigrating or insulting such icons and beliefs.

Altruism and self-sacrifice

Perhaps strangely, many people see their involvement with an extremist movement as a pro-social activity, and altruism has been identified as a potential factor in radicalisation.[36] Altruistic tendencies can be increased by stressing similarities with others. The stronger a person can identify with others the more they care about what happens to them. In contrast, stressing the differences weakens such bonds and interest and concern declines.

Altruism is likely to have an impact on support for extremism when it is considered within the context of identity. Individuals who feel their identity is closer to the militant group, and score higher on altruistic measures, are arguably the ones who will express and feel the strongest support for the group, including the group's use of extreme measures. Potentially, they will also be more likely to act on these sentiments.

Importantly, studies show that measures of altruism correlate closely with measures of psychological willingness to self-sacrifice.[37] Both of these factors also match closely with measures of having a commitment to higher causes — causes which provide meaning in people's lives. Self-sacrifice is also linked to an increased willingness to engage in extreme actions, to endure personal suffering and hardship on behalf of a cause, and feelings of anger towards people who do not respect that cause.

Radicalisation and Children and Teenagers

Many individuals can become engaged with violent extremist movements at a very young age, and adolescence, in particular, seems to be a critical period. Why adolescence is so important appears to relate to issues of identity and negative emotions. Establishing a clear sense of identity is a normal part of adolescence. The concern with radicalisation is when identity gravitates towards an ideology-based violence and is shaped by this.

This is more likely to happen in cases where the young person has a strong identification with an (ethnic and religious) in-group; where they perceive this in-group as superior; yet, where they also perceive this in-group to have been humiliated by others.[38] The psychological background can be marked by negative emotions and a quest for significance. Self-esteem may be low at the start of the process, but can rise as the individual embraces the radical ideology and increasingly incorporates this into their own sense of identity.

Young people with high personal uncertainty (e.g., who experience higher levels of anxiety and confusion) can be more inclined to support ideology-based violence. Researchers argue that uncertainty is a distressing feeling, and that people are fundamentally motivated to achieve a sense of certainty about themselves and their social worth. This can make extremist ideologies that provide a clear "black and white" worldview which minimises ambiguity and uncertainty very attractive, and indeed, studies show that people gravitate towards radical beliefs when they experience high levels of uncertainty. Also, young people who have a higher sense of agency (i.e. feel that they understand themselves and their roles) appear more willing to actually act on violent intentions. Important background environmental factors which contribute to all this can be negative situations at home, the presence and endorsement of the ideology among their peers and family, and negative key events in their personal lives.[39]

Gender and Radicalisation

Recent research shows that the recruitment of young men and women to terrorist causes can be highly gendered and operates on two levels.[40] How this happens can be well illustrated by examining recent developments with regard to militant jihadist radicalisation, particularly with regard to the Islamic State (IS). At the first level, recruitment focuses on critiquing gendered globalised societal patterns and norms, and second, targeting individual lives. These two layers of propaganda and recruitment reinforce each other, and provide a broad alignment of public values with private aspirations.

The first globalised narratives are produced on a mass scale and distributed via a range of media and platforms, from Ask.fm, Instagram, Facebook and Twitter, to online video channels and dedicated websites. Klaussen's in-depth analysis of IS online material reveals less than ten percent of material is concerned with violence.[41] Although different communities are targeted in unique ways there are common trends. Generally, the material focuses on the failings of Western states to allow Muslims to live according to their faith, points to the violence of Western governments and state agencies against Muslims, and emphasises the faults of Muslims who adopt alternative understandings of an Islamic way of life and particularly targeting Shia and Sufis. These claims are highly gendered and declare it an obligation on Muslim men to defend 'rightly believing' women from such attacks. Reinforcing this perception of threat, they allege that European men are emasculated by European state agencies, and are not 'real men' because of their failures to defend the 'appropriate' gender order. For example, the French language magazine, Dar Al-Islam, which supports ISIS, in the edition entitled, "Qu'Allah Maudisse La France", argued that:

> The laws banning the hijab, [and] the anti-terrorist laws which allow the imprisonment of any Muslim without any serious evidence are all slapping the face of every Muslim who still believes that it is possible to live with the disbelievers or worse to live Islam under the authority of the disbelievers ...

They highlight perceived discrimination in stop and searches by police that appear to disproportionately target Asian/Muslim men, as well as different sentencing and prosecution outcomes for Muslims compared to Caucasians.[42] Female supporters of ISIS talk about 'jihadi-hotties', or 'hipster jihadis', that fighters are more manly, and therefore better Muslims, and more attractive than Western Muslim men.[43] Correspondingly, they contend that women in the West are not respected, and the roles of wife and mother are not valued.[44] They present the IS as an opportunity for young men to demonstrate their 'manhood', by becoming a fighter/hero, by supporting and defending women, and by following God's requirement that they live under Islamic law. Avatars of ISIS men and their online personas emphasise their commitment to fitness, to guns, and to having sufficient income to provide for a family as the primary breadwinner. Fatherhood is also emphasised; for example, there is an online video from ISIS made in summer of 2015 showing men playing with children in a well-equipped playground, and fathers training young boys in combat and shooting.[45] The young boys are called 'little cubs" or 'little bears'.[46]

Correspondingly, they ask women to demonstrate their commitment to God and Islamic law by providing 'support' to their (future/current) husbands in the IS and by bringing up the next generation of Muslims in the 'correct' manner.[47] Women are told to expect a 'protected' but 'purposeful' life in Iraq and Syria under ISIS, and are encouraged to think about life as part of the 'sisterhood', facilitating belonging and commitment to the new cause. The interview with the girlfriend of one of the Charlie Hebdo attackers emphasised the need for women to be the 'base' and 'rocks' for men in ISIS.[48] Online material uses particular gendered motifs to exalt individual behaviours and traits. For women, modesty, piety and complementarity with men is emphasised through images of a lion and lioness, or a 'green bird'; images of romantic love do emerge, but these are presented as the 'beginning' of a new life rather than an end in itself. Notions of 'purity' therefore become important — purity in the sense of femininity/masculinity tied to morality and of faith.

The Online Environment and Social Media

The past decade has seen enormous attention focused on questions around the role the online environment and social media play in radicalisation.[49] While the online environment is hugely diverse and public platforms are used for propagating messages, recruitment of members (rather than merely sympathisers) requires more personalised forms of communication. They often use closed forum and messaging platforms, such as Telegram and WhatsApp. IS 'groups' are increasingly suspicious of unsolicited requests, and some reports suggest they require a 'recommendation' from a 'known'/'trusted' individual. This became evident in the Channel 4 Dispatches programmes aired in November 2015, where the undercover reporter had considerable difficulty accessing groups that 'met in real life' and she was finally ousted from a meeting because she could not allay the lead woman's fears that she was not carrying a camera in her bag.[50] Closest links seem to be with siblings.[51] Recruiters exploit their extensive knowledge of an individual by targeting any existing vulnerabilities in the young person's identity and life experiences. Peer-to-peer recruiters also encourage young women to distrust friends and family or 'traditional' authority figures, arguing 'they don't understand'. Moreover, they argue that those in the West follow an Islam that has been 'perverted' by culture and traditions that are not Islamic, or that those in authority have become corrupted by working for European authorities. This process of isolating young people from those around them and generating thick bonds of trust between them is essential to convincing them to make the move from belief to action (moving to IS territories). NGOs working in de-radicalisation anticipate spikes in recruitment during summer holidays, winter and Easter breaks.[52] This is because the intensity and volume of interaction is higher, as young people have fewer 'distractions', but also because travel is less suspect. Further, we see a spike in travel over the summer as young women seek to avoid 'holidays' to Pakistan or India. There are reports of some young couples travelling to the IS together after their families had denied their union.

They target individual lives in specific recruitment, and offer 'hope' through direct material reward, status and privilege.[53] Additionally, they tap into disappointment with life in the West; women's experiences, opinions and lives are shown 'not to matter' to the 'outside world' (whether that is Western politicians, state agencies or Muslim communities) and recruiters point to the failure of others to take potential recruits' actions or words seriously. At the individual level, they appear to focus on the lack of control and voice young women have in their lives — whether at home, the community or at school. They then link these personal experiences of disappointment back to a worldwide phenomenon of victimisation and oppression, for their global narrative that Muslims cannot live side by side with non-Muslims.

They offer a 'new life' belonging to IS young women, in which they are given 'choices' (IS allege) regarding marriage, work and education — providing they abide by the strict rules of gender segregation. Recruiters emphasise how 'meaningful' life is, and that hardships (in terms of electrical or medical shortages) are the burden they must endure in order to become better Muslims. Importantly young women are presented with an illusion of 'choice' in future husbands, providing their 'wali' (guardian) approves of the match. In marrying a fighter, women are given status and prestige, something recruiters allege they will not get while living in the West.[54] Furthermore, Western women are 'prized' potential wives (over local women) because they have shown their commitment to the cause by undertaking the journey, and because they have higher levels of education and maybe linguistically closer to their future husbands. The material is replete with decontextualised verses from the Quran and the Hadith (stories of the Prophet Mohammed's life). They aim to show how men can emulate the life of the prophet if they live in their caliphate.

However, in contrast to carrying out these domestic roles in the UK, in the IS it is alleged women can unite their private faith and life with their public/political goals. IS make it clear they do not anticipate women contributing to the 'battlefield', rather they are to provide supporting and domestic roles, but this is a 'political choice' as much as a personal one.[55] Images of women with weapons or dressed as a suicide bomber are signalled as a sign of defence but also to signify their support of violent 'jihad' and to show off the capability and weaponry available to fighters of the IS. Women are 'trained' in the use of light weaponry but only to defend themselves or their children, or to serve in two female-only moral police forces in IS territory — such as the Al-Khansaa Brigade.[56]

As the discussions show, the material offers a utopian vision[57] of itself — it identifies a problem with the world and living in the West, it presents an awe-inspiring and grand solution (itself), argues that young Muslims are responsible for its realisation, and offers 'hope' for a future. There is an underlying tension with this approach whereby it emphasises a new 'good life' for potential recruits while simultaneously highlighting their belief in an imminent apocalypse. However, this does not render IS a 'death cult': rather, death and violence is for a purpose — the protection of the new proto-state, and its 'citizens'. They link these global narratives of masculinity, politics and femininity to ideas about individuals' behaviours, by bridging the individual or private world, with public global narratives. The IS has been more successful in that than other groups.

Conclusion

Our understanding of how people become involved in terrorism and violent extremism has transformed since the turn of the century. That transformation occurred at the same time that 'radicalisation' took over as the dominant framework for considering questions around terrorist psychology, motivation and recruitment. Yet, is it the case that the major breakthroughs in understanding have happened because 'radicalisation' is a genuinely useful concept that has facilitated this progress? Or is it simply the inevitable result of the massive amount of research which has been focused on terrorism and terrorists in the wake of 9/11?

While radicalisation as a concept has troublesome baggage, it has nevertheless worked as an overarching theme for research on questions looking at support for and involvement in violent extremism. In this regard, it has arguably proven both more flexible and more cohesive than the previous frameworks. It has almost certainly made it easier to connect disparate research findings across a range of academic disciplines. Combined with the huge and sustained increase in scientific research across the area, significant progress seems almost inevitable.

Yet, while progress has been made, there are still very significant gaps in our understanding. Much of the evidence base remains seriously weak. Good quality studies have trickled in, but more are still needed. At this stage, it is clearly critical to remember that radicalisation is the result of many factors, some of which are about the individual involved, and some of which relate to their environment (including family and community). The range of factors involved is extensive, and the result is that radicalisation processes are complex and varied. Radicalisation itself is not a fixed state, but is dynamic, and changing events and factors can either deepen radicalisation or bring about de-radicalisation.

We also need to be careful in terms of how we think about the broader role of radicalisation. A subtle assumption has spread that 'radicalisation' as a phenomenon is the major root cause of terrorism. Yet, it is surely more accurate to see radicalisation as the recruitment processes. Other causes drive these processes, and it is these causes which merit attention and intervention. Added to this, many models of radicalisation seem weakly linked to the evidence we have regarding the structural causes of terrorism.[58] When different models are used to design or justify a variety of counter-terrorism policies and programmes, care is needed to look beyond the headline banner of radicalisation and pay attention to the causes identified *within* that model as key factors. Failing to do so, risks leading counter-terrorism and countering violent extremism down false roads.

Endnotes

1. See for example Silke, A. (2003). Becoming a Terrorist. In Silke, A (ed.). *Terrorists, Victims and Society: Psychological Perspectives on Terrorism and Its Consequences*, Chichester: Wiley, pp. 29–53.

2. Sedgwick, M. (2010). The Concept of Radicalization as a Source of Confusion, *Terrorism and Political Violence*, 22(4), 479–494.

3. Horgan, J, & Braddock, K. (2010). Rehabilitating the Terrorists? Challenges in Assessing the Effectiveness of De-radicalization programs, *Terrorism and Political Violence*, 22(2), 267–291.

4. Schmid, A. (2013). Radicalisation, De-Radicalisation, Counter-Radicalisation: A Conceptual Discussion and Literature Review, *ICCT Research Paper*, 97, 22.

5. See, for example, Richards, A. (2015). *Conceptualizing Terrorism*, Oxford: Oxford University Press.

6. For some good reviews of some of the most relevant models see: Borum, R. (2011). Radicalization into Violent Extremism II: A Review of Conceptual Models and Empirical Research, *Journal of Strategic Security*, 4(4), 7–62; King, M., & Taylor, D. (2011). The Radicalization of Homegrown Jihadists: A Review of Theoretical Models and Social Psychological Evidence, *Terrorism and Political Violence*, 23(4), 602–622; Allan, H., Glazzard, A., Jesperson, S., Reddy-Tumu, S., & Winterbotham, E. (2015). *Drivers of Violent Extremism: Hypotheses and Literature Review*, London: Royal United Services Institute.

7. Moghaddam, F. (2005). The Staircase to Terrorism: A Psychological Exploration, *American Psychologist,* 60(2), 161.

8. Silke, A., & Schmidt-Petersen, J. (2015). The Golden Age? What the 100 Most Cited Articles in Terrorism Studies Tell Us, *Terrorism and Political Violence.*

9. The model was first outlined in: McCauley, C., & Moskalenko, S. (2008). Mechanisms of Political Radicalization: Pathways Toward Terrorism, *Terrorism and Political Violence,* 20(3), 415–433; with an expanded description provided later in McCauley, C, & Moskalenko, S. (2011). *Friction: How Radicalization Happens to them and Us,* Oxford: Oxford University Press.

10. *Ibid.,* p. 416.

11. C McCauley, C., & Moskalenko, S. (2010). Individual and group mechanisms of radicalization. *Protecting the homeland from international and domestic terrorism threats: Current multi-disciplinary perspectives on root causes, the role of ideology, and programs for counter radicalization and disengagement,* pp. 82–91.

12. Kruglanski, A., Gelfand, M., Bélanger, J., Sheveland, A., Hetiarachchi, M., & Gunaratna, R. (2014). The Psychology of Radicalization and Deradicalization: How Significance Quest Impacts Violent Extremism, *Political Psychology,* 35(1), 69–93.

13. Dugas, M., & Kruglanski, A. (2014). The Quest for Significance Model of Radicalization: Implications for the Management of Terrorist Detainees, *Behavioral Sciences & the Law,* 32(3), 423–439.

14. Kruglanski, A., Gelfand, M., & Gunaratna, R. (2012). Terrorism as Means to an End: How Political Violence Bestows Significance. In Shaver, P. R., & Mikulincer, M. (eds.). *Meaning, mortality, and choice: The social Psychology of Existential Concerns,* Washington, DC: American Psychological Association, pp. 203–212.

15. *Op. cit.*

16. University of Amsterdam, *Empirical Study (revised). SAFIRE: Scientific Approach to Finding Indicators for & Responses to Radicalisation.* (2013). http://www.safire-project-results.eu/deliverables.html.

17. Marret, J., Feddes, A., Mann, L., Doosje, B., & Griffioen-Young, H. (2013) An Overview of the SAFIRE Project: A Scientific Approach to Finding Indicators of and Responses to Radicalisation, *EXIT-Deutschland: Zeitschrift für Deradikalisierung und demokratische Kultur,* 1, 123–148.

18. *Op. cit.*

19. Silke, A. (2008). Holy Warriors Exploring the Psychological Processes of Jihadi Radicalization, *European Journal of Criminology*, 5(1), 99–123.

20. Sageman, M. (2011). *Leaderless Jihad: Terror Networks in the Twenty-First Century*, University of Pennsylvania Press.

21. Bakker, E. (2006). *Jihadi Terrorists in Europe*. Clingendael Security Paper No. 2, Haag: Netherlands Institute of International Relations.

22. Kule, A., & Gül, Z. (2015). How Individuals Join Terrorist Organizations in Turkey: An empirical study on DHKP-C, PKK, and Turkish Hezbollah, *The Global: A Journal of Policy and Strategy*, 1(1).

23. Borum, R. (2014). Psychological Vulnerabilities and Propensities for Involvement in Violent Extremism, *Behavioral Sciences & the Law*, 32(3), 286–305.

24. Silke, A. (2010). *The Psychology of Counter-terrorism*, Oxon: Routledge.

25. See for example, Horgan, J. (2008). From Profiles to Pathways and Roots to Routes: Perspectives from Psychology on Radicalization into Terrorism, *The ANNALS of the American Academy of Political and Social Science*, 618(1), 80–94; *op. cit.*

26. See, for example, Bandura, A. (1990). Mechanisms of Moral Disengagement in Terrorism. In W, Reich. (ed.). *Origins of Terrorism: Psychologies, Ideologies, States of Mind*, Washington DC: Woodrow Wilson Center Press, 161–191; Pyszczynski, T., Abdollahi, A., Solomon, S., Greenberg, J., Cohen, F., & Weise, D. (2006). Mortality Salience, Martyrdom, and Military Might: The Great Satan Versus the Axis of Evil, *Personality and Social Psychology Bulletin*, 32(4), 525–537; and Silke, A. (2014). *Terrorism: All That Matters*, London: Hodder and Stoughton.

27. *Op. cit.*

28. *Ibid.*

29. Bhui, K., Everitt, B., & Jones, E. (2014). Might Depression, Psychosocial Adversity, and Limited Social Assets Explain Vulnerability to and Resistance against Violent Radicalisation?' *PLoS ONE*, 9(9), e105918. doi:10.1371/journal.pone.0105918.

30. See for example, Dean, C. (2014). The Healthy Identity Intervention: The UK's Development of a Psychologically Informed Intervention to Address Extremist Offending. In Silke, A. (ed.). *Prisons, Terrorism and Extremism: Critical Issues in Management, Radicalisation and Reform*, Oxon: Routledge; Liht, J., & Savage, J. (2008). Identifying Young Muslims Susceptible to Violent Radicalisation: Psychological Theory and Recommendations. In Sharpe, M. (ed.). *Suicide Bombers: The Psychological, Religious and Other Imperatives*, Amsterdam, Netherlands: IOS Press, 5–25 and Schwartz, S.,

Dunkel, C., & Waterman, A. (2009). Terrorism: An Identity Theory Perspective, *Studies in Conflict & Terrorism*, 32, 537–559.

31. Lub, V. (2013). Polarisation, Radicalization and Social Policy. Evaluating the Theories of Change, *Evidence and Policy*, 9, 165–183.

32. Feddes, A., Mann, L., & Doosje, B. (2015). Increasing Self-Esteem and Empathy to Prevent Violent Radicalization: A Longitudinal Quantitative Evaluation of a Resilience Training focused on Adolescents with a dual Identity, *Journal of Applied Social Psychology*, 45, 400–411.

33. *Op. cit.*

34. Pyszczynski, T., Solomon, S., & Greenberg, J. (2002). *In the Wake of 9/11: The Psychology of Terror* Washington, DC: American Psychological Association.

35. *Op. cit.*

36. See for example, O'Gorman, R., & Silke, A. (2015). Terrorism as Altruism: An Evolutionary Model for Understanding Terrorist Psychology. In Taylor, M., Roach, J., & Pease, K. (eds.). *Evolutionary Psychology and Terrorism*, Oxon: Routledge, 149–163; and Reeve, Z. (2015). Terrorism as Parochial Altruism. Paper presented at the *Annual Convention of the American Political Science Association*, San Francisco, 3–5 September 2015.

37. Bélanger, J., Caouette, J., Sharvit, K., & Dugas, M. (2014). The Psychology of Martyrdom: Making the Ultimate Sacrifice in the Name of a Cause, *Journal of Personality and Social Psychology*, 107(3), 494–515.

38. *Op. cit.*

39. *Ibid.*

40. See for example, Bloom, M. (2010). Death Becomes Her: The Changing Nature of Women's Role in Terror, *Georgetown Journal of International Affairs*, 91–98.

41. Klausen, J. (2015). Tweeting the Jihad: Social Media Networks of Western Foreign Fighters in Syria and Iraq, *Studies in Conflict & Terrorism*, 38(1), 1–22.

42. The Return of Khilafah. Dabiq. No.1. http://media.clarionproject.org/files/09-2014/isis-isil-islamic-state-magazine-Issue-1-the-return-of-khilafah.pdf.

43. http://www.telegraph.co.uk/news/worldnews/middleeast/11011634/Islamic-States-new-icon-is-a-hipster-jihadi.html.

44. Smith, M., & Saltman, EM. (2015). Til Martyrdom do us part: gender and the ISIS phenomenon, *Strategic Dialogue*. http://www.strategicdialogue.org/Till_Martyrdom_Do_Us_Part_Gender_and_the_ISIS_Phenomenon.pdf.

45. See for example, http://www.washingtonpost.com/sf/life-in-the-islamic-state/2015/10/01/overview/

46. For example, https://v.storyful.com/production/44/62/85/9f/syfl-27656-e43ecf78.mp4

47. From the Battle of Al-Ahzab to the War of Coalitions. Dabiq. No. 11. http://www.clarionproject.org/docs/Issue%2011%20-%20From%20the%20battle%20of%20Al-Ahzab%20to%20the%20war%20of%20coalitions.pdf.

48. http://www.longwarjournal.org/archives/2015/02/new-issue-of-dabiq-features-interview-with-widow-of-paris-gunmen-2.php.

49. See for example, Conway, M. (2012). From al-Zarqawi to al-Awlaki: The Emergence of the Internet as a New Form of Violent Radical Milieu, *CTX: Combatting Terrorism Exchange*, 2(4), 12–22; and Silke, A. (2010). The Internet & Terrorist Radicalisation: The Psychological Dimension. In Dienel, H., Sharan, Y., Rapp, C., & Ahituv, N. (eds.). *Terrorism and the Internet: Threats, Target groups, Deradicalisation Strategies*, Amsterdam: IOS Press, 27–40.

50. http://www.channel4.com/info/press/news/new-undercover-investigation-into-british-women-supporting-isis.

51. RAN. (2015). Briefing Notes: Gender and Islamic State, *Women and Radicalisation* Conference Proceedings, Copenhagen, 2nd November 2015.

52. Research private correspondence with de-radicalisation workers with Dr K. E. Brown.

53. Deeb, SE. (2015). For an IS fighter, a paid Honeymoon in the Caliphate's Heart, *Associate Press* 26 May 2015. http://bigstory.ap.org/article/56445f3cc1ca4f51af716c71d54ed483/fighter-paid-honeymoon-caliphates-heart.

54. Smith and Saltman (2015) *op. cit.* See also K. Brown, 'Utopian Vision in Jihadi Gender Politics'. *Durnstein Symposium*, Austria, 2015. https://www.academia.edu/11637582/Utopian_Visions_in_Jihadi_Gender_Politics.

55. http://www.telegraph.co.uk/news/worldnews/islamic-state/11429118/What-is-luring-Western-women-to-Syria-to-join-Isil.html.

56. "Women's Manifesto of the Al-Khansaa Brigade' Translated by the Quilliam Foundation January 2015

57. Brown, K. (2015). Utopian Vision in Jihadi Gender Politics. *Durnstein Symposium*, Austria, 2015. https://www.academia.edu/11637582/Utopian_Visions_in_Jihadi_Gender_Politics.

58. See for example, Lia, B., & Skjolberg, K. (2004). *Causes of Terrorism: An Expanded and Updated Review of the Literature*, Norwegian Defence Research Establishment.

Chapter 10

Radicalisation into Violent Extremism: A New Synthesis?[1]

Kumar Ramakrishna

The horrific terrorist attacks of November 13, 2015 in Paris that killed about 130 people and soon claimed by the notorious Islamic State of Iraq and Syria or ISIS, underscored in tragic fashion, yet again, the importance of a better understanding, on the part of governments and civil societies, of the processes resulting in radicalisation into violent extremism (RIVE). To be sure, ever since the epochal September 11, 2001 al-Qaeda attacks that killed almost 3,000 civilians in New York and Washington DC, much ink has been spilled in scholarly and policy circles on this very issue. However, consensus on what the terms "radicalisation" and "extremism" mean remains elusive. As terrorism scholar Peter R. Neumann puts it, the meaning of the term "radicalization" is "ambiguous" because to be radical does not automatically mean being violent. For instance, in the Royal Canadian Mounted Police, radicalisation is seen as a purely cognitive phenomenon, comprising "'the movement of… individuals from moderate mainstream beliefs to extremist views".[2] Other interpretations however suggest that the

Assoc Prof Kumar Ramakrishna is Head of Policy Studies in the Office of the Executive Deputy Chairman, S. Rajaratnam School of International Studies. He is also the immediate past Head of CENS.

end-state of radicalisation is most certainly terrorist violence.[3] Complicating matters moreover is the fact that, as Robin L. Thompson suggests, at times "radicalization is good and radicalized persons motivate others to take action for the good of humanity".[4] Hence "radical groups" should not be hastily stigmatised as dangerous.[5] Neumann notes nevertheless that despite the ambiguities swirling around the term, it is still likely to dominate "public discourse, research and policy agendas for years to come".[6] Similar concerns surround the term "extremism". The United Kingdom's well-known Contest Strategy, for instance has argued for effective strategies to counter "violent extremism".[7] Across the Atlantic, meanwhile, in August 2011, the Obama Administration similarly declared its intent to "prevent violent extremism in the United States".[8] However, like the term "radicalisation", there remains ongoing debate on what the term "extremism" actually means. The key issue once again is that to be extremist in one's views does not necessarily mean to be violent. Moreover, as in the case of radicalisation, political scientist Cass Sunstein insists that when "people shift from indifference to intense concern with local problems, such as poverty and crime", then "extreme movements are good, even great".[9] On the other hand, influential commentators such as Maajid Nawaz of the UK-based Quilliam Foundation have warned of the inherently violent potentials within extremism. To Nawaz and others like him, there is no such thing as "non-violent" extremism. Instead they suggest that a symbiotic relationship exists between ostensibly non-violent extremism and its violent manifestations.[10]

This chapter seeks to make a modest contribution to the ongoing debate. It will argue that a new conceptual synthesis may be possible that offers a fresh way to make sense of the process of radicalisation into violent extremism. To this end, the chapter will argue that two key analytical distinctions need to be made: between the *processes* of cognitive and behavioural (or violent) radicalisation; and between the *end-states* of radicalism and extremism. In sum, it will be argued that while the process of cognitive radicalisation may result in either radicalism or extremism; behavioural or violent radicalisation manifested in the form of terrorist violence, is more likely to be the outcome of the psychological end-state of extremism. To this end, the chapter will unpack the argument as follows: the first section will provide a concise review of various extant interpretations of the terms "radicalisation" and "extremism". The second section will then offer a new conceptual synthesis, arguing that cognitive radicalisation should be seen as the process of *drastic identity simplification* on the part of in-group members that perceive themselves to be under collective threat by an out-group. That is, in the process of cognitive radicalisation, in-group members will depluralise their many social and even personal identities in favour of a single overarching in-group identity. At the same time, in-group members will simultaneously depluralise the multiple social and personal identities of out-group members on the other side of the conflict dyad, in favour of a single overarching out-group identity. The psychological end-result of cognitive radicalisation therefore would be the resolution by in-group members of the multiple social and personal identities on both sides of the conflict dyad in favour of a *single axis of collective identification*: Christian versus Muslim; Serb versus Croat, Tamil versus Singhalese; in short the proverbial Us-versus-Them — the essence of cognitive radicalisation. Cognitive radicalisation, however, it will be argued in the subsequent section, does not necessarily and automatically lead to out-group violence in the form of terrorism. This is where the chapter will, following the recent seminal work of the eminent terrorism scholar Alex Schmid, argue for a distinction to be made between the psychological end-states of radicalism and extremism. It will show that while radicals can on occasion resort to violence, the real threat of violence emanates not from radicals but rather extremists. Hence, the policy concern should not really be radicalisation into radicalism *per se*, but rather *radicalisation into extremism, with its inherent violent potentials.*

Radicalisation and Extremism: Contending Interpretations

There have been as mentioned many interpretations of the term "radicalisation". One typical suggestion is that it "means the process of adopting or promoting an extremist belief system for the purpose of facilitating ideologically based violence to advance political, religious, or social change".[11] Another definition suggests that it is the "process by which individuals come to undertake terrorist activity, or directly aid or abet terrorism".[12] A seminal and much-cited 2007 report by the New York Police Department (NYPD) Intelligence Division isolates four phases of radicalisation: a "pre-radicalisation" stage; a "self-identification" stage, where individuals first become attracted to violent ideologies through a "cognitive opening caused by some personal, socio-economic or political crisis"; an "indoctrination" stage, in which a gradual intensification of violent beliefs occurs, principally through intensive contact with a "spiritual sanctioner" and a small group of "like-minded" individuals; and finally the *jihadisation* stage, where the individual has reframed his self-identity as a *jihadist* committed to terrorist violence. In a nutshell "the progression of searching, finding, adopting, nurturing, and developing" this extreme religious belief system "to the point where it acts as a catalyst for a terrorist act" characterises radicalisation.[13] There have been other interpretations. Fathali Moghaddam has outlined a Staircase to Terrorism model. This comprises six stages an individual would typically pass through before engaging in terrorist acts. The process starts from a situation where an individual, unable to alleviate a perceived adversity, undergoes profound frustration, develops aggressive sentiments that are displaced onto a target group, joins a terrorist organisation, embracing its us-versus-them ideological paradigm, and ultimately crosses the moral threshold into, as well as surmounts inhibitory mechanisms against, violence.[14] Meanwhile Randy Borum proposes a Four-Stage Model of the terrorist mindset, in which an individual first frames a particular event, condition or grievance ("it's not right") as being unjust ("it's not fair"). The radicalising individual then attributes the unjust situation to a target person, group or nation ("it's your fault"), and ultimately vilifies and demonises that responsible party ("you're evil"). Borum's view is that the last stage reached tends to coincide with "justification or impetus for aggression".[15]

While the aforementioned models of radicalisation are *stage* models, so-called *process* models that essentially seek to isolate the factors or mechanisms that promote RIVE also exist. The U.S. National Counter-Terrorism Center (NCTC) model is representative of this group. This model emphasises the interaction between personal, group, community, socio-political and ideological factors.[16] Another process model is the author's own Radical Pathways Framework, which seeks to tease out how radicalisation can be the product of the complex interaction between human nature, culture, ideology, small-group dynamics and the individual personality.[17] In a sort of mixed stage and process framework, Joshua Sinai first divides the overall radicalisation process into three stages: a radicalisation, mobilisation and action phase. He then identifies six factors that influence the radicalisation phase: personal, political and socioeconomic, ideological, community, group and enabling factors. Sinai argues that the mobilisation phase is influenced by the three factors of opportunity, capability and readiness to act. Finally, the action phase is dominated by target selection activity.[18]

Like the term "radicalisation", the word "extremism" has had several interpretations. In essence, extremism suggests "being at the margins, of existing on the boundaries or of functioning at the edges", and only tenuously linked to the normative core or centre.[19] Klein and Kruglanski likewise argue that extremism should be seen as a "deviation from the norm or the majority".[20] They add that from another angle, extremism can also be interpreted as "zeal or profound conviction" for "a particular position or attitude on a given issue".[21] Douglas Pratt offers yet another nuance, suggesting that extremism "takes its own wider group identity — be it religion or tradition — to an extreme; not by a move away from the centre, but rather by intensifying its self-understanding and self-proclamation as representing, or being, the centre".[22] Peter Neumann for his part suggests that extremism can be viewed at two levels: at the level of *"political ideas"* — as has been discussed — it may represent beliefs "that are diametrically opposed to a society's core values, which — in the context of a liberal democracy — can be various forms of racial or religious supremacy, or ideologies that deny basic human rights of democratic principles".[23] Neumann — following the philosopher Roger Scruton — adds however that extremism can also be manifested in another sense, at the level of the "methods by which actors seek to realise any political aim, namely by 'show[ing] disregard for the life, liberty, and human rights of others'".[24] In fact as we shall soon see, this perspective of extremism as a *violent method* hints at the opportunity for a fresh conceptual synthesis of the whole issue of RIVE.

A New Synthesis: Cognitive Radicalisation Re-interpreted

Neumann makes a valid point in asserting that much of the ambiguity surrounding the meaning of the term "radicalisation" emerges from a "principal conceptual fault-line": on the one hand, "notions of radicalisation that emphasize extremist beliefs" — or "'cognitive radicalization'" — and ideas that "focus on extremist behavior" — "'behavioural radicalisation'".[25] Lorenzo Vidino offers perhaps a typical understanding of the relationship in much of the literature.[26]

> Cognitive radicalization is the process through which an individual adopts ideas that are severely at odds with those of the mainstream, refutes the legitimacy of the existing social order, and seeks to replace it with a new structure based on a completely different belief system. Violent radicalization occurs when an individual takes the additional step of using violence to further the views derived from cognitive radicalism.

Vidino adds that while violent radicalisation poses an immediate threat to society that governments should of course address, a more basic issue is what to do about "cognitive radicalism", which is "widely understood to be the logical antecedent to behavioural radicalism".[27] This assumed link between cognitive and behavioural radicalisation has not gone unchallenged however. Terrorism scholars such as John Horgan and Randy Borum assert that the "assumption that extremist beliefs are the precursor to violent action" is "fundamentally flawed".[28] They posit rather that because "terrorists do not always hold strong political beliefs", there is really "no inevitable link between (extremist) political beliefs and (violent) political action, and that the two phenomena should be studied separately".[29] In like vein, Clark McCauley and Sophia Moskalenko agree that "bad ideas are not like a dose of salts that must produce bad actions" and hence there is *"no 'conveyor belt' from extreme beliefs to extreme action"*.[30] In other words, cognitive radicalisation is a distinct phenomenon from violent radicalisation and the two should not be conflated.

Such a viewpoint has nevertheless in turn been discounted by scholars who cling to the stance that there *is* a link. Peter Neumann for example admits that while it cannot be said that "ideology is always the principal reason for people joining terrorist groups", the historical record — whether one is examining violent Irish Republicanism, Tibetan non-violent separatist resistance or the current wave of *jihadist* terrorism — strongly suggests that "the role of beliefs and ideology" — the cognitive element — "in behavioural radicalisation is obvious and well documented".[31] Moreover, citing research from social movement theorists, Neumann avers that in a terrorist network not everyone need be an intellectually sophisticated ideologue, as there is instead "a good sense of, and commitment to, core principles and ideas".[32] Further support for the idea that cognitive radicalisation and violent radicalisation are intertwined come from recent research on "dangerous speech". Susan Benesch has argued that when "an act of speech has a reasonable chance of catalysing or amplifying violence by one group against another, given the circumstances in which it was made or disseminated, it is Dangerous Speech".[33] In the view of Benesch, dangerous speech — *which is from our perspective, a verbal expression of internalised beliefs and attitudes, in short cognitive factors* — occurs when the following key "variables" are all present, *inter alia*: a charismatic speaker holding sway over a particular audience; a community that is vulnerable and wracked by a combustible combination of socioeconomic and political anxieties that can be exploited; speech content that evinces linguistic dehumanisation of out-group members "as vermin, pests, insects or animals" and justifies violence against them as a legitimate exercise of self-defence; an enabling environment of poor governance and weak rule of law; and finally a dearth of countervailing sources of information. Benesch argues that recent empirical evidence from the 1994 Rwandan genocide confirms the validity of the dangerous speech construct.[34] In other words, given the right conditions, cognitive radicalisation expressed in the form of dangerous speech can under certain conditions generate out-group violence. By implication, therefore, cognitive radicalisation is intertwined with behavioural radicalisation.

It is suggested here moreover that cognitive radicalisation contributes to its violent, behavioural manifestation in yet another way. Cognitive radicalisation, quite apart from the process of internalising extremist beliefs as Vidino and others suggest, also involves a *drastic identity simplification dynamic* that depending on *the intensity with which anti-social beliefs about out-group members are held*, may generate terrorist violence. This requires elaboration. Nobel laureate Amartya Sen has articulated what can be seen as the normal, "steady state":

> The same person can, for example, be a British citizen, of Malaysian origin, with Chinese racial characteristics, a stockbroker, a nonvegetarian, an asthmatic, a linguist, a bodybuilder, a poet, an opponent of abortion, a birdwatcher, an astrologer, and one who believes that God created Darwin to test the gullible.[35]

However, when the members of a religious (or ethnic or national) in-group collectively perceive that their religious and cultural distinctiveness is under physical and especially existential threat, all the diverse social identities described by Sen are drastically simplified to *a single axis of collective identification that is perceived to be at risk*. Slavenka Drakulic alludes to this psychological dynamic of drastic identity simplification in her description of the cognitive impact on Croats of Serb violence during the Balkan wars of the early 1990s:

> Along with millions of other Croats, I was pinned to the wall of nationhood — not only by outside pressure from Serbia and the Federal Army but by national homogenization within Croatia itself. *That is what the war is doing to us, reducing us to one dimension: the Nation.* The trouble with this nationhood, however, is that whereas before, I was defined by my education, my job, my ideas, my character — and yes, my nationality too — now I feel stripped of all that (emphasis mine).[36]

Meanwhile Lord Alderdice, a trained psychiatrist and politician deeply involved in forging the Good Friday agreement between Catholics and Protestants in Northern Ireland in April 1998, observed a similar phenomenon during the Troubles in Northern Ireland:

> The community had regressed from a myriad of individual differences maintained in a broad mosaic of relationships, to a narrower frame of reference where the single difference between Protestant Unionist and Catholic Nationalist assumed pre-eminence.[37]

Another example of cognitive radicalisation understood as a process or dynamic of drastic identity simplification, is articulated by Yossi Klein Halevi, an American Jew who was once associated with the Jewish Defence League, an American Jewish extremist organisation. Referring to how his father, a survivor of the Holocaust in World War Two, had brought him up, Halevi recounted:

During the war Jewishness had become the central — the only — fact of a Jew's existence. And so if one could be killed for being a Jew, then one simply had to live as a Jew. There was no joy in that decision, but neither was there regret. To reject one's Jewishness made as much sense as to reject one's gender (emphasis mine).[38]

The cognitive radicalisation of American Orthodox Jews — who like Halevi — became extremists in the 1960s, was evinced by drastic identity simplification *not just within the in-group, but also across the conflict dyad to encompass out-group members*, in this case Germans. As Halevi recalls:

I hated Germans. All Germans. Children, old people, anyone who spoke that language and lived that culture. Nazis couldn't possibly hate Jews, I thought, as much as I hated Germans. If I inadvertently touched some product made in Germany, my hand recoiled, repelled by intimacy with Germanness.[39]

In other words and to reiterate, cognitive radicalisation can also be manifested as a process of drastic identity simplification. That is, as seen, the multiple social identities within a community are reduced to a single overarching in-group: *Us,* while the multiple identities in the other community are simplified to a single adversarial *Them,* the out-group. Cognitive radicalisation within communities as just described occurs, to reiterate, where significant inter-group tensions, prejudices and conflict are a deeply intrinsic part of historical or contemporaneous experience. As it turns out, psychologist Michael J. Stevens has aptly captured the identify simplification dynamic at the core of this understanding of cognitive radicalisation: "during inter-group contestation and conflict, group identity becomes more salient than individual identity; concern with ingroup welfare replaces individual concerns; there is a heightened sense of shared grievances; and importantly, ingroups tend to become aggressive behaviorally and engage in outgroup stereotyping".[40]

It is worth noting that the cognitive radicalisation process described here also corresponds with the first three phases of social psychologist Anthony Stahelski's five-stage "social psychological conditioning" model, which from our perspective could be seen as a RIVE model as well: first, in-group *depluralisation*, in which all other competing group identities are stripped away; *self-deindividuation*, in which in-group members' personal identities are eliminated and *other-deindividuation*, in which the personal identities of out-group members are stripped away.[41] There are two further clarifications that should be made at this point. First, thus far we have been speaking of cognitive radicalisation as a process of drastic identity simplification on both sides of a conflict dyad (for instance, Sunni versus Shia) from the perspective of *members of the in-group only*. If however this process occurs on both sides of conflict dyad — that is from the perspective of members of the in-group as well as members of the out-group, *mass radicalisation* could be said to be occurring. Radicalisation "can occur", Alex Schmid agrees, "on both sides of a conflict dyad".[42] Mass radicalisation is incidentally a phenomenon that needs further research.[43]

There is a second clarification: radicalisation can occur not just to individuals but also small groups and larger collectivities.[44] In the view of McCauley and Moskalenko "radicalization is a psychological trajectory that, given the right circumstances, can happen to any person, group or nation".[45] Hence, whether we are talking about Irish Catholics and Protestants during the Troubles in Northern Ireland; Serbs, Croats and Bosnian Muslims in the war-torn Balkans of the 1990s and Shia and Sunni in ISIS-scourged Syria and Iraq today, what unites these various conflict dyads — despite their differing circumstances and issues — is the fact that these were and are all in the throes of mass radicalisation.

The End-State of Cognitive Radicalisation: Radicalism or Extremism?

It was earlier suggested that cognitive radicalisation involving a drastic identity simplification dynamic may ultimately generate terrorist violence depending on *the intensity with which anti-social beliefs about out-group members are held.* This leads us to an important distinction between the psychological end-states of "radicalism" and "extremism". Alex Schmid in this connection has argued in recent seminal work that one should in fact distinguish analytically between "(open-minded) radicals and (closed minded) extremists".[46] Based on close analysis of decades of research on the psychology of Fascism and Communism, Schmid avers that *extremists are more than mere radicals.* While radicals advocate sweeping political change and their "system-transforming" solutions may at times become "violent and non-democratic", Schmid cautions that "it does not follow that a radical attitude must result in violent behavior". Instead radicals have been known to be "open to rationality and pragmatic compromise", as well as to evince that they can be "tolerant, pluralist and anti-authoritarian". Most importantly, Schmid opines that "radical militants can be brought back into the mainstream".[47] The latter analysis sheds some light on how certain well-known Islamist radicals such as Maajid Nawaz of the Quilliam Foundation in the UK as well as ex-Quilliam member and former Islamist Ed Husain were able to re-enter the democratic mainstream.[48] Extremists on the other hand, are perhaps a different kettle of fish. *One may say that the intensity with which the extremist clings to his beliefs significantly exceeds that of the radical.* Hence, Schmid notes that the extremist "state of mind tolerates no diversity", is intolerant, dogmatic and adheres to an "ideology" emphasising "a simplified monocausal interpretation of the world where you are either with them or against them". Most crucially, *perhaps arising from the greater and more profound zeal with which they espouse their anti-social beliefs* compared to radicals, extremists are much more "positively in favour of the use of force to obtain and maintain political power, although they may be vague and ambiguous in their public pronouncements, especially when they are in a position of weakness".[49] In this respect, the notorious UK-based Islamist activist Anjem Choudary, who was jailed in September 2014 for allegedly promoting support for ISIS and for circulating material that could be interpreted as urging terrorist violence — and whose supporters have included individuals who have actually carried out terrorist acts — appears to exemplify extremism rather than merely radicalism.[50]

Furthermore it could be proffered that the ideal-type *radical mindset* in some ways corresponds with the first three stages of Stahelski's aforementioned RIVE model: to recapitulate, *in-group depluralisation*, in which all other competing group identities are stripped away; *self-deindividuation*, in which in-group members' personal identities are eliminated; and *other-deindividuation*, in which the personal identities of out-group members are stripped away. The ideal-type *extremist mindset*, on the other hand appears to correspond rather neatly with the final two stages of Stahelski's model: *dehumanisation,* in which out-group members are seen as "subhuman" or "inhuman", and finally *demonisation*, in which they are regarded as "evil".[51] This is sobering: what existing RIVE models are clear about is when out-group members are dehumanised as disgusting or evil, out-group violence may just be around the corner, other supporting conditions permitting.[52] It is worth noting as well that it is certainly possible for an individual to start off as a radical but then later, thanks to a confluence of factors such as the perceived failure to impact state policy; state repression and external events, to radicalise further into extremism.[53] In a 2014 analysis Schmid goes even further, suggesting that it may be a mistake to describe extremists who promote a violent ideology as "non-violent" even if they neither directly incite nor personally participate in acts of violence themselves. In his assessment, non-violence suggests a principled philosophy, such as the Tibetan separatism Neumann mentions. Schmid would much prefer extremists to be labeled as "not-violent" or "not-now-violent", because the reason they do not employ violence is for cynically tactical rather than profound philosophical reasons.[54]

Concluding Remarks

This chapter has attempted to provide a new synthesis of the process of RIVE. Affirming the view that RIVE has both behavioural and very important cognitive components that are intertwined, it does so chiefly by going beyond extant understandings of cognitive radicalisation as the process of adopting an extremist belief system that legitimates out-group violence, to encompass an additional, complementary perspective. That is, cognitive radicalisation is equally the process of drastic identity simplification that depending on the intensity with which anti-social beliefs about out-group members are held, may generate terrorist violence. As discussed, from the perspective of members of an in-group, cognitive radicalisation can be seen as a process of drastic identity simplification on both sides of a conflict dyad. If this process occurs on both sides of conflict dyad — that is from the perspective of members of the in-group as well as members of the out-group, mass radicalisation is underway. Moreover, cognitive radicalisation can occur not just with individuals but also small groups and larger collectivities. Additionally, we saw that there are two possible psychological end-states of cognitive radicalisation: radicalism and extremism. While radicals can on occasion be violent, they can be negotiated with and brought back into the mainstream; hence perhaps the greater policy challenge is posed by extremists, whose profound zeal in attaching themselves to the anti-social beliefs embedded in their ideologies arguably make them a relatively greater threat to public order in globalised, multicultural societies. In short, further research on how cognitive radicalisation leads to its violent, behavioural manifestations; ways to distinguish more clearly between radicals and extremists; and the ensuing implications for national and regional counter-terrorist and rehabilitation programs, are perhaps amongst the key policy challenges that need to be addressed.

Bibliography

Alderdice, J. (2007). The Individual, the Group and the Psychology of Terrorism, *International Review of Psychiatry,* 19, 201–209.

Bartlett, J., Birdwell, J. & King, M. (2010). *The Edge of Violence: A Radical Approach to Extremism,* London: Demos.

Benesch, S. (2013). Dangerous Speech: A Proposal to Prevent Group Violence, http://dangerousspeech.org/guidelines/. (Retrieved 24 November 2015).

Borum, R. (2011). Radicalization into Violent Extremism II: A Review of Conceptual Models and Empirical Research, *Journal of Strategic Security,* 4(4), 37–62.

Collins, L. (9 September 2011). Former Extremist Warns Against Post-Bin Laden Triumphalism, *The National.* http://www.thenational.ae/arts-culture/books/former-extremist-warns-against-post-bin-laden-triumphalism (Retrieved 4 December 2015).

Dodd, V., & Halliday, J. (25 September 2014). Anjem Choudary among nine arrested in London anti-terrorism raid, *The Guardian.* http://www.theguardian.com/uk-news/2014/sep/25/nine-arrested-london-anti-terrorism. (Retrieved 17 November 2015).

Empowering Local Partners to Prevent Violent Extremism in the United States. (2011). Washington D.C: The White House.

Halevi, Y. K. (2014). *Memoirs of a Jewish Extremist: The Story of a Transformation,* New York: Harper Perennial.

Husain, E. (2007). *The Islamist: Why I Joined Radical Islam in Britain, What I Saw Inside and Why I Left,* London: Penguin.

Klein, K. M., & Kruglanski, A. W. (2013). Commitment and Extremism: A Goal Systemic Analysis, *Journal of Social Issues,* 69(3), 419–435.

Kressel, N. J. (2002). *Mass Hate: The Global Rise of Genocide and Terror,* revised and updated edition, Cambridge, MA: Westview Press.

McCauley, C. & S. Moskalenko. (2014). Some Things We Think We Learned Since 9/11: A Commentary on Marc Sageman's 'The Stagnation in Terrorism Research'. *Terrorism and Political Violence,* 26: 601–606.

McCauley, C., & Moskalenko, S. (2011). *Friction: How Radicalization Happens to Them and Us,* New York and Oxford: Oxford University Press.

Moghaddam, F. M. (2006). *From the Terrorists' Point of View: What they Experience and Why They Come to Destroy,* Westport and London: Praeger Security International.

Nawaz, M., with Bromley, T. (2012). *Radical: My Journey from Islamist Extremism to a Democratic Awakening,* London: W.H. Allen.

Neumann, P. R. (2013). The Trouble with Radicalization. *International Affairs,* 89(4), 873–893.

Pratt, D. (2010). Religion and Terrorism: Christian Fundamentalism and Extremism. *Terrorism and Political Violence,* 22(3), 438–456.

Radicalization Dynamics: A Primer. (2012). Washington D.C.: National Counterterrorism Center.

Ramakrishna, K. (2004). *Constructing' the Jemaah Islamiyah Terrorist: A Preliminary Enquiry,* Singapore, Institute of Defence and Strategic Studies Working Paper 71.

Ramakrishna, K. (2009). *Radical Pathways: Understanding Muslim Radicalization in Indonesia,* Westport and London: Praeger Security International.

Ramakrishna, K. (2015). *Islamist Terrorism and Militancy in Indonesia: The Power of the Manichean Mindset,* Singapore: Springer.

Schmid, A. P. (2013). *Radicalisation, De-Radicalisation, Counter-Radicalisation: A Conceptual Discussion and Literature Review.* The Hague: International Center for Counterterrorism (ICCT) Research Paper.

Schmid, A. P. (2014). *Violent and Non-Violent Extremism: Two Sides of the Same Coin?* The Hague: International Center for Counterterrorism (ICCT) Research Paper.

Scruton, R. (2007). *The Palgrave Macmillan Dictionary of Political Thought,* Third Edition, Basingstoke: Palgrave Macmillan.

Sen, A. (2006). *Identity and Violence: The Illusion of Destiny*, London: Allen Lane.

Silber, M. D. & Bhatt, A. (2007). *Radicalization in the West*: *The Homegrown Threat,* New York: NYPD Intelligence Division.

Sinai, J. (2012). Radicalization into Extremism and Terrorism: A Conceptual Model, *The Intelligencer: Journal of US Intelligence Studies,* 19(2), 21–25.

Stahelski, A. (2005). Terrorists are Made, Not Born: Creating Terrorists Using Social Psychological Conditioning, *Cultic Studies Review,* 4(1), 1–11.

Stevens, M. J. (2002). The Unanticipated Consequences of Globalization: Contextualizing Terrorism. In Stout, C. E. (ed.). *Psychology of Terrorism*: Vol. 3 — *Theoretical Understandings and Perspectives*, London and Westport, Connecticut: Praeger, pp. 31–56.

Sunstein, C. R. (2009). *Going to Extremes*: *How Like Minds Unite and Divide* New York: Oxford University Press.

Thompson, R. L. (2011). Review of Clark McCauley and Sophia Moskalenko, *Friction: How Radicalization Happens to Them and Us*, New York: Oxford University Press, *Journal of Strategic Security* (2011). 4(4), 195–196.

Vidino, L. (2010). *Countering Radicalization in America*: *Lessons from Europe,* Washington D.C: United States Institute of Peace Special Report 262.

Violent Radicalization and Homegrown Terrorism Prevention Act, *gov.track.us,* October 24, 2007. https://www.govtrack.us/congress/bills/110/hr1955/text (Retrieved 4 December 2015).

Endnotes

1. Portions of the material in this chapter are adapted from the longer analysis in Kumar Ramakrishna, (2015). *Islamist Terrorism and Militancy in Indonesia*: *The Power of the Manichean Mindset*, Singapore: Springer.
2. Neumann, P. R. (2013). The Trouble with Radicalization, *International Affairs* 89(4), 873–874.
3. Silber, M. D. & Bhatt, A. (2007). *Radicalization in the West*: *The Homegrown Threat,* New York: NYPD Intelligence Division.
4. Thompson, R. L. (2011). Review of Clark McCauley and Sophia Moskalenko, *Friction*: *How Radicalization Happens to Them and Us*, New York: Oxford University Press, *Journal of Strategic Security* (2011). 4(4), 195–196.

5. Sunstein, C. R. (2009). *Going to Extremes: How Like Minds Unite and Divide*, New York: Oxford University Press, p. 149.
6. Neumann, The Trouble with Radicalization.
7. Bartlett, J., Birdwell, J., & King, M. (2010). *The Edge of Violence: A Radical Approach to Extremism*, London: Demos, p. 57.
8. *Empowering Local Partners to Prevent Violent Extremism in the United States.* (2011). Washington D.C: The White House.
9. Sunstein, *Going to Extremes*, p. 149.
10. Collins, L. (9 September 2011). Former Extremist Warns Against Post-Bin Laden Triumphalism, *The National.* http://www.thenational.ae/arts-culture/books/former-extremist-warns-against-post-bin-laden-triumphalism (Retrieved 4 December 2015).
11. Violent Radicalization and Homegrown Terrorism Prevention Act, *gov.track.us,* October 24, 2007. https://www.govtrack.us/congress/bills/110/hr1955/text (Retrieved 4 December 2015).
12. Bartlett, Birdwell & King. *Edge of Violence*, London: Demos, p. 8
13. Silber and Bhatt. *Radicalization in the West.*
14. Moghaddam, F. M. (2006). *From the Terrorists' Point of View: What they Experience and Why They Come to Destroy,* Westport and London: Praeger Security International.
15. Borum, R. (2011). Radicalization into Violent Extremism II: A Review of Conceptual Models and Empirical Research, *Journal of Strategic Security,* 4(4), 38–39.
16. *Radicalization Dynamics: A Primer.* (2012). Washington D.C.: National Counterterrorism Center.
17. Ramakrishna, K. (2009). *Radical Pathways: Understanding Muslim Radicalization in Indonesia,* Westport and London: Praeger Security International.
18. Sinai, J. (2012). Radicalization into Extremism and Terrorism: A Conceptual Model, *The Intelligencer: Journal of US Intelligence Studies,* 19(2), 21–25.
19. Pratt, D. (2010). Religion and Terrorism: Christian Fundamentalism and Extremism, *Terrorism and Political Violence*, 22(3), 440.
20. Klein, K. M., & Kruglanski, A. W. (2013). Commitment and Extremism: A Goal Systemic Analysis, *Journal of Social Issues,* 69(3), 422.
21. *Ibid.*
22. Pratt, Religion and Terrorism.
23. Neumann, The Trouble with Radicalization, pp. 874–875.
24. *Ibid.*, p. 875. See also Scruton, R. (2007). *The Palgrave Macmillan Dictionary of Political Thought,* Third Edition, Basingstoke: Palgrave Macmillan.

25. Neumann, The Trouble with Radicalization, p. 873.
26. Vidino, L. (2010). *Countering Radicalization in America: Lessons from Europe,* Washington D.C: United States Institute of Peace Special Report 262, 2010, p. 4.
27. *Ibid.*, pp. 4–5.
28. Neumann, The Trouble with Radicalization, p. 878.
29. *Ibid.*, p. 879.
30. McCauley, C. & Moskalenko, S. (2014). Some Things We Think We Learned Since 9/11: A Commentary on Marc Sageman's "The Stagnation in Terrorism Research", *Terrorism and Political Violence*, 26, 604.
31. Neumann, The Trouble with Radicalization, p. 880.
32. *Ibid.*, pp. 880–882.
33. Benesch, S. (2013). Dangerous Speech: A Proposal to Prevent Group Violence, http://dangerousspeech.org/guidelines/. (Retrieved 24 November 2015).
34. *Ibid.*
35. Sen, A. (2006). *Identity and Violence. The Illusion of Destiny,* London: Allen Lane, p. 24.
36. Drakulic in Kressel, N. J. (2002). *Mass Hate: The Global Rise of Genocide and Terror,* revised and updated edition, Cambridge, MA: Westview Press, p. 28.
37. Alderdice, J. (2007). The Individual, the Group and the Psychology of Terrorism, *International Review of Psychiatry,* 19, 201–209.
38. Halevi, Y. K. (2014). *Memoirs of a Jewish Extremist: The Story of a Transformation,* New York: Harper Perennial, pp. 19–20.
39. *Ibid.*, p. 61.
40. Ramakrishna, K. (2004). *Constructing' the Jemaah Islamiyah Terrorist: A Preliminary Enquiry,* Singapore, Institute of Defence and Strategic Studies Working Paper 71, 39. See also Stevens, M. J. (2002). The Unanticipated Consequences of Globalization: Contextualizing Terrorism. In Stout, C. E. (ed.). *Psychology of Terrorism:* Vol. 3 — *Theoretical Understandings and Perspectives,* London and Westport, Connecticut: Praeger, p. 45.
41. Stahelski, A. (2005). Terrorists are Made, Not Born: Creating Terrorists Using Social Psychological Conditioning, *Cultic Studies Review,* 4(1), 1–11.
42. Schmid, A. P. (2013). *Radicalisation, De-Radicalisation, Counter Radicalisation: A Conceptual Discussion and Literature Review,* The Hague: International Center for Counterterrorism (ICCT) Research Paper, pp. 18–19.
43. McCauley, C., & Moskalenko, S. (2011). *Friction: How Radicalization Happens to Them and Us,* New York and Oxford: Oxford University Press, pp. 145–148.

44. Schmid, *Radicalisation, De-Radicalisation, Counter-Radicalisation,* 39.
45. McCauley and Moskalenko, *Friction,* p. 4.
46. Schmid, *Radicalisation, De-Radicalisation, Counter-Radicalisation,* p. 10.
47. *Ibid.,* pp. 8–10.
48. Nawaz, M., with Bromley, T. (2012). *Radical: My Journey from Islamist Extremism to a Democratic Awakening,* London: W.H. Allen.; Husain, E. (2007). *The Islamist: Why I Joined Radical Islam in Britain, What I Saw Inside and Why I Left,* London: Penguin.
49. Schmid, *Radicalisation, De-Radicalisation, Counter-Radicalisation,* 9–10.
50. Dodd, V., & Halliday, J. (25 September 2014). Anjem Choudary among nine arrested in London anti-terrorism raid, *The Guardian.* http://www.theguardian.com/uk-news/2014/sep/25/nine-arrested-london-anti-terrorism. (Retrieved 17 November 2015).
51. Stahelski, Terrorists are Made, Not Born.
52. For instance, Borum, Radicalization into Violent Extremism II.
53. P. R. Neumann, talk, Singapore, February 20, 2013.
54. Schmid, A. P. (2014). *Violent and Non-Violent Extremism: Two Sides of the Same Coin?,* The Hague: International Center for Counterterrorism (ICCT) Research Paper, pp. 13–14.

Part IV

Strategic and Crisis Communications

Chapter 11

The 21st Century Strategic Communication Landscape and its Challenges for Policymakers

Steven R. Corman

I don't know what the hell this [strategic communication] is that Marshall is always talking about, but I want some of it.

Admiral Ernest King[1]

Strategic communication can be straightforwardly defined as organisational communication to purposefully advance a mission.[2] The concept has been around for hundreds or even thousands of years. Christopher Paul notes that the Romans had educational exchange programs.[3] Sun Tzu's dictum that "excellence consists in breaking the enemy's resistance without fighting" is an example of recognition by military leaders that action has a communicative effect that influences the attitudes and behaviours of an adversary. Napoleon Bonaparte engaged in strategic communication when he "spoke as a [Muslim]" and discussed conversion with clerics while in Egypt; "to do so was essential to his success, to the safety of his

Steven R. Corman is a Professor in the Hugh Downs School of Human Communication and Director of the Center for Strategic Communication at Arizona State University.

army, and, consequently, to his glory. In every country he would have drawn up proclamations and delivered addresses on the same principle. In India he would have been for Ali, at Thibet for the Dalai-lama, and in China for Confucius".[4] The epigram suggests that strategic communication has origins as a distinct concept dating to around World War II. Indeed, efforts to influence military engagements through strategic communication first became institutionalised during the first and second World Wars,[5] as mass communication channels flourished.

Strategic communication as a concept has come into common use only in the last 15 years. It encompasses a number of related activities. In the business domain, marketing, advertising and public relations are all examples of strategic communication. In government and the military, analogous activities fall within the scope of strategic communication. Defined by Gullion in the mid-60s, public diplomacy is "the influence of public attitudes on the formation and execution of foreign policies".[6] It incorporates efforts including international broadcasting and educational exchange programs. In the military, strategic communication includes functions such as public affairs, civil-military operations and information operations.

This essay focuses on the growing importance of strategic communication in the government and military sectors in the present century. I argue that this is the result of two factors: the increasing role of non-state actors in conflict, and globalisation effects on states. In the next section, I examine the dependence of non-state actors on strategic communication because of the asymmetric advantages it affords in terms of recruitment, terrorism and intimidation and maintaining the identification of supporters and followers. Then I discuss the effects of globalisation on state actors and the importance of strategic communication in establishing and maintaining their legitimacy. After that, I address the key challenges policymakers need to consider in the strategic communication realm, before concluding with comments on the ways strategic communication will likely affect the national security domain in the foreseeable future.

Strategic Communication and Non-state Actors

Violence by non-state actors (NSAs), particularly terrorist groups, is an increasing problem (though mainly in countries where those groups are based). The latest available data shows a 61 percent increase in deaths from terrorist attacks from 2013 to 2014.[7] Other violent non-state groups are increasing their activity too: in Africa, attacks by communal militias, rebel forces and political militias have trended upward since around 2010.[8]

Such groups use unconventional tactics in an attempt to offset disadvantages in military power by using strategies and tactics not available to their state-based adversaries.[9] This results in some asymmetries that work to their advantage. For example, they lack concentrated assets like permanent bases and they do not depend on institutional infrastructure to operate. Both of these realities limit targets that are available in a conventional war. Because of this, and because they tend to be smaller in number than conventional forces, they are harder to geo-locate and therefore harder to attack.

However, the lack of a permanent presence and institutional infrastructure also presents at least one important disadvantage. Unlike state-based actors, they cannot depend on government institutions to recruit members, gain legitimacy or influence targeted populations to support them. They cannot (at least in most cases) build recruiting centres, visit schools, establish widespread conscription or use mass communication channels that are monopolised by the state.

Accordingly, skilled strategic communication through new media channels is critical to the success of their enterprise. Amble explains its importance for terrorist groups:

> While combatant groups employ propaganda for varying purposes, its value for terrorists specifically lies in the magnification of public attention to their cause and their activities. Militarily weak organizations cannot hope to achieve strategic objectives by force alone. Their chances for success, and indeed their very relevance, hinge enormously on earning and maintaining popular support, making the psychological battle supremely important for jihadists. For them, a failure to adopt powerful new weapons can have catastrophic impacts. As such, terrorists have embraced new media technologies to spread their messages.[10]

New media is essentially free of cost, difficult to trace, reaches a broad audience and is especially popular with NSAs' target demographic. Weimann cites another advantage, that it supports "narrowcasting".[11] This is a term originally applied to television programming,[12] but has come to mean marketing to niche audiences with specifically tailored messages.

Niche marketing is important because a main aim of recruiting by NSAs is cultivation of identification with the organisation and its movement. This is something every state-based military force does too, but is particularly important for irregular groups:

> Another way of understanding and differentiating NSAs is the extent to which they rely on identity and resources in order to organise and mobilise their members. ... NSAs become the only organisational identity of the members, at the expense of other identities (family, communities, and so forth).[13]

Another indication of the importance of strategic communication via new media is the extent to which it is controlled and managed by groups that use it. Studying the so-called Islamic State, Klausen found clear evidence that its media efforts, despite appearances, are not bottom-up affairs. Instead, a few key individuals are responsible for transmitting messages through a network that is carefully managed to create reach and redundancy.[14]

Thus strategic communication — especially though new media channels — is extremely important to the success of NSAs, and this is one reason it has become increasingly important over the last decade or so. Strategic communication is not just the province of NSAs, though; it is also of increasing importance to state actors because of forces of globalisation.

Strategic Communication and State Actors

Strategic communication through vehicles like propaganda and diplomacy has been an element of statecraft since ancient times. However, recent trends toward globalisation have pushed its importance to new levels. Growing dependencies in trade and finance have increased the potential leverage of economic sanctions against countries who behave in ways viewed as unacceptable by the international community, making efforts to legitimise state actions more important than ever before. Waters[15] argues that the political and cultural exchanges inherent in globalisation place unprecedented importance on communicative, symbolic exchange.

There are numerous examples that illustrate the resources states expend on legitimising their actions through strategic communication to a global audience. One is the recent Russian incursion into Ukraine. This conflict followed a pattern established in the earlier conflict in Georgia, wherein Russia would issue passports to former USSR citizens, stir-up discontent among these groups, then use this as a pretext for intervention.[16]

A signature strategic communication tactic in this playbook is framing the intervention as an effort to protect "human rights" of Russian-speaking "citizens" in the affected countries. In May 2014, the Russian Foreign Ministry released a white book detailing what it said were large-scale human rights violations in Ukraine,[17] including discrimination against religious and ethnic minorities. In an earlier speech to the Russian Parliament, Vladimir Putin complained, "we hoped that Russian citizens and Russian speakers in Ukraine, especially its southeast and Crimea, would live in a friendly, democratic and civilised state that would protect their rights in line with the norms of international law. However, this is not how the situation developed".[18] By framing the intervention in terms of protecting citizens and human rights, Russia legitimises its actions through appeal to accepted international norms, and forestalls retaliation that might occur if its actions were interpreted as simply an effort to recapture territory lost in the fall of the former Soviet Union.

The South China Sea conflict is another contemporary example of states using strategic communication to legitimise their actions to an international audience. China is in a territorial dispute with several other nations claiming sovereignty over islands and other geographic features in the South China Sea. It makes extensive legal arguments for sovereignty over the area, citing ancient documents describing its discovery and naming,[19] as well as a map produced by the Nationalist government of the Republic of China 1947 purportedly showing claims to the territory.[20] In addition to this strategic communication appealing to international legal norms, China has recently begun development and reclamation projects on the islands, and challenging military incursions into the 12 mile zone that, by international convention, protects a nation's air and sea space. All of these are symbolic acts that communicate its claim of sovereignty to other nations. China's adversaries also engage in strategic communication around this conflict, making contravening legal arguments and presenting physical challenges to China's claimed exclusion zones.

The South China Sea dispute is but one example of the importance China places on its image and legitimacy with outside audiences. It considers public opinion in the west so important that it has clandestinely acquired ownership of a radio station holding company in the U.S. and editorial influence over the reporting of member stations (and has made similar efforts in Europe and Australia).[21] This is part of a concerted and explicit strategic communication campaign, declared publicly in 2014 when President Xi Jinping said: "We should increase China's soft power, give a good Chinese narrative, and better communicate China's messages to the world".[22]

Key Challenges for Policymakers

The increasing importance of strategic communication and the evolving context of the media system in which it operates present several key challenges for policymakers in government and military sectors. The most important have to do with how strategic communication efforts are conducted and assessed. One issue is that current policies and doctrines are based on outdated ideas. In a widely circulated white paper,[23] my colleagues and I argued that present day strategic communication practice is based on a *message influence model* that was state-of-the-art in the 1950s but fails in the present day context.

This model, based on an engineering concept of electronic communications (specifically telephone systems) developed in the 1940s, holds that sources encode messages that are transmitted to receivers, where they are decoded and received. When this process fails it is because something interferes with the transmission process. In the absence of such interference, messages travel to receivers uncorrupted and have their intended effects. Modern communication theory holds that communication is a matter of engagement rather than transmission. The exchange of meaning is a complex process of simultaneous adjustment rather than control, and this means that modern communicators must embrace uncertainty and complexity.

From a policy perspective, this requires a different approach to strategic communication than the control-oriented one common in government and military institutions. In complex communication systems, careful planning of interventions is rarely fruitful because actions have unintended consequences. While there can be goals and strategies, the tactics used to implement the strategies must be fluid. Strategic communication, in other words, is a rugged landscape,[24] where the best efforts evolve rather than being engineered. This means deploying varying solutions,[25] assessing their fitness, retaining elements that produce good outcomes, but testing continued variation on the other elements. Developing good communication systems is therefore a long-term incremental process, and one in which a significant amount of failure is to be expected along the way to finding a fit solution. Neither government nor military culture supports this kind of process. But to confirm with contemporary realities, it should be changed to do so.

One policy challenge of this evolutionary approach is that there must be some good way of assessing fitness. Measures of effectiveness (MOEs) are a staple of strategic communication in all contexts; however, government and military organisations face special problems in this regard. For business strategic communication, MOEs are typically built-in. For example, if Toyota launches a new marketing campaign, it can easily measure its effectiveness because the company automatically knows how many cars are sold before and after the fact. Public sector strategic communicators often do not enjoy access to such measures. If a military information operations unit launches a campaign to discourage support for a terrorist group in a certain area, it may not have good measures of how many people support such illicit and covert groups, and few options for collecting relevant data.

Good MOEs in these contexts require designing strategic communication efforts with measurement in mind, and deploying them in ways that allow for quasi-experimental control. For instance, I recently spoke with a military psychological operations officer who described a campaign to encourage the target audience to report certain kinds of activities to local police. They worked with police to be sure reports were logged and classified in a useful way. They deployed their campaign in a limited area and collected police logs, both from this "test" area and another "control" area where the campaign was not deployed, creating a valid test of the effectiveness of their campaign. Policy should require this kind of testing where it is practical, and train strategic communication personnel to design and conduct it.

Another policy challenge of an evolutionary approach has to do with leading efforts that are loosely structured. The kind of creative variation advocated above demands a less centralised approach to strategic communication, but how can efforts be strategic if they are not directed and controlled? Thomas Nissen proposes the concept of *narrative led operations* as a way to ensure consistency and coherence in a decentralised operation. He argues that leadership intent should be expressed through a narrative account of the problem the effort is trying to solve, the desire created by the problem, and a projected resolution of the desire. Those executing this narrative vision are then required to make sure that whatever actions they propose are coherent within an arc of locations, events, actions and participants leading form the desire to the resolution:

> The narrative helps provide the tone and guides the planning, decision-making, communication, and actions of every single member of the organisation — from strategic to tactical level. Every decision, operation, activity, and communication should first be compared to the narrative to ensure it is consistent with the overarching tone and intent of the strategic narrative.[26]

In this way, people executing a communication strategy are free to exercise decentralised, creative judgment about messages they produce, but within constraints established by the narrative. This admittedly requires policymakers to relinquish considerable control to policy implementers. As discussed above, the cultures of military and government organisations resist this. However, it is the only path to success given demands of the complex operating environment of contemporary strategic communication.

Impacts in the Near Future

In summary, I have shown that strategic communication, which has been party of the military and government operational environment for centuries, has taken on special importance in this century because of the special needs of non-state actors and globalisation and globalisation pressures on state actors. This presents special challenges for military and government policymakers, whose institutions were shaped by ideas and requirements that have recently changed. New policies are needed that take account of the complexity of the present day strategic communication operating environment, including cultural change, new procedures and doctrine and a new leadership model. In closing, I discuss cases where strategic communication will likely have significant impacts in the next few years.

In terms of non-state actors, violent Islamist groups will continue to use strategic communication to influence the hearts-and-minds of contested populations all over the world. The so-called Islamic State is the major threat, and is spreading its influence beyond Iraq and Syria to Afghanistan and North Africa,[27] and the Caucasus,[28] and is actively recruiting educated Westerners to join their cause.[29] This group has a sophisticated strategic communication operation in which "[m]ore than half of the messages are true propaganda, portraying a utopian civil society in which children are taken for idyllic days out by fighters and clean hospitals are run by Australian doctors as part of the 'IS Health Service' (mirroring the colours and font of Britain's National Health Service)".[30]

The intent of such messaging is to legitimise the group as an actual state, a cornerstone of its recruiting and branding strategy. Their aggressive promotion of a Caliphate narrative and an End Times narrative focused on Dabiq[31] are part of the same strategy. There are options for challenging these messages,[32] but so far, there seems to be little systematic effort to do so. As long as their narratives remain unchallenged, and governments and media continue to frame them as "the Islamic State", we can expect the group to continue to gain influence, recruit more supporters and members, and spread geographically.

In terms of state actors, the main near-future concern is rekindling of superpower conflict. The South China Sea situation, mentioned above, is one potential flash point. Both China and the United States are testing one another, and this creates the potential for unintended consequences that could escalate to a military engagement. Strategic communication is a crucial factor here because it frames actions and influences interpretations by each side of what the other is doing.

The situation with Russia is perhaps a greater concern. Its entry into the Syrian conflict has created the appearance of a proxy war.[33] The situation in Ukraine remains unsettled, and Russia now appears to be setting its sights on the Baltic States. It recently began a legal review questioning the 1991 decision granting them independence from the Soviet Union,[34] and has taken provocative actions in Estonia and Latvia. Both countries are NATO member countries, have NATO military centres on their soil, and have Russian speaking minorities who are subject to the kinds of interventions to protect "human rights" described above. Thus, we can expect actions taken by Russia, the framing of these and subsequent NATO responses, to be significant strategic communication factors in inter-state conflict in the near future.

Endnotes

1. As paraphrased by Admiral James Stavridis; see Murphy, D. M. (2008). *The trouble with Strategic Communication*. Issue paper 2-08, Center for Strategic Leadership, U.S. Army War College.

2. Hallahan, Kirk, Holtzhausen, Derina, van Ruler, Betteke, Verčič, Dejan and Sriramesh, Krishnamurthy (2007) 'Defining Strategic Communication', *International Journal of Strategic Communication*, 1, 1, 3–35

3. Paul, C. (2011). *Strategic communication: Origins, concepts, and current debates*. Santa Barbara, CA: Praeger.

4. de Bourrienne, L. A. F. (1889). *Memoirs of Napoleon Bonaparte*, Phillips, R. W. (ed.). New York: Charles Scribner.

5. Paul, Chapter 3.

6. Cull, N. J. (2009). Public Diplomacy before Gullion: The Evolution of a Phrase. In Snow, N., & Taylor, P.M. (eds.). *Routledge Handbook of Public Diplomacy*, New York: Routledge, p. 19.

7. Institute for Economics & Peace (2014). *Global Terrorism Index*. http://static.visionofhumanity.org/sites/default/files/Global%20Terrorism%20Index%20Report%202014_0.pdf (Retrieved 22 October 2015).

8. See Armed Conflict Location & Event Data Project http://www.acleddata.com/agents-of-violence-in-2014/ (Retrieved 22 October 2015).

9. Tomes, R. R. (2004). Relearning Counterinsurgency Warfare, *Parameters*, 34(1), 16–28.

10. Amble, J. C. (2012). Combating Terrorism in the New Media Environment, *Studies in Conflict & Terrorism*, 35, 342.

11. Weimann, G. (2014). *New Terrorism and New Media*, Washington, DC: Commons Lab of the Woodrow Wilson International Center for Scholars.

https://www.wilsoncenter.org/sites/default/files/STIP_140501_new_ terrorism_F.pdf (Retrieved 22 October 2015).

12. Parsons, P. (2003). The Evolution of the Cable-Satellite Distribution System. *Journal of Broadcasting & Electronic Media,* 47(1), 1–16.

13. DCAF, (2015). *Armed Non-State Actors: Current trends & future challenges.* Geneva Centre for the Democratic Control of Armed Forces, Working Paper No. 5, p. 10. http://www.dcaf.ch/content/download/53925/812465/file/ansa_ final.pdf (Retrieved 22 October 2015).

14. Klausen, J. (2015). Tweeting the Jihad: Social Media Networks of Western Foreign Fighters in Syria and Iraq, *Studies in Conflict & Terrorism,* 38(1), 1–22.

15. Waters, M. (1995). *Globalization,* New York: Routledge.

16. Sherwin, E. (3 August 2014). Caucasus History Almost Repeats Itself In Crimea, *Deutsche Welle.* http://www.dw.com/en/caucasus-history-almost repeats-itself-in-crimea/a-17482549 (Retrieved 22 October 2015).

17. ITAR–TASS (5 May 2014). Russian Foreign Ministry Presents White Book on Human Rights Abuses in Ukraine, *TASS Russian News Agency.* http:// en.itar-tass.com/russia/730463 (Retrieved 23 October 2015).

18. Washington Post (18 March 2014). *Transcript: Putin says Russia will protect the Rights of Russians Abroad,* https://www.washingtonpost.com/world/ transcript-putin-says-russia-will-protect-the-rights-of-russians-abroad/2014/ 03/18/432a1e60-ae99-11e3-a49e-76adc9210f19_story.html (Retrieved 23 October 2015).

19. Shen, J. (2002). China's Sovereignty over the South China Sea Islands: A Historical Perspective, *Chinese Journal of International Law,* 1(1), 94–157.

20. Office of Ocean and Polar Affairs (5 December 2014). Maritime Claims in the South China Sea, *Limits in the Seas,* No. 143. U.S. State Department. http://www.state.gov/documents/organization/234936.pdf (Retrieved 23 October 2015).

21. Crovitz, G. (8 November 2015). China's "Soft" Power Exposed, *The Wall Street Journal.* http://www.wsj.com/articles/chinas-soft-power-exposed-1447019906 (Retrieved 23 October 2015).

22. Shambaugh, D. (2015, July/August). China's Soft Power Push, *Foreign Affairs.* https://www.foreignaffairs.com/articles/china/2015-06-16/china-s-soft-power-push (Retrieved 23 October 2015).

23. Corman, S. R., Trethewey, A., & Goodall, B. (April 2007). *A 21st Century Model for Communication in the Global War of Ideas: From Simplistic Influence to Pragmatic Complexity.* Report No. 0701. Consortium for Strategic Communication, Arizona State University. http://csc.asu.edu/ wp-content/uploads/pdf/114.pdf (Retrieved 23 October 2015).

24. Corman, S. R., & Dooley, K. J. (January 2008). *Strategic Communication on a Rugged Landscape: Principles for Finding the Right Message*. Report No. 0801, Consortium for Strategic Communication, Arizona State University. http://csc.asu.edu/wp-content/uploads/pdf/121.pdf (Retrieved 23 October 2015).

25. In biological systems these variations are literally random; in a communication context it is best to think of them as creative — i.e. random within limits.

26. Nissen, T. (2013). Narrative led operations, *Militært Tidsskrift*, 141(4), 72.

27. Schmitt, E., & Kirkpatrick, D. D. (14 February 2015). Islamic State Sprouting Limbs beyond Its Base, *The New York Times*. http://www.nytimes.com/2015/02/15/world/middleeast/islamic-state-sprouting-limbs-beyond-mideast.html (Retrieved 23 October 2015).

28. Joscelyn, T. (3 September 2015). Islamic State's Caucasus "province" Claims First Official Attack on Russian Forces, *Long War Journal*. http://www.longwarjournal.org/archives/2015/09/islamic-states-caucasus-province-claims-first-official-attack-on-russian-forces.php (Retrieved 23 October 2015).

29. Scarborough, R. (1 June 2015). Islamic State recruits Westerners with promise of Muslim utopia, *The Washington Post*. http://www.washingtontimes.com/news/2015/jun/1/islamic-state-recruits-westerners-with-promise-of- (Retrieved 26 October 2015).

30. Economist Data Team (8 October 2015). The IS Media Machine, *The Economist*. http://www.economist.com/blogs/graphicdetail/2015/10/tracking-islamic-states-media-output (Retrieved 26 October 2015).

31. McCants, W. (2015). *The ISIS apocalypse*: *The History, Strategy, and Doomsday Vision of the Islamic State*, New York: St. Martins.

32. Furlow, R. B., Fleischer, K., & Corman, S. R. (27 October 2014). *De-romanticizing the Islamis State's vision of the Caliphate*. Report No. 1402, Center for Strategic Communication. http://csc.asu.edu/wp-content/uploads/pdf/csc1402-deromanticizing-islamic-state-caliphate.pdf (Retrieved 26 October 2015).

33. Barnard, A., & Shoumali, K. (12 October 2015). U.S. Weaponry Is Turning Syria Into Proxy War with Russia, *The New York Times*. http://www.nytimes.com/2015/10/13/world/middleeast/syria-russia-airstrikes.htm (Retrieved 26 October 2015).

34. Grigas, A. (4 July 2015). How Russia sees Baltic Sovereignty, *The Moscow Times*. http://www.themoscowtimes.com/opinion/article/how-russia-sees-baltic-sovereignty/525643.html (Retrieved 26 October 2015).

Chapter 12

Digital Naturals and the Effects of Social Media on Disaster Communication

W. Timothy Coombs

The southern California wildfires of 2007, the 2010 earthquake in Haiti, Hurricane Sandy in 2013, the Boston bombings in 2013 and the 2011 earthquake and tsunami in Japan are all examples of disasters that are linked to social media. The five examples all caused people to re-think the way social media is used during a disaster. More precisely, each of these disasters provided evidence to government officials, non-government agencies (NGOs) and researchers about the benefits social media channels can provide during a disaster communication. The re-thinking included how people in disaster use social media and how disaster responders (government officials and NGOs) might use social media to enhance disaster communication and improve disaster management as a whole. This chapter identifies key ways that those responding to disasters and those affected by disasters can utilise social media to maximise the benefits it offers for disaster communication. To develop these points in detail, it is first instructive to examine the new digital context for disaster communication.

W. Timothy Coombs is a Professor in the Department of Communication at Texas A&M University.

After exploring this new context, the lessons learned by responders and researchers are presented along with the lingering concerns both have with using social media as part of disaster communication.

Changing Context for Disaster Communication: Publics and Communication Technology

In 2001, Marc Prensky coined the terms digital natives and digital immigrants. The idea was to distinguish generations by their technology use. Digital immigrants has been raised in the analogue world and were now new to the digital world, hence they were immigrants struggling in a new world. Digital natives were born in the digital age of the internet and were comfortable in that environment. Researchers Young and Åkerström (2015)[1] argue that today the distinction between digital natives and digital immigrants is no longer valid. People of all ages are comfortable, to varying degrees, with the digital environment and engage it daily, what Young and Åkerström (2015) call digital naturals. The key characteristic is that people are using the digital environment because they have the skills (some are more skilled than others) to work in and are comfortable (some more so than others) in the digital environment. Evidence of the emergence of the digital naturals are older adults increasingly using various social media and most adults making smart phones an extension of their own bodies.

The digital naturals reflect the idea of the networked society. The idea of the networked society originates in 1981 and holds that the digital connections that arise in society will create significant social, political and cultural changes. For our purpose, the digital naturals are connected to one another and to many of the organisations in their lives through social media channels. These networked individuals create new opportunities and challenges for disaster communication. One of the hallmarks of the digital naturals would be the mobile phone and other mobile devices. Increasingly, people are connected to others and the world around them through their mobile phones. Roughly four in seven people globally have mobile phones and the number of mobile phone users is greater than the number of people using toothbrushes. In the U.S., 82 percent of U.S. adults have cellphones and 25 percent of Americans only use mobile devices to access the internet. Marketers were quick to realise that mobile devices were the future for reaching people as they quickly moved to the development of mobile apps (applications) to reach potential consumers.[2]

Researchers and practitioners have found the same mobile trends hold for disaster communication as well. People take to their mobile devices to learn about impending and actual disasters. There is a heavy reliance on the social media channels of Facebook and Twitter, both of which have mobile apps, during disasters. In fact both social media channels now have special features designed for disaster situations and disaster communication. It is important to consider how each of these two social media channels has expanded into disaster communication.

Facebook is a social networking site where people connect with friends and family — it was designed to share information among people who were connected in some fashion. Disaster communication shares the same idea of sharing information so there is a natural link, but Facebook was not developed specifically as a delivery system for disaster situations. In 2014, Facebook announced a new app called Safety Check. Safety Check is a way to learn if people in your Facebook network are safe when a disaster hits near where they live. A Facebook user has to sign up for the service. When there is a natural disaster near where they live, a notification is sent to the user asking if he or she is alright. If the person is okay, he or she clicks on the "I'm Safe" button. Notifications are then sent to the user's friends telling them the person is safe. Only your friends can see the notifications. The Safety Check was inspired by Disaster Message Board created by Facebook engineers in Japan to people in the earthquake and tsunami to reconnect with friends and family. Facebook demonstrated the flexibility of the Safety Check by activating it during the November 2015 terror attacks in Paris. It was the first time Safety Check was used for an event other than a natural disaster and Facebook's management acknowledged the company was trying something new with the system.

Twitter is a social media designed to let your "followers" know what you are doing or thinking — it is designed to send messages to others. Twitter developed a more elaborate disaster communication in 2013 with its Twitter Alerts. Twitter Alerts is designed to allow organisations to send disaster-related messages to Twitter users who subscribe to the feature. According to Twitter, Twitter Alerts is "available to local, national and international institutions that provide critical information to the general public".[3] Eligible institutions include public safety agencies, law enforcement, local governments, county and regional agencies, emergency management agencies, and certain national, state and federal agencies and NGOs. Over 100 organisations in U.S., Japan and Korea are using the system. In the U.S., the American Red Cross, The Centers for Disease Control and Prevention and the Federal Emergency Management Agency are all users of Twitter Alerts.[4] Twitter Alerts is designed for messages about the following information: imminent danger warnings, instructions about preventive measures, directions for evacuations, urgent safety alerts, information about how to access key resources, information about utility and transportation outages and crowd and misinformation management.[5] Clearly this list covers a number of essential tasks for disaster communications.

At the heart of Twitter Alerts is a specialised Tweet composer that allows approved users to create and specially tag messages from any computer or mobile device. The Tweet is then instantly sent to subscribers as a push notification or a text message. Twitter has the ability to transmit messages in SMS to help overcome some of the telecommunication problems encountered in disaster areas. The Tweets are unique from normal Tweets and designed to standout from other Tweets and to be noticed on timelines whether the user is on a computer or a mobile device. Twitter also provides the organisational user with custom, easy-to-remember URLs for the Alerts. Given the 140 character limit of Twitter, it is vital to have URLs that link people to additional information and resources. Twitter notes the product allows users to create a message on the go, makes the message easy to identify and recommends organisations encourage their followers to subscribe.

The differences between the Facebook and Twitter disaster uses reflect the nature of the social media channels themselves. Facebook is about social networking, hence, its disaster app is about people telling one another if they are okay during a natural disaster. Twitter is a microblog designed to share information with wide range of followers (those who have chosen to receive messages from another user). The Twitter Alert can be used for a variety of disaster-related communication goals such as informing, debunking and organising. The next section of the chapter will examine the various communicative functions of disaster communication more closely.

The rise of the digital naturals and their propensity for mobile devices and social media channels has implications for how governments approach emergency management and communication. That has become evident by how people around the world have been using social media during disasters over the past eight years. The implications for communication can be felt significantly during the final three phases of emergency management: preparedness, response and recovery. The next section identifies some of the key points that governments and NGOs must consider when revising emergency communication for the digital age.

Disaster Communication in the Networked Society of the Digital Naturals

Experts on disaster communication in government, NGOs and academics all agree that social media changes the process and to be effective, responders must understand and utilise social media.[5] This section considers that potential advantages social media offer during the preparedness, response and recovery phases of disasters along with a consideration of the liabilities social media brings to disaster communication.

Preparedness advantages

Disaster communications cannot simply begin using social media during a crisis. Disaster communications must establish a social media presence and voice well before a crisis begins. Social media channels, especially Twitter and Facebook, require people to be aware of and attentive to the channels. For instance, if no one is following a disaster communicator on Twitter, their Tweets will have little effect during a disaster because no one is reading the Tweets. Governmental and NGO disaster communicators can build a social media presence and following through preparedness. During non-disaster times, social media can be used to build preparedness capacity. The disaster communicators can post messages designed to educate people about preparedness actions and to persuade them to engage in preparedness. An example would be CDC's use of social media as part of its zombie apocalypse campaign designed to get citizens to create family preparedness plans. The pre-disaster helps to establish the social media outlets as places to go for disaster information.

Social media provides an additional channel for sending warning messages about possible disasters. This would give information about the likely path of a hurricane and warnings about conditions being favourable for the development of tornados. As the Red Cross notes, social media should never be the only warning channels but serve to amply transmit the warning messages and to increase the reach of the warning messages.[2] Social media also can be monitored for warning signs of a crisis because people may post messages about the start of a disaster. However, using social media as part of disaster warnings raises issues about verification of information, a point that is addressed in more detail in the liability discussion. Finally, disaster communicators can try to train people in the effective use of social media during disasters including the use of hashtags to allow for information to be located more easily.

Response

Similar to warnings, social media provide additional channels for providing disaster-related information to people. This would include updates on the spread of the disaster, evacuation routes, aid centres, the capacity of local community health care, etc. Given how much the digital naturals rely upon their mobile devices, social media is an excellent tool for delivering disaster-related information to this audience. Moreover, the SMS feature of Twitter provides a more reliable delivery method than relying just on internet access or mobile phone messages. Sometimes misinformation is disseminated, even in social media. The Red Cross notes how social media is a useful tool to detect and to combat rumours (misinformation).[2]

Responders can use social media to aid in the development of situational awareness, especially in using geotags to map the disaster[6,7] and for locating aid requests.[8] Again, veracity of evidence is a concern for both situational awareness and aid requests. Responders can use social media for collaboration and managing knowledge through wikis and collaborative workspaces. The 2010 earthquake in Haiti was the first time the U.S. government used social media to help with knowledge management and the results suggested a faster decision cycle but using social media does create security and privacy concerns.[9] Social media can be used to document events in the disaster and as a continued means to enhance situational awareness and locate those people in need keeping in mind issues of verifying information.[10] Guan and Chen (2014)[11] found that Twitter provided useful data to chart the temporal and special effects of a hurricane.

Recovery

Social media has proven to be a valuable channel for volunteers and donations. Social media is useful for both actual and digital volunteers. Actual volunteers go to the site of the disaster and help while digital volunteers collect, synthesise and share disaster-related information. Social media is helpful in recruiting and organising actual volunteers. In addition, social media are the channels digital volunteers utilise for providing their unique form of aid in the disaster.[8] Sylvester *et al.* (2014)[12] found a direct connection between the number of Tweets and the amount of donations during Hurricane Irene. Social media are extremely valuable channels for reaching volunteers and generating donations as well as being useful outlets for updating disaster information.

Social media can be used to facilitate healing during a crisis. Social media has been used for online memorials that help with grieving and the need to express emotions, for online support groups and to connect people with mental health professions, and to help people find friends and family members as well as reconnect communities.[13] The early example from Facebook in Japan illustrates the ability to reconnect people.

It should be noted that the various benefits of social media reflect both how social media allow people to connect with one another and how social media allows disaster responders to connect with publics. That means some of the disaster communication is under the control of disaster responders and some is beyond their control. The nature of social media means that disaster responders have to relinquish some control over the communication process.

Liabilities of Social Media

The concern about veracity of information arose at a number of points in the benefits section. People can accidentally or purposefully misreport disaster information. Misinformation can lead to mistakes in establishing situational awareness and decisions about deploying aid resources. Hence, it is vital that disaster responders have various means of verifying information they receive through social media. Whatever methods are used, veracity of information must be a central concern.[9]

A larger concern is the digital divide or how the use and non-use of the internet reflects larger social inequalities in society. When studying a typhoon in the Philippines, Madianou (2015)[14] found that the reliance on social media intensified social inequalities. Essentially those with access to social media received greater aid than those that did not. Moreover, those who did not have access to social media were those who were already socially disadvantaged. Disaster communicators must think on the intentional and unintentional consequences of incorporating social media into their practice.

Conclusion

Today, digital naturals and the use of social media have led to a re-thinking of disaster communications. Governments and NGOs are finding ways to integrate social media into disaster preparedness, response and recovery. However, the enthusiasm must be tempered with lingering concerns such as verification of information. Still, it seems the potential assets of social media outweigh the liabilities in the disaster communication context.

Endnotes

1. Young, P. & Åkerström, M. (2015). Meet the Digital Naturals. In Coombs, W.T., Falkheimer, J., Heide, M. & Young, P. (eds.). *Strategic communication, Social Media and Democracy: The Challenge of the Digital Naturals*, Routledge: London, pp. 1–10.
2. Bernier, S., (2013). Social Media and Disaster: Best Practices and Lessons Learned. https://www.redcross.org/images/MEDIA_CustomProductCatalog/m22442828_Social_Media_-_Suzanne_Bernier_-_SB_Crisis_Consulting.pdf (Retrieved 22 October 2015).
3. Twitter Alerts (2013). https://media.twitter.com/best-practice/twitter-alerts. (Retrieved 22 October 2015)
4. Miners, Z. (2013). Twitter partners with FEMA, Red Cross of Emergency Alert Feature. http://www.computerworld.com/article/2485120/social-media/

twitter-partners-with-fema--red-cross-for-emergency-alerts-feature.html (Retrieved 22 October 2015).

5. Sutton, J., Palen, L., & Shklovski, I. (2008). Backchannels on the Front Lines: Emergent Uses of Social Media In the 2007 Southern California wildfires. In *Proceedings of the 5th International ISCRAM Conference*, Washington, DC, pp. 624–632.

6. Middleton, S. E., Middleton, L., & Modafferi, S. (2014). Real-Time Crisis Mapping of Natural Disasters using Social Media. *Intelligent Systems, IEEE*, 29(2), 9–17.

7. Yin, J., Lampert, A., Cameron, M., Robinson, B., & Power, R. (2012). Using Social Media to Enhance Emergency Situation Awareness, *IEEE Intelligent Systems*, (6), 52–59.

8. Christian Reuter, Thomas Ludwig, Marc-André Kaufhold, and Volkmar Pipek. 2015. XHELP: Design of a Cross-Platform Social-Media Application to Support Volunteer Moderators in Disasters. In *Proceedings of the 33rd Annual ACM Conference on Human Factors in Computing Systems* (CHI '15). ACM, New York, NY, USA, 4093-4102. DOI=http://dx.doi.org/10.1145/2702123.2702171

9. Yates, D., & Paquette, S. (2011). Emergency Knowledge Management and Social Media Technologies: A Case Study of the 2010 Haitian Earthquake, *International Journal of Information Management*, 31(1), 6–13.

10. Vieweg, S., Castillo, C., & Imran, M. (2014). Integrating Social Media Communications into the Rapid Assessment of Sudden Onset Disasters. In *Social Informatics*, Springer International Publishing, pp. 444–461.

11. Guan, X., & Chen, C. (2014). Using Social Media Data to Understand and Assess Disasters. *Natural Hazards*, 74(2), 837–850.

12. Sylvester, J., Healey, J., Wang, C., & Rand, W. M. (2014). Space, Time, and Hurricanes: Investigating the Spatiotemporal Relationship among Social Media Use, Donations, and Disasters. Robert H. Smith School Research Paper No. RHS, 2441314.

13. Houston, J. B., Hawthorne, J., Perreault, M. F., Park, E. H., Goldstein Hode, M., Halliwell, M. R., & Griffith, S. A. (2015). Social Media and Disasters: A Functional Framework for Social Media Use in Disaster Planning, Response, and Research. *Disasters*, 39(1), 1–22.

14. Madianou, M. (2015). Digital Inequality and Second-Order Disasters: Social Media in the Typhoon Haiyan Recovery. *Social Media + Society*, 1(2), 2056305115603386.

Chapter 13

The Evolution, Impact and Future of Social Media for National Security

Damien D. Cheong

Introduction

The evolution and growth of social media over the last decade has been phenomenal. Developed and conceptualised originally as an alternative medium for communication, it has now become a valuable resource for information-gathering as well. The ability to use social media in such diverse ways is being leveraged by both state and non-state actors for both positive as well as malicious purposes. State actors are often disadvantaged by the fact that they cannot exploit new technologies quick enough in light that policies (e.g., legislation), approaches and strategies often lag behind technological advancements.[1] The use of social media by violent extremist groups and the challenges created for law enforcement is a case in point.

The Islamic State group's (IS) use of social media channels to disseminate propaganda, facilitate recruitment and mobilise support has proven to be highly effective. The large number of supporters (fanboys) drawn to IS, as well as the number of foreigners who have made their way to Iraq/Syria to join the group is, arguably, testament to this.[2] In comparison,

Damien D. Cheong is a Research Fellow and Coordinator, Homeland Defence Programme at CENS.

state-sanctioned approaches to counter violent extremism in the online realm have shown to be less effective.[3] For instance in terms of messaging, an internal U.S. State Department memo from June 2015 admitted that state-initiated counter narratives are "being trumped" by IS.[4]

The solution is, unfortunately, not as simple as shutting down the social media accounts of IS supporters and fighters. This is because the data from such accounts is useful for investigators and analysts. Such data has been used to track, monitor and in some cases disrupt the organisation's networks on the ground. For example, the United States Air Force (USAF) tracked and bombed an IS position via intelligence obtained from a fighter's social media post.[5] In fact, social media data has become so valuable that security agencies have reportedly asked companies not to shut down the accounts of IS supporters/fighters.[6] Another reason against the shutting down of accounts is that monitoring would be more difficult as users employ more secure methods to mask their activities and/or go underground (dark web).[7]

A key challenge of analysing these large data sets is how to do so efficiently and effectively. In many countries, particularly in the West, this issue is further compounded because policies are often unclear as to what investigative actions should be permitted given the need to protect data privacy. As CIA Director John Brennan argued at a CSIS seminar following the Paris attacks in November 2015:

> And as I mentioned, there are a lot of technological capabilities that are available right now that make it exceptionally difficult, both technically as well as legally, for intelligence and security services to have the insight they need to uncover it. And I do think this is a time for particularly Europe, as well as here in the United States, for us to take a look and see whether or not there have been some inadvertent or intentional gaps that have been created in the ability of intelligence and security services to protect the people that they are asked to serve.
>
> And in the past several years because of a number of unauthorised disclosures and a lot of handwringing over the government's role in the effort to try to uncover these terrorists, there have been some policy and legal and other actions that are taken that make our ability collectively internationally to find these terrorists much more challenging. And I do hope that this is going to be a wake-up call, particularly in areas of Europe

where I think there has been a misrepresentation of what the intelligence security services are doing by some quarters that are designed to undercut those capabilities.[8]

Nevertheless, the ability to employ social media data in relation to dealing with national security threats is promising. In fact, there are already attempts to use such data to predict incidents, attacks and even natural disasters. Although still in its infancy, the ability to predict with reasonable levels of accuracy would result in new methods of threat detection and prevention.

Continued Growth of Social Media

Social media can generally be defined as online websites and/or mobile phone applications that facilitate "participation, openness, conversation, community and connectedness" among individuals.[9] "The *social* nature comes from the active and *live* interaction with other people, some of whom remain anonymous, while the term *media* constitutes the content that is generated as participants publish or broadcast information, share personal and professional data, and collaborate in online communities of interest".[10] The different types of social media include: social networks (Facebook), blogs (*Bertha Harian*),[11] wikis (Wikipedia), podcasts (iTunes), microblogging (Twitter), forums (Unofficial Microsoft Windows Forum)[12] and content communities (YouTube).[13]

Global social media usage is expected to grow with "global penetration rates now in excess of 30%".[14] This trend is bolstered by the popularity and adoption of SMART phones that facilitate social media usage on the go.[15] In Singapore, trends are similar with more than 90 percent of the population active on social media, and 80 percent active on mobile social media.[16] Expectedly, "as Internet users continue to grow their networks online, social media becomes an essential channel for information dissemination, consensus seeking, collective action and decision making".[17]

The continued growth and evolution of social media will inevitably have an impact on national security. As more opportunities are created by new technologies, the associated risks will increase as well. And as technological changes often alter human behaviour, behavioural vulnerabilities will likely be exploited. For example, when location-based applications like Foursquare became popular, criminals were able to burgle the homes of some users as their whereabouts were publicised on the application.[18]

Social Media as a Communication Tool

Social media was designed originally as a communication tool to facilitate relationship-building between peers. *Six Degrees*, established in 1997, was the first social media site that enabled users to befriend each another, and within a short time, weblogs or blogs appeared as did other social networking sites like Friendster in 2002. These sites not only provided users with platforms to share their thoughts publically but also enabled them to further develop their networks. The beginning of the 21st century saw more communication and socialisation sites like MySpace (2003), Facebook (2004) and Twitter (2006) emerge.[19] Sites soon began to offer bespoke communication options adding to the array of available applications. For example, individuals preferring to communicate though photos could use Instagram, while those wishing to communicate "in short bursts of information" could use Twitter.[20]

The popularity of social media as a communication tool can, arguably, be attributed to three main factors: (a) user-generated content; (b) wide reach and (c) influencing power.

User-generated content

The main advantage of social media is that it liberalises content production by enabling any individual to become an author/content producer. This has an empowering effect on the individual as he/she can freely write and publicise whatever he/she wants. The ability to express oneself unhindered can produce lively and meaningful debate as well as facilitate the exchange of ideas.

However, unrestricted expression can, in some circumstances, create national security challenges too. For instance, the anti-Islam video *The Innocence of Muslims* that was disseminated on YouTube in 2012, provoked violent protests around the world.[21] In addition, social cohesion, which countries like Singapore consider to be crucial for national security, can be undermined when individuals or groups advocate: (a) violence against other individuals or groups based on differences of ethnicity or religion; (b) violence against the state and (c) hatred of other individuals or groups based on differences of ethnicity or religion.[22] It is for this reason that the Singapore government regards attempts to provoke ethnic or religious discord by individuals or groups as a serious matter. The authorities often move quickly against such entities regardless of whether they are in the online or offline realms. In 2010 for example, Singapore's Internal Security Department questioned and counselled a Christian pastor for "making insensitive comments about Buddhism"[23] in several online video clips.[24]

Wide reach

The ability to transmit content quickly to local as well as global audiences has many advantages. Individuals have used social media to warn others of hazards and/or provide life-saving information in natural disasters and other types of crises. The Quakemap.org website for instance, was created in the wake of the 2015 Nepal earthquake to bridge the "information gap so that rescue and relief efforts could be informed and expedited by reports from the ground".[25] Users could: (a) report earthquake damage in real-time; (b) populate a map of affected areas and (c) identify the type of relief assistance required.[26]

One of the disadvantages of this global reach is that it has also facilitated the recruitment of terrorist fighters from across the world (as discussed in the IS example above). It has also become easier to mobilise global action and support for negative campaigns against individuals or companies. Greenpeace for instance, utilises "existing online communities", "marketing materials (videos, logos)" to generate awareness and promote the campaign, as well as issues "calls to action" to mobilise supporters to participate on the ground.[27] In their 2014 campaign against Burberry for example, Greenpeace activists not only created a "social media storm" by flooding the company's Twitter, Facebook and Instagram accounts with calls to use non-toxic chemicals in the manufacturing of children's clothes, but also coordinated street protests outside several stores around the world.[28]

Another benefit of social media's ability to reach audiences is tapping the wisdom of the crowds or crowdsourcing. Information, funds and innovations can be derived from multiple and diverse sources to solve puzzles or problems quickly. Even law enforcement agencies recognise the benefits of crowdsourcing, and have begun using it in investigations. The Federal Bureau of Investigation's (FBI) appeal for crowdsourced information during the Boston Marathon bombing in 2013 is a case in point.[29]

On the negative side, the hurried dissemination of information without verification is extremely problematic. Sunil Tripathi, an undergraduate, was misidentified as one of the suspects of the Boston Marathon bombing, which led to a manhunt for the wrong person. Tripathi had been reported missing before the attack, and was later found dead, an apparent suicide unconnected with the bombing or the subsequent manhunt.[30] Crowdsourcing as a result of or organised for such 'witch hunts' can result in excessive harassment of the individual(s) regardless of whether he/she/they are responsible or not. Moreover, such harassment may constitute a criminal offense as it is often taken to extremes in many of these online vigilantism cases.

Influencing power

Marketing professionals have, for many years, leveraged on the persuasive abilities of parents, best friends, journalists and other 'influential' people to help sell products/services to their target audience. As these influencers are perceived as "authentic, credible and trustworthy" by their peers, employing them to advocate a particular product or service significantly increases the likelihood of a sale.[31] Similarly, when attempting to alter or champion a particular viewpoint and/or behaviour, collaborating with influencers can increase the chances of success.[32]

Social media can increase the power of influencers as speeches, videos, publications and so on are disseminated to a wider audience. It can also create 'social media influencers' who blog about particular socio-political issues in order to persuade followers to adopt a specific point of view. Brandon Stanton, originator of the popular *Humans of New York* photo blog for example, was able to raise awareness and funds for a Pakistani charity through a special feature on Pakistan. It was reported that the "photographer's fans responded to these people's stories by heaping money onto a fundraising page".[33]

Influencers can be extremely useful in the national security domain as well.[34] In the area of community resilience for example, Risa Lavizzo-Mourey, the president and CEO of the U.S.-based Robert Wood Johnson Foundation (RWJF), is, arguably, one such influencer. She is a strong advocate of improving public health to enhance community resilience,[35] and writes blogs, gives speeches as well as engages a variety of stakeholders in support of this issue.[36] She uses these avenues to champion other issues related to public health as well. Her leadership of the RWJF increases her influence as the Foundation's donations and activities are geared toward improving public health and increasing overall community resilience tangibly. For example, the RWJF designed a community resilience framework for the Los Angeles County Department of Public Health in 2013 to "augment public health preparedness and reinforce longer standing public health approaches to improving community health and wellbeing".[37] Resilience tool kits and online/offline resources were produced as part of the project. For her efforts and accomplishments in public health, Lavizzo-Mourey has been recognised as a notable Influencer by LinkedIn and one of the World's 100 Most Powerful Women by Forbes.[38]

It must be noted, however, that if an influencer is seen to be too closely-linked with the state or the authorities, he/she will lose credibility and his/her message/advocacy adversely affected.

Debate Over Social Media Account Takedowns

The use of social media for malicious activities, especially by terrorist groups, has prompted calls for law enforcement to take decisive action against offenders by having accounts suspended or taken down. This is envisaged to prevent the spread of undesirable content as well as impair online activities as account holders are forced to create new accounts and re-build disabled networks.[39] In June 2015, EUROPOL announced the establishment of a Europe-wide cyber unit that would work in tandem with social media providers to take down IS sympathiser accounts.[40]

However, research by the UK think-tank DEMOS has shown that such an approach may not be effective. This is because users can simply switch to alternative platforms with enhanced encryption or use different technologies to bypass account suspensions.[41] For instance, when mobile and internet services were temporarily suspended by the Chinese government in the wake of the Umbrella protests in Hong Kong in 2014, activists in China and Hong Kong used the FireChat app (which is based on Bluetooth technology) to communicate.[42]

The take-down approach also complicates law enforcement investigations especially since the user's activities can potentially be a valuable source of data and intelligence. With the user moving to better encrypted platforms to conceal his/her activities, intelligence-gathering, in most instances, inevitably becomes more challenging.[43]

Leveraging Social Media Data

In addition to counter-terrorism investigations, data from social media can be used to assist in other national security-related purposes such as: (a) event detection; (b) early warning and (c) problem-solving.

Event detection

Social media data can be used for event detection including social disturbances and natural disasters. The analyst attempts "to identify and characterise events by observing the profiles of word or phrase usage over time — usually anomalous spikes of certain words and phrases together — that indicate that an event may be occurring".[44] The LastQuake application and website, for example, detects earthquakes by monitoring web traffic, photos and Tweets.[45]

Early warning (via sentiment analysis)[46]

"Monitoring [sentiment on] social media to spot emerging issues and trends" as well as assessing "public opinion concerning topics and events" can provide "early warning" for "extremist-related" events and/or social disturbances.[47] To improve the accuracy of sentiment analysis, natural language processing systems are constantly being improved to decipher sentiments more accurately. The *early Pursuit against Organized crime using envirOnmental scanning, the Law and IntelligenCE systems* (ePOOLICE) uses sentiment analysis as one of its main data sources when assessing threats from organised crime.[48]

Problem-solving (during crises)

Crowdsourcing is "the practice of obtaining information, ideas and services from large (often online) groups of people" for the purposes of generating or analysing data.[49] Crowdsourced data have been used in relief efforts of many disasters such as the 2015 Nepal earthquake mentioned above. Authorities were able to use maps and derive other useful insights from data provided by people who had first-hand knowledge of the area and/or were on the ground.[50]

Challenges of using social media data

As with any data source, using social media data is not without challenges. These include: (a) preserving data integrity; (b) analysing data sets quickly and reliably and (c) limitations of machine-generated insight.

Preserving data integrity

Even with self-correcting mechanisms on social media, ensuring data integrity is extremely challenging. This is because of the difficulties in detecting misinformation and rumours as well as the existence of social bots that generate false/misleading information on purpose. Misinformation dissemination, especially during a crisis, can exacerbate an already volatile situation as well as create new problems.[51] For instance, Veerender Jubbal, a Canadian of Sikh heritage, was misidentified as one of the perpetrators of the 2015 Paris Attacks when a doctored image of him in a suicide vest went viral.[52] Until new methods of accurately detecting misinformation quickly become available, it will be incumbent on social media users to correct any misinformation during time-sensitive events. Unfortunately, it is these very users that may inadvertently be generating and disseminating the erroneous information.

The emergence of social bots, which are essentially computer programmes designed to mimic human social media users, can also generate and spread misinformation. They are so 'real' that telling them apart from a human user can be difficult. Such social bots can be used to influence public opinion, "inflate follower counts, push spam or malware, and even to skew political discourse".[53] This is a serious issue for analysts as the data that they collect may be contaminated, which adversely affects the overall analysis. Methods to accurately detect sophisticated bots are still in development, as such, analysts should be cautious when attempting to derive insights from social media data.

Analysing big data sets quickly and reliably

The inherent challenges of analysing big data include: (a) volume: processing large data sets require adequate software/hardware and is time-consuming; (b) velocity: processing streaming data brings about similar issues and (c) variety: the different forms of data make processing and analysis more complex.[54]

Limitations of machine-generated insight

The technical limitations of existing software can impair the generation of insights especially when attempting to interpret Tweets or Facebook posts. This is because the software cannot: (a) effectively analyse "embedded linguistic clues concerning the certainty (truth) of the statements"; and (b) determine the "context" of a specific sentence.[55]

Future of Social Media Usage and Data Usage

Even with these limitations, the field of social media analytics is expected to grow as technology evolves and new ways of improving social media data processing are introduced. It is anticipated that developments in the following areas will occur in the foreseeable future:

Privacy/encryption enhanced services

The Centre for the Analysis of Social Media (CASM) at DEMOS predicts that there will be "growth in the availability of default encrypted social media services, anonymous social networks and decentralised distributed social networks".[56] Such services will operate "without centralised servers or administrators" and premised on a "distributed trust network".[57] This would certainly make censorship and monitoring more difficult, which suggests that policies will have to be tweaked to ensure that the balance between privacy and security is maintained and that efforts of law enforcement are not hindered.

Predictive analytics

Predictive analytics is being steadily advanced, with the accuracy of predictions expected to improve over time. EMBERS (Early Model Based Event Recognition using Surrogates) for instance, "is an automated 24×7 continuous system for forecasting significant societal events" that employs open source social media data. It was reported that "an average of 80–90 percent of the forecasts it generates have turned out to be accurate–and they arrive an average of seven days in advance of the predicted event".[58] EMBERS was credited with successfully predicting the June 2013 protests in Brazil and Feb 2014 violent protests in Venezuela.[59]

Information sharing for disasters and emergencies

Improvements are also being made in social media tools to help crisis responders and law enforcement. For example, the EU-funded Athena Project "aims to develop technical applications or 'apps' for smart phones and mobile digital media devices, which will capture real-time information from the public during crisis situations". [60] It "seeks to make the public part of the crisis team" and will attempt to improve information-sharing and advice between the authorities and the public.[61]

In the Philippines, Project Agos was developed as "a collaborative platform that combines top-down government action with bottom up civic engagement to help communities mitigate risks and deal with climate change and natural hazards. Using mobile and web technologies and social media, it ensures the flow of critical and actionable information to those who need it before, during, and after disasters and connects those who need help directly with those who can truly help".[62]

More holistic approaches to analyse social media data for crises are forthcoming. An example is the European Union-funded SUPER Programme that combines behavioural sciences, virtual spaces, rumour tracking, event detection, fusion and reasoning over social sensors and real-time search to assist law enforcement agencies during crises.[63]

Conclusion

This discussion concludes with some observations pertaining to the operational and policy-related dimensions of social media usage and social media data usage. First, the operability and resiliency of communication and critical infrastructure is important. As the ability to use social media is highly dependent on mobile phone towers, transmission networks as well as power grids, the inoperability of such infrastructure particularly during a crisis would prevent people from using social media on their smart devices to provide information. Backups of critical infrastructure and processes to restore power/communication quickly will have to be taken into account and carefully planned for.

Second, the demand and emergence of more secure/encrypted social media applications/platforms will intensify the existing debate over commercial interests versus security needs. From a commercial viewpoint, the development of better-encrypted platforms is commercially sound, but from the standpoint of law enforcement, this is an operational hindrance especially in counter-terrorism operations. At the moment, there is no clear answer on how the balance between commercial interests and security interests will be struck, but if private–public cooperation in the cyber realm is to be improved, then an acceptable solution must be found sooner rather than later.

Third, as human behaviour will invariably alter as a result of new communication platforms, the exploitation of behavioural vulnerabilities will likely increase as well. Online sex-predators, scammers, hackers, terrorist operatives and affiliates and other criminals are proficient in using various social engineering techniques to manipulate their victims. For instance, in a Credit-for-Sex scam, "scammers normally befriend their victims through social media platforms such as Wechat, iAround or Facebook and will communicate with them through online messaging and phone calls.

They try and convince male victims to buy purchase cards, online shopping credits or Money Line (MOL) in exchange for a meet-up, date, massage, sexual or escort services".[64] Once the credits have been transferred to the scammer, the expected 'meeting' does not take place. Further research into behavioural sciences and technology is therefore needed to help develop better policies and approaches.

Finally, the debate over privacy versus security will persist. Scandals involving misuse and/or breaches of data privacy would expectedly increase public opposition to and suspicion of investigatory powers of law enforcement agencies. Yet, such investigations are critical in dealing with today's national security threats. Public trust can be increased by: (a) ensuring that such powers are not abused/misused; (b) demonstrating tangible results in terms of solving crimes or preventing security incidents and (c) severely punishing officials who are convicted of misusing their powers.

Endnotes

1. Simon, C. (7 March 2015). Law Plays Catch-Up with Technology, *Straits Times*. http://www.straitstimes.com/opinion/law-plays-catch-up-with-technology (Retrieved 15 December 2015).

2. Bibi, T. v. G. (2015). *Responding to Cyber Jihad: Towards an Effective Counter Narrative*, ICCT Research Paper, p. 1. http://www.icct.nl/download/file/ICCT-van-Ginkel-Responding-To-Cyber-Jihad-Towards-An-Effective-Counter-Narrative-March2015.pdf (Retrieved 11 December 2015).

3. When asked if US government efforts had been successful in countering IS in "cyberspace or social media", Admiral Michael S. Rogers, Commander of the U.S. Cyber Command, Director of the National Security Agency and Chief of Central Security Services replied "no". See Ernst presses witnesses on US Counter-ISIS effort in Cyberspace (29 September 2015). *Senator Joni Ernst Webpage*. http://www.ernst.senate.gov/content/ernst-presses-witnesses-us-counter-isis-effort-cyberspace (Retrieved 11 December 2015).

4. Richard, S. (9 June 2015). Note for the Secretary, US Department of State. Cited in Mark, M., & Michael R. G. (12 June, 2015). ISIS Is Winning the Social Media War, U.S. Concludes, *New York Times*. http://www.nytimes.com/2015/06/13/world/middleeast/isis-is-winning-message-war-us-concludes.html?_r=0 (Retrieved 10 December 2015).

5. Walbert, C. (June 2015). Air Force Intel uses ISIS 'moron' Post to Track fighters, *CNN*5. http://edition.cnn.com/2015/06/05/politics/air-force-isis-moron-twitter/ (Retrieved 10 December 2015).

6. Colin, D., & Lorenzo F.-B. (11 July 2014). U.S. Intelligence Officials Want ISIL Fighters to Keep Tweeting, *Mashable*. http://mashable.com/2014/07/11/us-wants-iraq-radicals-to-tweet/#u9drk4DMLsqT (Retrieved 11 December 2015).

7. Pamela, E. (21 November 2015). Inside the App that's become ISIS' biggest Propaganda Machine, *Business Insider*. http://www.businessinsider.sg/telegram-isis-app-encrypted-propagandar-2015-11/#.VlUUt9nosdU (Retrieved 15 December 2015).

8. Ryan, T. B. (November 2015). Read the CIA Director's thoughts on the Paris Attacks, *TIME*. http://time.com/4114870/paris-attacks-cia-john-brennan/ (Retrieved 15 December 2015).

9. Anthony, M. *What is Social Media*, iCrossing ebook, p. 5. http://www.icrossing.co.uk/fileadmin/uploads/eBooks/What_is_Social_Media_iCrossing_ebook.pdf (Retrieved 15 December 2015).

10. Infocomm Technology Roadmap. (2012). IDA Singapore, p. 3. https://www.ida.gov.sg/~/media/Files/Infocomm%20Landscape/Technology/TechnologyRoadmap/SocialMedia.pdf (Retrieved 15 December 2015).

11. *Bertha Harian* is a socio-political blog by Bertha Henson, a veteran journalist from Singapore who has held various portfolios in Singapore Press Holdings' stable of newspapers.

12. This forum helps users of Windows with their software problems.

13. Mayfield, *What is Social Media*, p. 5.

14. Global Digital Statshot: August 2015, *We Are Social* website. http://wearesocial.net/blog/2015/08/global-statshot-august-2015/ (Retrieved 15 December 2015).

15. It is estimated that 2 million SMARTPHONE devices are sold every day around the world. See Global Digital Statshot: August 2015.

16. Simon, K. (November 2015). Southeast Asia Digital in 2015, *We Are Social*. http://www.slideshare.net/wearesocialsg (Retrieved 15 December 2015).

17. Infocomm Technology Roadmap.

18. Dan, F. (18 February 2010). Please Rob Me: The Risks of Online Oversharing, *TIME*. http://content.time.com/time/business/article/0,8599,1964873,00.html. (Retrieved 16 December 2015).

19. History of Social Media, *History Cooperative* website. http://historycooperative.org/the-history-of-social-media/ (Retrieved 16 December 2015).

20. *Ibid.*

21. Seven Dead as Anti-Islam Film Protests Widen (14 September 2012). *BBC News*. http://www.bbc.com/news/world-africa-19602177 (Retrieved 16 December 2015).

22. A key lesson from the Charlie Hebdo shooting in 2015 where the magazine's editor and several employees were killed by Islamists for publishing satirical cartoons of the Prophet Muhammad is that although freedom of speech/expression varies from country to country, certain topics, such as religion and race are personal and remain highly sensitive. As such, they should be treated respectfully online as well as offline. See Charlie Hebdo shooting: 12 people killed, 11 injured, in attack on Paris offices of satirical newspaper. (8 January 2015). *ABC News*. http://www.abc.net.au/news/2015-01-07/charlie-hebdo-satirical-newspaper-shooting-paris-12-killed/6005524 (Retrieved 16 December 2015).; Charlie Hebdo and Free Expression. (2015). *New York Times Editorial*. 18 January, 2015. http://www.nytimes.com/2015/01/19/opinion/charlie-hebdo-and-free-expression.html?_r=0 (Retrieved 16 December 2015).

23. Yen, F. (2010). ISD calls up Pastor for Insensitive Comments, *AsiaOne News*, 9 February, 2010. http://news.asiaone.com/News/the+Straits+Times/Story/A1Story20100209-197516.html (Retrieved 29 December 2015).

24. Singapore raps Evangelical Pastor for Ridiculing Buddhists, Taoists (10 February 2010). *Reuters*. http://blogs.reuters.com/faithworld/2010/02/10/singapore-raps-evangelical-pastor-for-ridiculing-buddhists-taoists/ (Retrieved 29 December 2015).

25. QuakeMap.org website. http://kathmandulivinglabs.org/project/details/quakemap-org (Retrieved 29 December 2015).

26. Siobhan, H. (18 August, 2015). Nepal earthquake: How open data and social media helped the Nepalese to help themselves, *ABC News*. http://www.abc.net.au/news/2015-08-16/nepal-earthquake-how-open-data-social-media-helped-rebuild/6700410 (Retrieved 16 December 2015).

27. Jeremiah, O. (19 July 2010). Greenpeace Vs. Brands: Social Media Attacks to Continue, *Forbes*, http://www.forbes.com/2010/07/19/greenpeace-bp-nestle-twitter-facebook-forbes-cmo-network-jeremiah-owyang.html (Retrieved 29 December 2015).

28. John, S. (7 August, 2014) Five Greenpeace Campaigns against Companies: Lego, Barbie and Shell, *The Guardian*. http://www.theguardian.com/sustainable-business/blog/greenpeace-campaigns-companies-lego-mattel-barbie-shell (Retrieved 29 December 2015).; How to Detox a fashion brand in 14 days, 6 cities and 10,000 tweets, Greenpeace website, 28 January 2014. http://www.greenpeace.org/international/en/news/Blogs/makingwaves/burberry-detox-victory/blog/48027/ (Retrieved 4 January 2016).

29. Tarun, W. (22 April 2013). Lessons from Crowdsourcing The Boston Bombing Investigation, *Forbes*. http://www.forbes.com/sites/tarunwadhwa/2013/04/22/lessons-from-crowdsourcing-the-boston-marathon-bombings-investigation/ (Retrieved 16 December 2015).

30. Man misidentified as Boston bomb suspect confirmed dead (25 April 2013). *The Associated Press*. http://www.cbc.ca/news/world/man-misidentified-as-boston-bomb-suspect-confirmed-dead-1.1343072. (Retrieved 21 December 2015).

31. John, R. (20 November 2015). 6 Critical Ways Social Media Influencers Can Expand Your Brand, *Huffington Post*. http://www.huffingtonpost.com/john-rampton/6-critical-ways-social-media-influencers-can-expand-your-brand_b_8606936.html (Retrieved 18 December 2015).

32. Ravi, G., & Hugh, B. (2013). *Using Social Media for Global Security*, Inn: John Wiley & Sons, p. 301.

33. Corinne, A., & Qasim, N. (24 August 2015). Humans of New York Helps Humans in Pakistan, *The Wall Street Journal*. http://blogs.wsj.com/indiarealtime/2015/08/24/humans-of-new-york-helps-humans-in-pakistan/. (Retrieved 6 January 2015).

34. For instance, governments can work directly or indirectly with such individuals in countering violent extremism (CVE) efforts. Influencers, according to a 2013 RAND report, can help promote government initiated or linked CVE programmes as well as negate the negative perceptions associated with such programmes. Todd C. H., Erin, Y., & Peter, C. *Promoting Online Voices for Countering Violent Extremism*, RAND Report RR-130-OSD, 2013, p. 8. http://www.rand.org/content/dam/rand/pubs/research_reports/RR100/RR130/RAND_RR130.pdf (Retrieved 18 December 2015). In such cases, it is important for the individual to have 'street cred' in order to be effective. Individuals such as Maajid Nawaz, a former member of the radical Islamist group Hizb ut-Tahrir, and Nasir Abbas, a former member of Jemaah Islamiya (JI), an al-Qaeda affiliate operating in Southeast Asia could be considered potential influencers.

35. Risa, L.-M. Building Healthy Communities after Disaster (23 May 2013). *LinkedIn*. https://www.linkedin.com/pulse/20130523144404-43742182-building-healthier-communities-in-the-aftermath-of-disaster?trk=eml-mktg-condig-0108-p3. (Retrieved 8 January 2016).

36. Mike H., (19 February 2015). A Minute with ... Commencement Speaker Risa Lavizzo-Mourey on Health Care Issues, Illinois News Bureau. https://insideillinois.info/blog/view/6371/208703 (Retrieved 7 January 2016).

37. Alonzo L. P., & Anita C. (27 August 2015). What Hurricane Katrina taught us about Community Resilience, *Robert Wood Johnson Foundation Culture of Health Blog.* http://www.rwjf.org/en/culture-of-health/2015/08/what_hurricane_katri.html (Retrieved 8 January 2016).

38. See Forbes' The World's 100 Most Powerful Women in 2015 website. http://www.forbes.com/profile/risa-lavizzo-mourey/ (Retrieved 8 January 2016).

39. Berger, J. M., & Jonathan M. (2015). The ISIS Twitter Census: Defining and Describing the Population of ISIS supporters on Twitter, *The Brookings Project on U.S. Relations with the Islamic World,* Analysis Paper, No. 20. http://www.brookings.edu/~/media/research/files/papers/2015/03/isis-twitter-census-berger-morgan/isis_twitter_census_berger_morgan.pdf, cited in Jamie Bartlett and Louis Reynolds, *The State of the Art 2015*: *A Literature Review of Social Media Intelligence Capabilities for Counter-Terrorism*, DEMOS, p. 19. http://www.demos.co.uk/wp-content/uploads/2015/09/State_of_the_Arts_2015.pdf (Retrieved 15 December 2015).

40. Vikram, D. (21 June 2015). Europol Web Unit to Hunt Extremists Behind Isis Social Media Propaganda, *The Guardian.* http://www.theguardian.com/world/2015/jun/21/europol-internet-unit-track-down-extremists-isis-social-media-propaganda (Retrieved 18 December 2015).

41. As the authors write: IS sympathisers immediately post it on text-based sharing boards like justpaste.it, dump.to or elsewhere, and alert everyone to its new location — from where it is very quickly downloaded and re-posted across multiple sites. See *The State of the Art 2015*, p. 18.

42. Jeff, Y. (3 October 2014). Hong Kong Protesters in Cyberwar, *CNN.* http://edition.cnn.com/2014/10/03/opinion/yang-hong-kong/ (Retrieved 5 January 2016).

43. It was alleged that the Chinese authorities in collaboration with hackers were able to gain access to the communications and personal data of the Umbrella protesters through Trojan horse programs. See Jeff, Y, Hong Kong Protesters in Cyberwar.

44. Jamie Bartlett and Louis Reynolds, *The State of the Art 2015: A Literature Review of Social Media Intelligence Capabilities for Counter-Terrorism*, DEMOS, September 2015, p. 19. Available: http://www.demos.co.uk/wp-content/uploads/2015/09/State_of_the_Arts_2015.pdf (Retrieved 15 Dec 2015)

45. Nsikan, A. (16 December 2015). This App spots Earthquakes before Seismic Reports, *PBS News Hour.* http://www.pbs.org/newshour/updates/lastquake-app-spots-earthquakes-early/ (Retrieved 20 December 2015).

46. Sentiment analysis or opinion mining "analyses people's opinions, sentiments, evaluations, appraisals, attitudes, and emotions towards entities such

as products, services, organisations, individuals, issues, events, topics, and their attributes". See Bing, L. (2012). *Sentiment Analysis and Opinion Mining*, San Rafael, California: Morgan & Claypool, p. 1.

47. Kristin, G., & Richard, C. (2012). Estimating the Sentiment of Social Media Content for Security Informatics Applications, *Security Informatics*, 1(1), p. 1.

48. ePOOLICE website. https://www.epoolice.eu/EPOOLICE/about.jsp. (Retrieved 20 Dec 2015)

49. Christian, D., & Patryk, P. (2013). Crowd-sourcing — Crisis Response in the Digital Age, *European Union Institute for Security Studies Issue Alert*. November 2013 http://www.iss.europa.eu/uploads/media/Alert_Crowd-sourcing.pdf (Retrieved 20 December 2015).

50. Shirley, S. W., Newley P., & Suryatapa B. (1 May 2015). Nepal Aid Workers Helped by Drones, Crowdsourcing, *The Wall Street Journal*. http://www.wsj.com/articles/nepal-aid-workers-helped-by-drones-crowdsourcing-1430483540 (Retrieved 20 December 2015).

51. World Economic Forum, Digital Wildfires in a Hyperconnected World, *Global Risks 2013*, Eighth Edition. http://reports.weforum.org/global-risks-2013/risk-case-1/digital-wildfires-in-a-hyperconnected-world/. (Retrieved 21 December 2015).

52. Kevin, R. (16 November 2015). Canadian Pictured as Paris Terrorist in Suspected Gamergate Smear, *The Guardian*. http://www.theguardian.com/world/2015/nov/16/canadian-pictured-as-paris-terrorist-in-suspected-gamergate-smear (Retrieved 21 December 2015).

53. Tom, S. (2015). Fake Persuaders, *MIT Technology Review*. 23 March, 2015. http://www.technologyreview.com/news/535901/fake-persuaders/ (Retrieved 21 December 2015).

54. For a comprehensive analysis see Richard J. S., & Dave, V. Tools and Technologies for the Implementation of Big Data. In Babak, A., Gregory, B. S., Hamid, R. A., Richard, H., Andrew, S., & Saskia, B. (eds.). *Application of Big Data for National Security: A Practitioner's Guide to Emerging Technologies*, Oxford, UK: Butterworth–Heinemann, an imprint of Elsevier Ltd. pp. 140–154.

55. Kellyn, R. (2015). Making Sense of Unstructured Natural Language Information. In Babak A., Gregory B. S., Hamid R. A., Richard H., Andrew S., & Saskia B. (eds.). *Application of Big Data for National Security: A Practitioner's Guide to Emerging Technologies*, Oxford, UK: Butterworth–Heinemann, an imprint of Elsevier Ltd. p. 182.

56. Jamie Bartlett and Louis Reynolds, *The State of the Art 2015: A Literature Review of Social Media Intelligence Capabilities for Counter-Terrorism*,

DEMOS, September 2015, p. 19. Available: http://www.demos.co.uk/wp-content/uploads/2015/09/State_of_the_Arts_2015.pdf (Retrieved 15 Dec 2015)

57. *Ibid*, p. 8.
58. Leah, M. G. (2015). The EMBERS Project can predict the Future with Twitter, *Newsweek*. 20 March, 2015 http://www.newsweek.com/2015/03/20/embers-project-can-predict-future-twitter-312063.html (Retrieved 22 December 2015).
59. Naren Ramakrishnan, Patrick Butler, Sathappan Muthiah*, Nathan Self, Rupinder Khandpur, Parang Saraf, Wei Wang, Jose Cadena, Anil Vullikanti, Gizem Korkmaz, Chris Kuhlman, Achla Marathe, Liang Zhao, Ting Hua, Feng Chen, Chang-Tien Lu, Bert Huang, Aravind Srinivasan, Khoa Trinh, Lise Getoor, Graham Katz, Andy Doyle, Chris Ackermann, Ilya Zavorin, Jim Ford, Kristen Summers, Youssef Fayed, Jaime Arredondo, Dipak Gupta, and David Mares, "Beating the News' with EMBERS: Forecasting Civil Unrest using Open Source Indicators', Proceedings of the 20th ACM SIGKDD International Conference on Knowledge Discovery and Data Mining, August, 2014. Available: http://www.cs.umd.edu/~srin/PDF/2014/embers-conf.pdf
60. The Athena Project website. http://www.projectathena.eu/project/ (Retrieved 22 December 2015).
61. *Ibid*.
62. Project Agos website. http://www.rappler.com/move-ph/issues/disasters (Retrieved 22 December 2015).
63. See The SUPER website. http://super-fp7.eu/ (Retrieved 22 December 2015).
64. 'Credit-for-Sex Scam', National Crime Prevention Council's Scam Alert Singapore website. http://www.scamalert.sg/scams/alipay-scam.html (Retrieved 25 December 2015).

Part V
Cyber

Chapter 14

Embracing Transformation: Success and Failure in Cybersecurity Implementation

Christian Lifländer

In reacting to the hacker attack against Sony Pictures Entertainment, CEO Michael Lynton was quoted as saying "there's no playbook for this, so you are in essence trying to look at the situation as it unfolds and make decisions without being able to refer to a lot of experiences you've had in the past or other peoples".[1] Google CEO Eric Schmidt, on the other hand, told programmers at a conference in San Francisco that "the Internet is the first thing that humanity has built that humanity doesn't understand, the largest experiment in anarchy that we have ever had."[2]

The two quotes from industry deal with different facets of cybersecurity, but accurately sum up the nature and state of play of the internet right now. This is new ground, it is messy and we are in many ways at

Christian Lifländer is Deputy Head for Policy at the Cyber Defence Section of the Emerging Security Challenges at NATO.

the beginning. In fact, if this moment in time were to be compared to a similarly seismic event, that of the Atomic Age,[3] we would probably be at the point where the first self-sustaining nuclear chain reaction took place in Chicago.

The aim of this paper is to scan the existing cyberthreat landscape in order to identify actors, their methods and possible objectives in order to understand what is taking place in the cyberecosphere. This brief summary is then followed by an overview of emerging and future issues that need to be considered by policy makers. Finally, the paper aims to sum up practices that the author on the basis of experience thinks have worked, for the benefit of those that are trying to understand how best to navigate the unchartered waters of cyberspace. After all, this new digital technology holds much promise, but it also raises concerns about real risks. One is reminded of the well-known aphorism, whereby you may not be interested in war, but war is certainly interested in you. Only this time it is the digital technology and developments in cyberspace that will increasingly be interested in us.

That Thing We Call Cyber

According to the World Economic Forum's 2015 report into global risks, cyberattacks are one of the most likely high-impact threats in the modern world (only behind water crises, interstate conflict and failure of climate-change adaptation).[4] That puts the phenomenon that we call cyber (be that cyberworld, cyberspace, cyberdomain or any other way of describing cyberspace) beyond the realm of William Gibson's science-fiction novels.[5] Quite simply, digital technologies are an integral part and parcel of our daily life and our planet is getting connected at an unprecedented speed.

Forecasts and numbers vary, with some claiming that around 5 billion connected things are in use this year, up more than 30 percent from 2014, which will then increase to about 25 billion by 2020.[6] Others have put the figure much higher saying that the number of devices and objects connected to the internet by 2020 will reach around 50 billion.[7] We will never know the exact figure, and in some ways it is also irrelevant.

What matters is that the interconnected and open character of cyberspace offers unprecedented opportunities for the global economy and is transforming the very fabric of our societies.

By the same token, this open and interconnected space makes us vulnerable as the rise of hyperconnectivity makes it difficult to secure ever more devices. To be more precise, attacks are taking place at a faster rate than we are building our defenses and we would be well advised to stop thinking of network defence as something similar to defending a castle with a distinct and hardened perimeter around it. Rather, one must assume that detection has replaced defence as a strategy.[8] To be effective, cyber-defences must be resilient and resourceful enough in order to detect anomalous behaviour early, limit its impact and recover to full system functionality as quickly as possible.

According to Symantec Internet Security Threat Report 2020 this is easier said than done since attackers are 'stepping up to exploit vulnerabilities, whereas our reaction time has not increased at an equivalent pace'.[9]

Tinker, Hacker, Soldier, Spy

Not surprisingly this fast developing ecosystem provides a formidable forum for all sorts of fraud, virtual robberies and blackmail, identity theft, but also for conducting digital attacks that have a political, ideological, religious or national cause.[10]

When it comes to the list of individuals, groups and organisations, domestic and international criminals, organised crime, hacktivists and governments as well as state-sponsored groups make up the list of usual suspects. While nation states remain the best resourced and most capable actors, non-state actors have also demonstrated an ability to launch significant cyberattacks. For example, the Islamic State is claimed to have sought the ability to launch cyberattacks against the U.S. government by trying to penetrate computers that regulate the electricity grid.[11] However, a lack of world-class expertise is likely to prevent terrorists from acquiring destructive capabilities for the time being and they are likely to be more prone to use the internet for propaganda purposes, for instance by issuing threats against military personnel or using campaigns tailored to its audience.[12]

The main tools in use include attempts by an attacker to obtain information about a user or to gain unauthorised access to the users' network by stealing the user name and password or installing malware. Social engineering that involves manipulating the user into performing certain actions or into unknowingly passing on confidential information is also used by cybercriminals and state-sponsored hackers. Similarly, software specifically designed to disrupt or damage a computer system, including viruses and Trojans, is increasingly on the rise. Particularly difficult are advanced, targeted and persistent hacker attacks that require substantial amounts of funding, technical expertise and specific knowledge of the target. These espionage activities, called Advanced Persistent Threats (APTs) are usually launched by states and targets include ministries of foreign affairs, embassies, parliaments, defence contractors and think tanks.[13]

Last, but not least, the ongoing Russo-Ukrainian conflict has shown examples of what appears to be a new kind of conflict called hybrid warfare. While there is no unanimity of views on the terminology, and whether it is really new at all, it is clear that by using military, economic, diplomatic, political and other mostly non-physical activities it may be possible to isolate and coerce a state, while intimidating and deterring more distant, and capable opponents. Cyberoperations have their role to play, and there is evidence of vigorous cyberespionage, as well as the use of old-fashioned bolt-cutters to sever lines of communication in Crimea, but a lack of attacks on critical infrastructure and defence systems raised the question of whether Russia actually used the full range of cybercapabilities at its disposal.[14] Indeed, based on recent reports that a Moscow-based hacking group caused unprecedented power outage on December 23 last year affecting 80,000 customers in Ukraine, it appears the cyberconflict in Ukraine is far from over.[15]

Grasping the Nettle

Much of what is happening in the cyberecosphere has not gone unnoticed by states and international organisations and significant steps have been taken in order to improve cybersecurity both at the national and international level.

On the military side, nations are increasingly putting cybersecurity and defence at a priority equivalent to defending land, sea, air and space. Many have recognised cyberspace as the fifth domain of warfare and are developing not only defensive, but also offensive cybercapabilities. Discussions are ongoing over implementation of proactive cyberdefence measures to counter attacks against networks. Also, national cybercommands have been created in several countries to reflect the need to organise the military differently for the digital battlefield. Additionally, the emphasis is increasingly on improving what could very well be the weakest link in the security chain, the human element, by incorporating necessary cyberelements into training, awareness and exercises.

On the civilian side, governments and the private sector rightly have identified the need to continue to focus on and grow capabilities. Consequently, national cyberstrategies have been developed, designating competent authorities and delineating authority, and identifying key government and commercial-sector entities. Similarly, national incident response capabilities have been established and the mapping of cross-sector dependencies has taken place.

Many have recognised the value and indeed the need to develop collaborative frameworks between industry and government. The United States Framework for Improving Critical Infrastructure Protection is perhaps the most well-known example of ways to help owners and operators of critical infrastructure to manage cybersecurity-related risks. Many have developed initiatives to improve information sharing between industry and government in order to increase overall situational awareness, such as the United Kingdom Cyber-security Information Sharing Partnership (CiSP).

Industry has also risen to the challenge as a first responder. For example, steps that have been taken by Microsoft to fight against cybercriminals by using traditional legal and court actions to dismantle criminal networks known as botnets testifies to the fact that the private sector role in dealing with cyberattacks has evolved. [16]

At the international level, various useful processes have emerged, such as the London process, which helps to raise awareness, provide a forum for debate and improve policy maker understanding. Not insignificantly, the most recent gathering in The Hague launched the Global Forum on Cyber Expertise (GFCE), meant to give political momentum to global cybercapacity building, make available technical expertise as well as new funding to strengthen cybersecurity, help fight cybercrime, better protect data and support e-governance.

Similarly, the agreement by the U.S. and China not to support or conduct cyber-enabled theft of intellectual property and to strengthen dialogue and cooperation is a step in the right direction, even if we have not seen it lead to concrete results and action yet.

In the same way, recent discussion in international fora such as the United Nations and the Organization for Security and Cooperation in Europe (OSCE) have the potential to make the internet less anarchical as rules of the road and norms of behaviour for states and individuals are set out. The Tallinn Manual, which examined the international law governing the resort to force by states as an instrument of their national policy, and the international law regulating the conduct of conflict in the cyberdomain, is now to be followed by the Tallinn 2.0 project, which will examine the international legal framework that applies to cyberoperations that do not rise to the aforementioned levels.[17] Also, with the soon to be approved Network and Information Security (NIS) Directive by the European Union, Europe is taking a step in the right direction.

Muddling Through

Despite this promising picture difficulties remain when it comes to operationalising and implementing cybersecurity.

Perhaps the biggest obstacle remains the view that cyber is a theoretical issue, which results in key decision makers treating the cost of cyberinsecurity as an abstract issue, thus making the language of force unconvincing. In other words, the primary difficulty of cybersecurity remains not the technology itself, but policy.[18]

Indeed, taking into account that the primary effects of a cyberattack are mainly 'intangible and informational, and are intended to manipulate data, create uncertainty, and shape opinion',[19] preparedness between countries and also companies continues to be uneven. Cyberattacks are viewed as somewhat of an abstract issue by both those in the public and private sector that perceive themselves to be less exposed or think that they can externalise the cost of an attack.[20]

Contributing to the splintering of cyberspace are different views regarding internet sovereignty, with Russia and China being willing to work with the international community, but only to the extent that this enshrines a consensus to rewrite governance along state lines and to define aggressions along territorial lines, which is in stark contrast to the idea of a free and open multi-stakeholder model of internet governance put forward by the West. Indeed, the Russian–Chinese idea of national sovereignty in cyberspace and their state-patrolled border approach coupled with a desire to forge a different world order is likely to have an impact not only on the future of the internet, but also for the future of how conflict and acts of war may be defined.[21]

Fragmentation also occurs at a national level as policy debates often emerge in response to a specific concern or a crisis that must be addressed, more often than not as a deliberate choice. Similarly, there might be a commitment to protect society against cybercrime, but there is weak political will to improve cyberhygiene, monitor for infections, update existing laws and improve regulatory governance mechanisms.[22] Some of it has to do with bureaucratic politics and a large part of it deals with how governments and corporations set and rank goals and deal with risks.

While public and government awareness and informed action remain crucial, private sector leaders have also quite often missed the opportunity to improve their understanding of the issue and pursue informed action. Delegating cybersecurity to the chief information security officers as is often the case, and without embracing it as part of a business strategy, has in many instances resulted in failure to protect critical business assets or processes. Last but not least, security is not often considered in product design, leading to a situation where even major international companies and government organisations find it difficult to test the security of services, software and devices.

Way Ahead

Cyber defence does not have a defined "end point" at which we are all secure. If you buy a helicopter, you will likely use it for 30 or 40 years almost unchanged, with only some modifications and upgrades. Even after 40 years, a helicopter might still be a very capable piece of military equipment. You cannot do the same in cybersecurity because things move much faster. Indeed, we are likely to be at the beginning of what promises to be a long and muddled journey, and our situation today might have very little to do with where we will end up.[23] Transformation, driven by technological innovation, is likely to take time and the path that innovation is going to take is difficult to predict. The end result is likely to be determined by how we interact with technology and the impact that culture, politics, economic arrangements, our values and regulatory mechanisms will have.

The fact that there have been no casualties caused by a cyberattack may for some time make it difficult to accept the notion that cyberattacks can 'compel the opponent to fulfill our will', to use Clausewitz's definition of war.

While this healthy scepticism based on absence of evidence is a perfectly natural first response, it is likely that failure to make 'cyber' and 'cyber security' part of an overall effort at the strategic level will result in countries missing the benefits of connectivity, at best. At worst, this could result in loss of revenue and political power, as countries are likely to find it more difficult to pursue security, prosperity or power itself.[24]

Indeed, looking ahead it is clear that the evolving threat landscape will continue to feature a combination of techniques that will include compromise of the supply chain, social engineering campaigns, new evolutions of malware and botnets, as well as exploitation of the vulnerabilities of mobile platforms. Given that the Internet of Things will bring with it a whole network of new physical objects, devices, vehicles and buildings, as well as new vulnerabilities, it is difficult to imagine any future event, conflict or crisis that would not include a cybercomponent. In fact, it is highly likely that cyberattacks by state and non-state actors will increase and more states will attempt to exploit the internet for offensive purposes, also as part of military operations. It is also likely that if a conflict were to erupt between states with significant cybercapabilities, national infrastructure supporting functions vital to society would become a target.

If there is one piece of advice to those that deal with policymaking, it is to become aware of the transformation and to embrace cybersecurity and resilience at the core of a modernisation strategy. In practical terms this means taking appropriate action at the political level through policy creation, adoption of laws, market incentives, implementing regulations and other mechanisms. Enhancing cyberdefence inevitably costs money. However, raising the general baseline by incorporating cyber-risks into risk management and governance processes, implementing industry standards and basic best practices, as well as coordinating cyberincident response planning, is likely to be cheaper than the cost of insecurity.

Finally, it would be wise to recognise that dealing with threats emanating from cyberspace is a cooperative effort, where no one, however powerful, can go it alone. With this in mind, one would be best served by thinking about cyberspace as a domain where military and civilian, military defence and homeland security, as well as public and private interests intertwine. Whether one is to improve supply chain management, share information on vulnerabilities, or build trust and solicit support in the event of cyberincidents, one cannot but take into account the role of the private sector, which owns most of the world's information systems and provides most of the technical solutions for cyberdefence. This should make public–private partnerships absolutely essential for ensuring a truly effective cyberdefence of any country or defensive organisation. Put differently, without a working public–private partnership any attempt to deliver cyberdefence will only succeed partially.

Endnotes

1. 'Sony's Computer Network is Still Down', Associated Press, January 9, 2015.
2. Jerome Taylor, Independent.co.uk, at http://www.independent.co.uk/lifestyle/gadgets-and-tech/news/google-chief-my-fears-for-generation-facebook-2055390.html. (Retrieved 26 February 2016)
3. Term coined by William Laurence, a New York Times journalist, who became the official journalist for the Manhattan Project.
4. Global Risks (2015), 10th Edition published by the World Economic Forum within the framework of The Global Competitiveness and Benchmarking Network. Available at http://www3.weforum.org/docs/WEF_Global_Risks_2015_Report15.pdf.
5. William Gibson is credited with having invented the term cyberspace in his novel *Neuromancer* (Gibson, 1984).
6. Gartner, Inc, Press Release at http://www.gartner.com/newsroom/id/2905717.
7. Cisco at http://www.cisco.com/web/solutions/trends/iot/portfolio.html.
8. For further reading please see Melissa E. Hathaway (2014) (Ed.). *Best Practices in Computer Network Incident Defence: Incident Detection and Response*, IOS Press.
9. Symantec 2015 Internet Security Threat Report, Volume 20, available at http://www.symantec.com/security_response/publications/threatreport.jsp

10. For further information on typology of different players, means and their methods please see Roland Heickerö (2013). The Dark Sides of the Internet. On Cyber Threats and Information Warfare, Peter Lang GmbH, Internationaler Verlag der Wissenschaften, Frankfurt am Main.

11. http://www.politico.com/story/2015/12/isil-terrorism-cyber-attacks-217179.

12. Danish Defence Intelligence Service Intelligence Risk Assessment (2015).

13. For further reading see F-Secure Labs Threat Intelligence White Paper on The Dukes, 7 years of Russian cyberespionage available at https://www.f-secure.com/documents/996508/1030745/dukes_whitepaper.pdf.

14. 'Kenneth Geers (Ed.), Cyber War in Perspective: Russian Aggression against Ukraine, NATO CCD COE Publications, Tallinn (2015).

15. http://www.reuters.com/article/us-ukraine-cybersecurity-sandworm-idUSK-BN0UM00N20160108.

16. Further reading please see Janine S. Hiller (2015), Civil Cyberconflict: Microfsoft, Cybercrime, and Botnets, 31 SANTA CLARA HIGH TECH. L.J. 163.

17. For further reading please see NATO Cooperative Cyber Defence Centre of Excellence at https://ccdcoe.org/research.html (Retrieved 26 February 2016).

18. Bruce Schneier (2013). Understanding the Threats in Cyberspace, September 27. Europe's World.

19. James Andrew Lewis (2015). Compelling Opponents to Our Will': The Role of Cyber Warfare in Ukraine, in 'Cyber War in Perspective: Russian Aggression against Ukraine, NATO Cooperative Cyber Defence Centre of Excellence, Tallinn, Estonia.

20. Global Risks (2015). 10th Edition published by the World Economic Forum within the framework of The Global Competitiveness and Benchmarking Network.

21. Nicholas Dynon (2015). The Future of Cyber Conflict: Beijing Rewrites Internet Sovereignty Along Territorial Lines, The Jamestown Foundation, Publication: China Brief, 15(17).

22. Robert K. Knake (2015). 'Cleaning Up U.S. Cyberspace', Council on Foreign Relations Cyber Brief.

23. See Internet Society, 'Internet Futures Scenarios', Internet Society, 6 October 2009. Alternatively see Jason Healey, 'The five Futures of Cyber Conflict and cooperation', Atlantic Council Issue brief, 2012, for further reading on different predictions regarding the future of cyberspace.

24. For further reading please see Alexander Klimburg (Ed.), 'National Cyber Security Framework Manual' by NATO CCD COE, Tallinn 2012.

Chapter 15

Singapore's Approach to Cybersecurity

Wong Yu Han

Introduction

In 2015, Singapore celebrated the 50th anniversary of our independence. Over these 50 years, Singapore has transformed into a high-tech city state, an internationally trusted business hub and a safe and secure home for our people.

The Smart Nation concept is Singapore's vision for the future. Through the Smart Nation, Singapore will use information technology to its fullest to enable people to achieve meaningful lives. By leveraging on technology, networks and data, Singapore wants to create solutions that address common challenges, such as the efficiency of the transportation network, ensuring an efficient and effective healthcare system and sustaining an aging population — problems that are inherent in many countries today.

In realising the Smart Nation vision, there would be a shift of essential functions and daily activities into the cyberrealm. The physical and cyber-worlds would be more densely interconnected, converging into a hybrid physical-cyberreality where cyber-risks are multiplied and can result in grave consequences in the physical world.

Wong Yu Han is Director/Strategy at the Cyber Security Agency of Singapore (CSA).

The cyberthreats are real. Conventional criminal activities have moved into cyberspace, with the likes of cheating through social media scams and stealing through banking trojans. Singapore's systems are constantly probed, regularly attacked and from time to time, compromised and penetrated.[1] Fortunately, our critical functions have not been disrupted by cyberattacks. Cybersecurity thus plays a critical role in realising our Smart Nation ambition and protecting our way of life.

Challenges

A complex problem

With modern economic and social life dependent on 24/7, global connectivity, cyberspace has evolved into a strategic asset for nations. Cybersecurity is not a purely technical issue, but one with technological, economic, political and social components. In this regard, cybersecurity is not a complicated system, but a complex system. Complicated systems have many inter-related components, but they are typically well-behaved and predictable, with a consistent output for a given input. On the other hand, complex systems cannot be adequately described in terms of cause and effect. Each of the cybersecurity's components is evolving in its own way and in response to each other as well as to new disruptions. Our approach to cybersecurity will have to adapt to the dynamic responses of the system.

Part of our challenge with cybersecurity today is the newness of the cyberspace and its explosive growth in one generation. Twenty years ago, the internet had only 16 million users. Today, there are more than three billion — a 200-fold increase. Institutions and policies were designed for the physical world with defined jurisdictions and established roles, and have not yet caught up with the trans-border cyberrealm. Businesses and citizens, who have honed their instincts to the dangers and criminal intent of the physical world, have poor awareness of the mentalities and behaviours to adopt for staying safe in cyberspace. On the other hand, cyberthreat actors have adapted far more rapidly, readily exploiting the vulnerabilities in both the technology and users.

The international community is still seeking consensus on cyberspace and cybersecurity. Issues that shape global development and cooperation — such as internet governance, rules of engagement, multi-jurisdictional cooperation — remain to be resolved, as participating actors seek to balance competing security, economic and social interests. Though consensus-building is a long journey, it remains nonetheless the pivotal condition for real advances in global cybersecurity.

Inter-connections and inter-dependencies

As systems are increasingly networked, there are more inter-connections across systems and industry sectors. Some of these inter-connections are intended, while others can result from poor implementation, leaving security gaps waiting to be found out.

This results in two challenges. First, organisations are exposed to vulnerabilities down their supply chain and vendor networks. These cracks allow attackers to enter one weak point and move across other systems laterally with great stealth. Second, there are new cyberinter-dependencies within and across the sectors, in addition to existing logical and physical ones, such that attacks in one sector can impact other sectors through cyberspace.

Signal-to-noise ratio

At the organisational level, many low level exploits succeed through known vulnerabilities. Not only do such incidents consume a disproportionate effort in after-incident response, they also increase the cyberbackground noise and can mask the activity of advanced, persistent threat actors.

Many such incidents can be reduced with investment in cyberdiscipline; this means instilling the practice to regularly patch vulnerabilities, applying well-documented and mature measures such as white-listing of applications, and ensuring sound governance. With organisations strengthening their cybersecurity posture, there can be an overall reduction in cyberincidents and increase in signal-to-noise ratio, thus enabling cyberdefenders to focus on detecting and responding to more serious threats.

Human capital

With a growing awareness of cyber-risks, there is a strong demand for talented and experienced cyberpractitioners to bring solutions and design security into our interconnected systems. This is a demand that will keep growing as cyberspace rapidly expands into to all parts of our lives. There is, however, a current shortage of cybersecurity practitioners.

Ramping up our professional cybersecurity workforce and building a sustainable pipeline of talent are challenges that are not unique to Singapore. Singapore would also have to devise schemes to attract talent and facilitate the development and transfer of talent not just across related professional fields, but also across the worlds of academia, government and industry. Each of these worlds is already building up their own cyber-security talent; movement across these worlds can engender innovation and alignment of purposes.

Beyond specialised cybersecurity professionals, developers and engi-neers should be required in general to have better security consciousness and skills. This would enable them to design security into their products at the outset.

Singapore's Approach to Tackle Cyberchallenges

The cyberspace is too vast and challenging for any single entity to have complete visibility or oversight. Singapore's approach to counter the cybersecurity challenges extends beyond the efforts of the Government, in what is termed as a "Whole-of-Society Approach to Cyber Security", where the industry, academia and research institutes are also key players.

Government

In April 2015, the Singapore government laid foundation for shared responsibility and central resolve by establishing the Cyber Security Agency (CSA). In an environment where there is increasing interde-pendencies and risks in cyberspace, CSA provides dedicated and central-ised oversight of Singapore's national cybersecurity functions. This includes developing strategies, setting policies and effecting plans for guiding the nation's cybersecurity efforts, strengthening operational and intelligence capabilities to support the management of national-level crises, and developing policies and providing support to increase the security posture of critical information infrastructure (CIIs). It will also focus on engagement and partnership to ensure the holistic development of Singapore's cybersecurity ecosystem.

Critical information sectors have been prioritised to strengthen the CIIs that deliver essential peacetime services to businesses and individuals, such as telecommunication services and banking transactions. Singapore adopts a "sector-led" model for CIIs, whereby CSA has oversight over national cybersecurity policies and functions, while each sector regulator is responsible for ensuring cybersecurity readiness within its sector. The sector regulator would direct CII operators to take adequate cybersecurity measures. This model allows sector regulators to take a risk-based approach that balances business demands with security needs.

Tackling cybercrime is a critical cross-cutting component for securing our cyberspace. The Ministry of Home Affairs is taking the lead to strengthen capabilities for dealing with cybercrime and engaging international and regional law enforcement bodies for cross-border cooperation.

With increasing security concerns surrounding the protection of an increasingly large amount of data that comes with the growth of our Smart Nation, policies need to be in place to ensure that data custodians remain responsible for the usage and distribution of the collected data. The Personal Data Protection Commission (PDPC) was established to enforce the Personal Data Protection Act (PDPA) and advance policies in data protection so as to foster an environment of trust among businesses and consumers.

To build up R&D expertise and capabilities in cybersecurity for Singapore, the National Cybersecurity Research and Development Programme Office Directorate, which is housed in the National Research Foundation, develops and implements initiatives to improve the trustworthiness of cyberinfrastructure for Singapore. It has set aside $130 million over 5 years to support research in areas including scalable trustworthy systems, resilient systems, threat detection and cyberspace governance and policy research.

Academia and research institutes

Academia and research institutes play a key role in the development of cybersecurity research expertise and capabilities to advance Singapore's position as a leading player in cybersecurity. These capabilities include engineering expertise to develop innovative solutions for security needs, as well as policy proficiencies to navigate legal and political complexities. In this regard, the focus on cybersecurity by the Centre of Excellence for National Security is a much welcome initiative.

Our universities are building research capabilities in cybersecurity. The iTrust cybersecurity research centre in the Singapore University of Technology and Design was set up in 2013 in collaboration with the Ministry of Defence with a focus on cyberphysical systems, enterprise networking and the Internet of Things. In 2016, a National Cybersecurity R&D Laboratory will become operational at the National University of Singapore.

Besides cybersecurity R&D capability development, academia is crucial in the growth and the strengthening of our cybersecurity workforce. Our Institutes of Higher Learning (IHL) provide continuous training and skill development through a wide range of cybersecurity training programs designed for individuals at both entry and professional levels.

Industry

Industry is another important contributor to our efforts in countering cybersecurity challenges. In a field that is still in its nascent stages of development, industry provides the critical pool of talent and speed of innovation for breakthroughs in practical and cost-effective solutions. They provide the vital training grounds where professionals can hone their skills through real-life scenarios and raise the overall quality of cybersecurity workforce. It is crucial for us to partner with leading industry players to enhance our cybercapability development and widen our cyberdefence mechanisms.

The willingness of local and international firms, as well as professional bodies, to step forward in levelling up our professionals has been encouraging. For instance, FireEye's Asia Pacific Centre of Excellence, in collaboration with Infocomm Development Authority of Singapore, provides manpower training programmes for expert level skills in the area of cyberthreat intelligence. Singtel has set up an Asia Pacific Cyber Security Competency Centre with the Economic Development Board of Singapore.

The Association of Information Security Professionals and CREST International are partnering the CSA of Singapore to set up a local certification centre to raise professional standards in penetration testing and incident response.

Singapore as a Leading Player in Cybersecurity

Beyond incorporating cybersecurity as an enabler for our Smart Nation ambitions, Singapore can aspire to be a leading player in cybersecurity and a venue for cybersecurity innovation, business and partnerships. Singapore is neutral and stable country, with strong rule of law. It has a tech-savvy workforce and students with a strong foundation in science and mathematics. It is also one of the leading financial centres of the world and a regional data hub. There is much that Singapore can offer the cybersecurity industry to seed new innovations and develop advanced capabilities for the region.

Conclusion

International studies have found that Singapore has made progress towards cybersecurity maturity. For example, the Australia Strategic Policy Institute's Cyber Maturity in the Asia-Pacific Region 2015 report stated that Singapore has done well to establish government structures and regulatory levers to support cybersecurity and tackle cybercrime. It has also been actively engaging international partners and businesses on cyberissues and raising citizens' awareness of cybersecurity.

Nonetheless, in view of a rapidly evolving cybersecurity and technology landscape, some cybersecurity researchers have assessed that no country is cyberready. Our legislation, policies and initiatives have to be continually updated to address emergent cybersecurity issues. Our capabilities have to be upgraded and expanded to enhance the detection of attacks, increase the robustness of our incident response and strengthen the protection of key assets. Our businesses and people have to be more savvy in managing risks and dangers in cyberspace.

There is no absolute certainty in cybersecurity; technologically sophisticated countries and organisations have found themselves victims of cyberattacks. Even as Singapore improves its cybersecurity posture, our nation must build up resilience such that we are able to defend ourselves in the event of successful cyberattacks and be able to operate in spite of these attacks.

Endnote

1.   Speech by Prime Minister Lee Hsien Loong at Founders Forum Smart Nation Singapore Reception on April 20, 2015. "There is one horizontal which is critical to nay Smart Nation, and that is cybersecurity. With more connectivity, with more systems going online and enabled by technology, we have to take cybersecurity very seriously. The threats are real. IT systems in Singapore are constantly probed, regularly attacked, and unfortunately, from time to time compromised and penetrated, just like IT systems anywhere".

Chapter 16

Regional Cybersecurity Policy Developments in Southeast Asia and the Wider Asia Pacific

Caitríona Heinl

This chapter highlights current and evolving developments relating to cybersecurity in the Southeast Asia and wider Asia Pacific region. It specifies factors and trends that are relatively unique to this region that have an impact on cyber-related policies. The article then analyses both recent and future development and implementation of cyber policy, including applied policy suggestions that are likely to be considered in the near future.

Region-specific Factors and Trends

Several trends are quite specific to the Southeast Asia and Asia Pacific region that have implications for the analysis and development of cyber-security policy. First, there has been a tendency to date in discussions related to cybersecurity policy development in the region to reference Asia without always clearly defining what this is understood to be. This means that analyses have sometimes been at cross-purposes when discussing

Caitríona Heinl is Research Fellow at the Centre of Excellence for National Security (CENS) with responsibility for cyber matters.

cybersecurity in the "region". The "region" is very large and it is extremely diverse. Countries differ significantly, and institutional structures like ASEAN, the ASEAN Regional Forum (ARF) and APEC, among others, also vary significantly. For instance, these mechanisms encompass very different country participants. The structures and policies of ASEAN are not the same as the ARF, even though they are often referred to as one and the same. For these reasons, policy analysis and negotiations on cybersecurity policies need to become slightly more nuanced and one's understanding of the region should be better clarified so as to better inform the development of policy for the region.

On a similar note, it is important that clear terminology be used more frequently for cybersecurity issues in order to better understand the meaning of terms that are being used frequently in official forums and analyses in the region. Otherwise, not only do discussions often seem at cross-purposes, but it ultimately leads to less effective negotiations. At the time of writing, when it comes to cybersecurity, it is not unusual that the understanding of a term or definition used by a country or an individual may differ significantly to another. By further developing a common understanding of terms utilised, this should better facilitate policy development across the region. Furthermore, by better clarifying or defining the meaning of terms at national level where these have not always been clearly defined, this should also benefit more fruitful discussions and understanding at both regional and international levels.

Third, given that the Asia Pacific is a very diverse region and countries vary significantly, this impacts the development and implementation of cybersecurity policy for a number of reasons. States are at different stages in terms of information and communication technologies (ICT) development and adoption, and they also face different types of threats. In addition, not only are they at different stages of development but they can also differ significantly in terms of culture and ideology. National level priorities for cybersecurity can then be quite different, thus impacting progress at regional level.

Fourth, there is a digital divide. In particular, the ASEAN region comprises some of the most advanced countries in terms of ICT but also several developing countries. While there are ongoing efforts to bridge this digital and development divide, reports often state that the extent of this digital divide is one of the most serious challenges to developing ICT infrastructure. A further evolving dynamic to consider is that the absolute number of internet users has recently become greater in developing countries than that in more developed countries. Nevertheless, these less digitally developed countries can potentially incorporate lessons within their plans for development from the experiences of other countries in this area. Such disparities in ICT development could in fact be an advantage for those countries with less developed ICT infrastructure and less connected critical infrastructure. They could, for instance, adopt practices on how to best counter cyber-related threats, they can implement good practice policies and measures, and incorporate security and data privacy by design from inception (although this would require both the political will to do so as well as financial and labour resources).

Another recent trend relates to the large volume of citizens who have been coming online across the Asia Pacific. In Southeast Asia specifically, this has been primarily occurring in the less digitally developed countries where internet penetration rates have not yet reached saturation. This has raised the likelihood that higher levels of cybercrime will ensue. One of the main reasons for this development has been the use of mobile smartphones, which has been game changing in how quickly it has facilitated the high increase of ICT use in the region over a relatively short period of time.

The difficulty that then arises however, and has already begun to become more apparent in the ASEAN region specifically, is that with such greater connectivity the probabilities of transnational and cross-border cyber-related incidents also becomes higher. The establishment of the INTERPOL Global Complex for Innovation (IGCI) in Singapore, although it has a global mandate, is therefore a very welcome and timely development for countering cross-border cybercrime and cyber-related criminal activities in these countries. It would be beneficial if law enforcement authorities' capability from regional and international bodies, including INTERPOL, could be leveraged. In addition, the Netherlands government recently launched the multi-stakeholder Global Forum on Cyber Expertise (GFCE) at the Global Conference on Cyber Space 2015 in order to address rule-building for a secure and open internet, confidence and trust building and capacity building by focusing on practical recommendations and best practices. At the time of writing, the GFCE has two cybercrime initiatives, one of which is a project to prevent and combat cybercrime in Southeast Asia focusing on assessing capabilities and training. The idea is that GFCE initiatives identify successful policies and multiply these on a global scale.

In addition, this trend of increasing levels of cybercrime across the region is worrisome for another reason — the sixth factor that needs particular attention is the link that exists between the domains of cyber-crime and cybersecurity. The concern is that, in Asia particularly, such growth in cybercrime could cause even further instability among states because of the nature of espionage and military activities in the cyber domain. State actors in this region have become more involved in attempting to obtain or develop their own cyber capabilities over the past few years, but strong legal and technical attribution is not easy yet. Subsequently, although attribution seems to be possible, some states believe that high levels of plausible deniability allow for engaging in more activity without penalty. And so, given that more non-state actors are acting regularly in this space across the region, there is now a higher possibility of mistakenly blaming the wrong party, perhaps leading to serious misunderstandings between states.

In light of the tensions that exist over territorial disputes in the South China and East China Seas, for instance, as well as the military build-up that has been occurring in the Asia Pacific, such an environment of insta-bility that is exacerbated by the activity of non-state actors is less than ideal. This is particularly concerning given that these cyber-related inci-dents can happen at great speed and often challenge traditional state responses. Moreover, strong regional cooperation mechanisms to deal with the nature of such incidents are not yet in place.

A further factor to consider is that the region is known for high national security sensitivities, interstate tensions and strategic competition. And where geopolitical tensions already exist or flare up, it is expected that cyber will also have a continuing role. One current example is the frequent display of cross-border politically motivated "hacktivism" that is often fuelled by grievances over state disputes like those related to the South China or East China Seas. This has been particularly prominent in the Philippines for instance, but more recent reports by think tanks in the region highlight that now corporations are often also targeted by politically motivated attacks. And this is not because of the data they hold but because these corporations are perceived to represent a certain state or government industry.

Regional Policy Development and Implementation

National and regional level efforts to implement comprehensive responses or develop cybersecurity strategies have so far been relatively fragmented. Nevertheless, at national level, there has been a remarkable shift in government awareness across the region in recent years. As a result, there have been many new national-level developments, which are likely to continue, such as the establishment of national cybersecurity agencies, the designation of cybersecurity coordinators and work on developing national cybersecurity policies and frameworks.

While these are welcome developments, the region also requires deepened regional level cooperation mechanisms for cross-border cyber-related matters. These should also take into account national needs and regional nuances as well as complement consensus reached at international level like the work of the UN Group of Governmental Experts (UN GGE) on norms, confidence building measures (CBMs), and capacity building.

Regional cooperation is particularly significant in this field at the moment since it helps to build common understanding, and it is also key to international discussions. Especially since it is now important to operationalise these international agreements by focusing on practical CBMs where there are often less ideological tensions between states. Given the varying cultural and ideological tensions in this region, CBMs are practical measures that do not focus on these issues too much.

In addition, regional responses can inform each other, as well as inform evolving international discussions such as those held by the UN GGE. For instance, good practices from the OSCE Decision on regional cyber CBMs in 2013 or the work of the Organisation of American States (OAS) could be considered at the ARF. In fact, the OSCE Decision in 2013 outlined that in implementing CBMs, states should consider discussions and expertise in other relevant international organisations working on these issues. It is important to avoid duplication of efforts and to build on knowledge already available.

In Southeast Asia, cooperation on cyber issues is essential to enhance security in the ASEAN region and to support the functioning of increasingly interdependent markets as well as economic and social development. Furthermore, given ASEAN plans for regional connectivity for transports systems, enhanced ICT infrastructure like the optical fibre network, and a regional energy security framework including regional grids as well as the ASEAN post-2015 agenda, critical infrastructure protection is vital. In such instances, different levels of development and adoption of ICT across ASEAN members should not be reason to deter enhanced cooperation.

Cyber has implications in most policy portfolios and so it is natural that there have been developments under the three ASEAN community pillars (political and security; economic and socio-cultural) over recent years, albeit to different degrees. Agreements by the ten ASEAN members have so far aimed to develop a common framework for network security; minimum standards for integrity of networks; best-practice models for business continuity in all sectors and the establishment of the multi-stakeholder ASEAN Network Security Action Council to promote computer emergency response team (CERT) cooperation. The 2012 Mactan Cebu Declaration outlined, among other items: (1) Promoting international and regional collaboration to enhance the security of information infrastructure for "sustainable economic and social development"; (2) Working towards a safe and trusted environment and harmonised rules that will promote trade, investment and entrepreneurship; (3) Facilitating resilient information infrastructure through implementing national frameworks on submarine cable connectivity protection; (4) Enhancing policy frameworks and sharing of best practices on data protection and (5) Continuing collaboration among ASEAN CERTs.

The ARF has also been active in working towards better cooperation on these issues. In 2012, the foreign ministers highlighted the need to coordinate to ensure security for ICT, a statement on cooperation was adopted, and agreement made to develop a work plan relating to cybersecurity. This work plan, the "ARF Work Plan on Security of and in the Use of ICTs", was subsequently adopted in September 2015 and several ARF workshops have been held over recent years that have focused on CBMs and capacity building measures. Most recently, China and Malaysia co-hosted the ARF Workshop on Cyber Security Capacity Building, and a joint seminar hosted by the U.S and Singapore was held on operationalising cyber CBMs in the ARF. It is now timely to begin implementing and clarifying what has been agreed by states in this field and to focus on translating agreements into action points.

Further Future Policy Recommendations

Although there have been positive developments in terms of national policy development and implementation, as well as some progress in regional cooperation, there is still a need for greater collaboration across the region. Those countries that have not yet developed or implemented cybersecurity strategies and policies, including national contingency and cyber crisis management plans, also realise that they need to move in this direction.

National CERTs need to be strengthened, but existing operational cooperation and information sharing among regional and international response teams equally needs to be enhanced. While there are a number of capacity building efforts across countries in the region, it is expected that there will be more emphasis in the near future on further capacity building for states that request technical, policy, legislative, organisational or law enforcement training. Such efforts should be coordinated where possible by states in order to avoid an unnecessary duplication of efforts that waste limited resources, whether financial or labour resources. It would also be beneficial if capacity building programmes were to be better tailored, and as specific as possible, so as to cater for the unique needs and circumstances of each country and the region itself.

The trust of citizens and their cooperation with government will most likely become increasingly critical if cybersecurity strategies are to function properly. This will likely challenge governments in the region where future security initiatives and fundamental rights measures relating to data privacy and freedom of expression, among others, should be proportionate. It is also probable that the private sector and large corporations will play more of a role in driving policies in this field over the near term in order to best suit the needs of the corporations themselves but also those needs and demands of their consumers. In the ASEAN region specifically, there is much that the private sector could do in terms of measures related to the economic and socio-cultural agendas.

In fact, the UN GGE 2015 report specifies that while states have a primary responsibility to maintain a secure and peaceful ICT environment, international cooperation would benefit from the appropriate participation of the private sector, academia and civil society. The ARF discussions seem slightly lacking in the level of private sector and civil society involvement. Private sector involvement is highly important in this field, especially to ensure that discussions between states are accurately informed. Possible ways to surmount this lack of inclusion might be to leverage regional trade associations, alliances or international chambers of commerce that can properly represent the interests of the private sector where there are concerns over which corporations should be included. Alternatively open consultations could be held so that the views of corporations may be submitted, perhaps even on an ongoing basis. The OSCE deals with this challenge by having a dedicated meeting once per year that includes all these stakeholders so that they are incorporated into the process.

The outcome of recent region-based meetings among the different stakeholders from government, academia and research institutes, law enforcement and the private sector have further highlighted the need to reduce what is described as default ambiguity in this region. This is identified as critical to this domain, especially since stakeholders argue that this could set the foundation for further dialogue and cooperation on cyber issues. There is still a continuing call for the better clarification of governance structures and doctrine shaping regional cyber policies in order to mitigate the risk of state misperceptions and misunderstandings. Several other steps can thus be taken to deal with such ambiguity like the regular publication of white papers or strategies; defining military doctrine in cyberspace; establishing contact points; clarifying national terminology; better international coordination; building trust and personnel exchanges.

Academia and research institutes in the region could become more active and conduct deeper applied policy analyses of the issues. Equally states could encourage such analysis on cyber policy and invest in the research capacity of their institutes since the literature on these debates within the region is relatively thin. The UN GGE 2015 report suggests exchanges of personnel between research and academic institutions (also in incident response and law enforcement), and this is a CBM where some collaborative work has already been conducted both in the region and across regions. For example, the ASPI Cyber Policy Centre has arranged exchanges and it has an informal network of fellows from across Asia. This type of cooperation could be continued and deepened by other institutions through establishing similar exchanges.

In terms of cooperation at regional ASEAN level, the central elements of the post-2015 agenda vision include aiming to increase cooperation between the three community pillars. This should be helpful when it comes to cyber policy issues that fall within each of these pillars, but have not in fact been sufficiently coordinated across the communities to date. The vision also calls for enhanced information sharing among ASEAN Plus One, ASEAN Plus Three, the East Asian Summit; the ARF; the ASEAN Defence Ministers' Meeting Process (ADMM) and ADMM Plus. Again, this should positively impact the development of policies that relate to cyber by reducing unnecessary duplication of efforts across these regional mechanisms. It is further envisaged that adherence to shared values and norms be promoted such as protection of human rights and fundamental freedoms, good governance, rule of law, anti-corruption and democracy.

Defence cooperation for cyber-related threats could be further strengthened in the near term. While there have been Defence Minister calls at ADMM meetings in the past to work together in order to restrain cyber threats, there has been little movement in discussions by officials in the ADMM process on how this can be achieved. Notably, the Philippines recently proposed to include these discussions in the ADMM Plus process by establishing an expert working group. Although it still remains to be seen whether there is political willingness for this to be pursued. In the meantime, there are several measures that could be considered over the near term that include, among others, the developing of military CBMs like hotlines, or regular exchanges of defence officials. Track 1.5 and Track 2 formal and informal initiatives could also be better leveraged to facilitate this type of progress, as could discussions on good practices that have been developed by other states in other regions on building cooperation on questions related to cyber defence like those that are outlined in the 2014 EU Cyber Defence Policy Framework.

In this region, there is often much value in hosting discussions at Track 1.5/Track 2 levels, or even informal roundtables, in order to facilitate greater understanding where discussions might be deemed sensitive or where official positions may not even be fully determined yet. This can often provide an excellent opportunity to discuss and debate key questions in an informal setting where officials are not held hostage to a position. It can additionally facilitate the creation of a community of interest and informal networks for future collaboration and information sharing.

The ARF Work Plan outlines future proposed activities including conducting workshops and seminars. It specifies 11 suggestions that could be focused upon in the near future. The purpose of which is to promote a peaceful, secure, open and cooperative ICT environment and to prevent conflict and crises by developing trust and confidence between states in the ARF region, and by capacity building. It rightly identifies that practical measures are needed to enhance the predictability of state activities and reduce national security risks.

First, it suggests the voluntary sharing of information on national laws, policies, best practices, strategies, rules and regulations plus procedures for this sharing of information. Related to this point the OSCE 2013 Decision outlines that states are encouraged to have modern and effective national legislation to facilitate on a voluntary basis bilateral cooperation and effective, time-sensitive information exchange between competent authorities, including law enforcement authorities. Second, discussion exercises could be held on how to prevent incidents becoming regional security problems. The ARF has been quite active in hosting a number of table-top and discussion exercises like the Workshop on CBMs co-hosted by Australia and Malaysia in 2014 which included a table-top exercise. Such discussions could be especially beneficial if clear action points could then be formed based on good practices to prevent incidents escalating to become regional security problems. Although it may be difficult to achieve in practice, there seems to be a desire to use the lessons and key takeaways from these workshops and discussions, and perhaps create a mechanism for their implementation.

A third suggestion is conducting surveys on lessons learnt in dealing with threats, and the creation of ARF databases on potential threats and possible remedies, taking into account the work already done in the commercial computer security sector and CERT community. It would be a mistake to not include material from the private sector and CERT community, and new initiatives should be careful not to reinvent the wheel by duplicating efforts. There is a lot of information that is available from the private sector, CERTs and law enforcement. Law enforcement in particular has been collating much information on threats and remedies, especially INTERPOL in its work across Southeast Asia more recently. It is worth considering whether these efforts can be further leveraged by the political security community in the ARF. A difficulty that might arise however is how to make this information both intelligible and actionable, given the large amounts of data available. It might perhaps be useful to also have a section within such databases where analysts identify threats that seem to be particular to the region itself, and where there may not be clear solutions yet. This means that it might be easier to then identify whether other regions may be experiencing such incidents and have best practice solutions. Alternatively, ARF participant countries may have some good practices that could then be shared in other regions.

The Work Plan further suggests the promotion of and cooperation in research and analysis on relevant issues. It would be particularly useful if more evidence-based conclusions were produced, and analysis conducted that is specifically relevant to the challenges in the region. Increasing cooperation between other research institutes is also another form of CBM and while this is already occurring on a somewhat informal basis, more cooperation and exchanges might facilitate progress. Furthermore, publicly available open-source publications that drive awareness of the issues and inform policy-makers would be equally beneficial. Another CBM that is suggested is discussion on rules, norms and principles of responsible behaviour plus the role of cultural diversity in the use of ICTs. There is a need to more deeply discuss respect for and the role of cultural differences, and most specifically how cultural differences should not mean that universal human rights are not valid or that they transcend fundamental freedoms.

Another interesting suggestion relates to introducing measures to promote cooperation against criminal and terrorist use of ICTs, including (among others) cooperation between law enforcement and legal practitioners, a possible joint task force between countries, crime prevention and information sharing on possible regional cooperation mechanism. Such a joint task force might be quite effective, especially since one of the challenges that face law enforcement authorities includes the formal mechanisms for cooperation such as the Mutual Legal Assistance Treaty (MLAT) procedures. A more informal solution like a joint task force might be one way to achieve concrete results and it is a solution that some law enforcement authorities in other regions are hoping to pursue to surmount this challenge.

It is also suggested that discussion be held on terminology to promote understanding of different national practices and usage. Rather than arguing for harmonisation of terminology for now, there is acknowledgement that there is an absence of agreed terminology and for reasons already discussed in the article, this should be addressed. Most notably, under the OSCE 2013 Decision, states agreed to voluntarily provide a list of national terminology with an explanation or definition of each term with a view to creating a glossary.

Such ARF workshops and seminars are in their own right a form of CBM in that they allow for an opportunity to establish relationships among authorities and to build cooperation on subjects under discussion. Building trust and relationships between the experts is key to this process of enhancing understanding and cooperation. The ARF Work Plan also mentions establishing senior policy points of contact to facilitate real time communication. The 2015 UN GGE report in fact recommends that contact points be identified at both policy and technical levels to address serious incidents and as well as a directory for these contacts. In establishing a contact database, manpower issues at the ARF Secretariat may have to be examined if it is to be hosted there, especially since the regular maintenance and updating of such a database can be quite challenging. Experts should also meet regularly, although staff rotations will not help where relationships are already established. The OSCE has agreed that in this instance states will update contact information annually and notify changes after 30 days if there is a change. National experts are also expected to meet approximately three times per year to discuss information exchanged and the development of CBMs.

Going forward, the UNGGE 2015 report suggests that states voluntarily provide national views of categories of infrastructure that they consider critical and national efforts to protect them, including information on national laws and policies for the protection of data and ICT enabled infrastructure. It also suggests that states try to facilitate cross-border cooperation to address critical infrastructure vulnerabilities that transcend national borders. Given connectivity plans for critical infrastructure in the region, especially in ASEAN, this is a CBM that could be more deeply examined in future by ASEAN members as well as by ARF participant countries.

In short, these are challenges that impact every state in the region and it is in the interests of each to continue to collaborate more effectively given the cross-border nature of the cyber field. There have been many developments in recent years, some of which are highlighted in this chapter, but much space still remains for deeper policy implementation at both national and regional level.

Index

www.ingramcontent.com/pod-product-compliance
Lightning Source LLC
LaVergne TN
LVHW022336060326
832902LV00022B/4071